Joseph Smith's AMERICA

HIS LIFE AND TIMES

Joseph Smith's
AMERICA

HIS LIFE AND TIMES

CHAD M. ORTON

WILLIAM W. SLAUGHTER

DESERET
BOOK

SALT LAKE CITY, UTAH

Library of Congress Cataloging-in-Publication Data

Orton, Chad M.
  Joseph Smith's America : his life and times / Chad M. Orton, William W.
Slaughter.
      p. cm.
Includes bibliographical references.
    ISBN 1-57008-979-5 (hardcover : alk. paper)
1. Smith, Joseph, 1805–1844. 2. Church of Jesus Christ of Latter-day
Saints—History. 3. Mormon Church—History. 4. United States—Church
history. I. Slaughter, William W., 1952– II. Title.
    BX8695.S6S53 2005
    289.3'092—dc22   2004029763

Printed in the United States of America   18961
R. R. Donnelley and Sons, Harrisonburg, VA

10 9   8   7   6   5   4   3   2

CONTENTS

We can no longer say there is nothing new under the sun.
For this whole chapter in the history of man is new.

—Thomas Jefferson, 1801

❧

Be not weary in well doing, for ye are laying the foundation of a great work.
And out of small things proceedeth that which is great.

—Doctrine and Covenants 64:33

❧

I hear America singing, the varied carols I hear,
Those of mechanics, each one singing his as it should be blithe and strong,
The carpenter singing his as he measures his plank or beam,
The mason singing what belongs to him in his boat, the deckhand singing on the steamboat deck,
The shoemaker singing as he sits on his bench, the hatter singing as he stands,
The wood-cutter's song, the ploughboy's on his way in the morning, or at noon intermission or at sundown,
The delicious singing of the mother, or of the young wife at work, or of the girl sewing or washing,
Each singing what belongs to him or her and to none else.

—Walt Whitman, "I Hear America Singing," from *Leaves of Grass*

❧

The past is a foreign country: they do things differently there.

—Lesley Poles Hartley, *The Go-Between* (1953)

"TO EVERY THING THERE IS A SEASON"

To every thing there is a season, and a time to every purpose under the heaven," wrote the author of the Old Testament book of Ecclesiastes. To the ancient Greeks, time was differentiated in terms of chronos and kairos. Chronos referred to the progression of time, while kairos meant the opportune moment or the right time for something to happen in the appropriate measure, thus bringing forth, or enabling, a wholeness. American theologian Paul Tillich stated that kairos "points to unique moments in the temporal process, moments in which something unique can happen or be accomplished." It is the "perfect now" in which events have meaning that might otherwise be lost or not understood. The infinite touches the finite; the "eternal breaks into the temporal."

Inventor, statesman, and entrepreneur
Benjamin Franklin (1706–1790)

Such was the case with the prophetic life of Joseph Smith, who came at a time and a place when and where he was most needed—a man with the right message at the right time. God did not randomly or accidentally pick the person, the place, or the time, to restore His gospel to His people.

Joseph Smith's America was uniquely situated to accommodate this prophet raised up to restore the fullness of the gospel in the latter days. The United States in the 1800s was largely a work-in-progress trying to define itself. America was young, fresh, open, and creative. By the 1840s, Americans were referring to their nation in a new way: Young America. This designation reflected a general mindset that greater things were yet to come. Populist movements were reshaping America's religious, social, and political landscape, while a blossoming of inventions affected every aspect of life. "The world is deriving vigour, not from that which is gone by, but from that which is coming," Sampson Reed wrote in 1826.

The Young America of Joseph Smith was a changing, evolving, and growing nation. In fact, widespread change was, for perhaps the first time in history, becoming the norm rather than the exception. Few aspects of the nation and society escaped change during the first half of the nineteenth century. Benjamin Franklin wrote shortly before his death in 1790, "I wish it had been my destiny to have been born two or three centuries [later]. For invention and improvement are everywhere. The present progress is nothing less than astounding." One modern think tank has estimated that prior to the birth of Jesus Christ, new ideas, including scientific inventions and improved ways of doing things, were produced annually at the rate of 39 a year. During Joseph Smith's lifetime, that number exploded to 3,840 a year—a nearly 1,000% increase. Today an estimated 110,000 changes occur each year—a 280% increase over the nineteenth century.

Young America was a time and place that brought forth Americans of incomparable talent, inventiveness,

It is by no means improbable that some future text-book, for the use of generations yet unborn, will contain a question something like this: What historical American of the nineteenth century has exerted the most powerful influence upon the destinies of his countrymen? And it is by no means impossible that the answer to that interrogatory may be thus written: Joseph Smith, the Mormon prophet. And the reply, absurd as it doubtless seems to most men now living, may be an obvious commonplace to their descendants. History deals in surprises and paradoxes quite as startling as this. The man who established a religion in this age of free debate, who was and is to-day accepted by hundreds of thousands as a direct emissary from the Most High,—such a rare human being is not to be disposed of by pelting his memory with unsavory epithets. Fanatic, imposter, charlatan, he may have been; but these hard names furnish no solution to the problem he presents to us. Fanatics and impostors are living and dying every day, and their memory is buried with them; but the wonderful influence which this founder of a religion exerted and still exerts throws him into relief before us, not as a rogue to be criminated, but as a phenomenon to be explained. . . . If the reader does not know just what to make of Joseph Smith, I cannot help him out of the difficulty. I myself stand helpless before the puzzle.

—Former Boston mayor Josiah Quincy in *Figures of the Past*, 1883. In a May 1844 letter Quincy described a recent visit with Joseph as "one of the most extraordinary conversations I ever participated in."

Nathaniel Hawthorne (1804–1864). One of the founding fathers of American fiction, his work explored spiritual and moral conflict

intellectual prowess, and artistic creativity. James Fenimore Cooper, Edgar Allen Poe, and Nathaniel Hawthorne helped forge American literature. Artists Thomas Cole and John Audubon created artistic expression of, and deep appreciation for, America's natural beauty. Ralph Waldo Emerson and Henry David Thoreau helped sculpt American intellectual and philosophical thought. Poets Henry Wadsworth Longfellow and Walt Whitman reflected America through their poetry. Businessmen such as Francis

Born in the lowest ranks of poverty, without book-learning and with the homeliest of all human names, he had made himself at the age of thirty-nine a power upon earth. . . . His influence, whether for good or for evil, is potent to-day, and the end is not yet.

—Josiah Quincy

Cabot Lowell pioneered the dawning of a new era of American manufacturing. Renaissance men like artist-inventor Samuel F. B. Morse and physician-author-professor Oliver Wendell Holmes Sr. were examples of the possibilities of life. Inventors John Deere and Cyrus McCormick changed farming forever. Social activists Frederick Douglas and Dorothea Dix worked to better humanity's everyday temporal condition. Women such as Sacagawea and Dolley Madison deeply affected the course of America, while best-selling

Abolitionist, novelist, and children's book writer Lydia Maria Child (1802–1880)

Walt Whitman
1849

Above: Henry Wadsworth Longfellow (1807–1882), whose sentimental and moralizing verse found a receptive audience as his fame grew with such narrative poems as "Paul Revere's Ride," "The Village Blacksmith," and the epic "Song of Hiawatha."

Right: Walt Whitman (1819–1892), whose poetry celebrated the individual, democracy and freedom, and the brotherhood of man

"Old Hickory," Andrew Jackson (1767–1845), gained a national reputation during the War of 1812. He was a non-aristocrat who believed in the common man

President Thomas Jefferson (1743–1826) was a Renaissance man who, in 1801, concluded, "We no longer can say there is nothing new under the sun."

author Lydia Maria Child profoundly influenced the way a generation of women maintained households and raised children. Political leaders such as Andrew Jackson molded a new populist political landscape.

When Joseph Smith was born on 23 December 1805, Thomas Jefferson, the third president of the United States, was in his second term; Lewis and Clark's Corps of Discovery was wintering on the coast of the Oregon territory; more than 90 percent of Americans lived on farms and in the country; and the nation consisted of fifteen states trying their best to be united. Internationally, Napoleon's ambitions were pitting France and Spain against Great Britain, Austria, Naples, Russian, and Sweden. America was feuding with Great Britain over international trade rights and borders. Egypt was beginning to establish itself as a

modern sovereign state. America's neighbors in South and Central America continued to struggle with European domination.

There were many "firsts" in America and the world during the Prophet's lifetime. The stethoscope was

Above: Lewis and Clark of U.S. Corps of Discovery holding council with Indians

AS IF IT WERE HOLY GROUND

Americans during the first half of the nineteenth century felt a strong sense of mission. They believed that their nation had been set aside by God for a specific purpose, a belief that was at least a century old. In 1742, the great American religious leader Jonathan Edwards wrote that "the latter-day glory; is probably to begin in America":

It is worthy to be noted, America was discovered about the time of the reformation, or but little before: which reformation was the first thing that God did towards the glorious renovation of the world, after it had sunk into the depths of darkness and ruin, under the great anti-Christian apostasy. So that, as soon as this new world stands forth in view, God presently goes about doing some great thing in order to make way for the introduction of the church's latter-day glory—which is to have its first seat in, and is to take its rise from, that new world.

It is agreeable to God's manner, when he accomplishes any glorious work in the world, in order to introduce a new and more excellent state of his church, to begin where no foundation had been already laid, that the power of God might be the more conspicuous; that the work might appear to be entirely God's, and be more manifestly a creation out of nothing. . . . When God is about to turn earth into paradise, he does not begin his work where there is some good growth already, but in the wilderness, where nothing grows, and nothing is to be seen but dry sand and barren rocks; that the light may shine out of the darkness, the world be replenished from emptiness, and the earth watered by springs from a droughty desert. . . .

. . . And if we may suppose that this glorious work of God shall begin in any part of *America,* I think, if we consider the circumstances of the settlement of *New England,* it must needs appear the most likely, of all *American* colonies, to be the place whence this work shall principally take its rise.

And, if these things be so, it gives us more abundant reason to hope that what is now seen in *America,* and especially in *New England,* may prove the dawn of that glorious day; and the very uncommon and wonderful circumstances and events of this work, seem to me strongly to argue that God intends it as the beginning or forerunner of something vastly great.

Although the American sense of mission had its roots in New England Puritanism, the idea spread throughout the nation. The topic was frequently mentioned in patriotic speeches, where the rhetoric was intended to inspire, with equal parts hyperbole and salesmanship. In 1823, Charleston, South Carolina, statesman Hugh Legaré proclaimed in his Independence Day oration sentiments that his audience would have readily embraced: "It is the proud distinction of Americans . . . that in the race of moral improvement . . . we have outstripped every competitor and have carried our institutions, 'in the sober certainty of waking bliss,' to a higher pitch of perfection than ever warmed the dreams of enthusiasm or the speculations of the theorist. It is that a whole continent has been set apart, as if it were holy ground, for the cultivation of pure truth."

invented in France (1816); England introduced both the passenger railway and the railway tunnel (1825–1826); Boston was the location for the first U.S. savings bank (Provident Institute for Savings, 1816); Louis Braille introduced his reading system for the blind (1829); an Italian synthesized salicylic acid, the basic ingredient in aspirin (1838); the rules for baseball were created (1839); a Scot produced the first bicycle (1839); the first useable photographic process, the daguerreotype, was introduced (1839); and the first Christmas card was created (1843).

In Joseph's last year of life, 1844, John Tyler was the tenth president of the United States; there were twenty-six states united in name only, and Americans living on farms had fallen to less than 70 percent. The change resulted largely from the fact that the population

"Remember the Alamo!" The bloody defeat at the battle of the Alamo in March 1836 rallied Anglo-Texan settlers in their fight for independence from Mexico

of the nation had nearly quadrupled in the years since Joseph was born, while the borders of the nation had changed relatively little during his lifetime. The nation was preparing to grow in a major way as Congress voted to annex the Republic of Texas. Eventually, the Republic would cede to the United States additional land that currently makes up parts of Colorado, New Mexico, Kansas, Oklahoma, and Texas.

Joseph Smith's life spanned the Second Great Awakening; the War of 1812; Napoleon's defeat at Waterloo; the development of American canals, roads, and railways; the fiftieth anniversary of American Independence; the abolition of slavery in Mexico and the British Empire; the volatile rise of the anti-slavery movement in the United States; the first settlers traveling the Oregon Trail; the Battle of the Alamo; the crowning of England's Queen Victoria; the independence of most Central and South American countries; the uniting of lower and upper Canada; and the beginnings of America's shift from an agrarian to an industrial economy.

Religion in Young America was changing as revival camp meetings swept through the country during the Second Great Awakening. Unleashing a wave of populist and democratic religion, the Second Great Awakening refocused American perception of religion. Few remained untouched during this time of religious originality and transformation, including the

Queen Victoria's (1819–1901) long reign as queen of the United Kingdom (1837–1901) witnessed the growth of Britain's commercial strength and maritime power

LAND OF OPPORTUNITY

"Ours is a country, where men start from a humble origin . . . and where they can attain to the most elevated positions, or acquire a large amount of wealth, according to the pursuits they elect for themselves," Calvin Colton wrote of Young America in 1844. "No exclusive privileges of birth, no entailment of estates, no civil or political disqualifications stand in their path; but one has as good a chance as another, according to his talents, prudence, and personal exertions. This is a country of self-made men, than which nothing better could be said of any state or society."

Four years after leaving Norway in June 1831 for new opportunities in America, Gjert Hovland wrote of the hope and success his adopted country afforded him in a letter to a Norwegian friend. Concerning his life in upstate western New York, Hovland wrote, "Nothing has made me more happy and contented than that we left Norway and came to this country. We have gained more since our arrival here than I did during all the time I lived in Norway, and I have every prospect of earning a living here for myself and my family, even if my family becomes larger, so long as God gives me good health."

While America was a land of opportunity, some immigrants were disappointed to find that the ground was not really or figuratively covered with gold. One German immigrant in Cincinnati wrote to relatives in Germany that success could be had—but it required an ability and a willingness to work hard:

A lot of people come over here who were well off in Germany but were enticed to leave their fatherland by boastful and imprudent letters from their friends or children and thought they could become rich in America. This deceives a lot of people, since what can they do here? If they stay in the city they can only earn their bread at hard and unaccustomed labor. If they want to live in the country and don't have enough money to buy a piece of land that is cleared and has a house then they have to settle in the wild bush and have to work very hard to clear the trees out of the way so they can sow and plant. But people who are healthy, strong, and hard-working do pretty well.

I the Lord, knowing the calamity which should come upon the inhabitants of the earth, called upon my servant Joseph Smith, Jun., and spake unto him from heaven, and gave him commandments;

And also gave commandments to others, that they should proclaim these things unto the world; and all this that it might be fulfilled, which was written by the prophets—

The weak things of the world shall come forth and break down the mighty and strong ones, that man should not counsel his fellow man, neither trust in the arm of flesh—

But that every man might speak in the name of God the Lord, even the Savior of the world;

That faith also might increase in the earth;

That mine everlasting covenant might be established;

That the fulness of my gospel might be proclaimed by the weak and the simple unto the ends of the world. (D&C 1:17–23)

— Revelation received by Joseph Smith, 1 November 1831

A DANIEL AND A CYRUS

Parley P. Pratt, 1807–1857

President Joseph Smith was in person tall and well built, strong and active, of a light complexion, light hair, blue eyes, very little beard, and of an expression peculiar to himself, on which the eye naturally rested with interest, and was never weary of beholding. His countenance was ever mild, affable, beaming with intelligence and benevolence, mingled with a look of interest and an unconscious smile, or cheerfulness, and entirely free from all restraint or affection of gravity; and there was something connected with the serene and steady penetrating glance of his eye, as if he would penetrate the deepest abyss of the human heart, gaze into eternity, penetrate the heavens, and comprehend all worlds.

He possessed a noble boldness and independence of character; his manner was easy and familiar; his rebuke terrible as a lion; his benevolence unbounded as the ocean; his intelligence universal, and his language abounding in original eloquence peculiar to himself—not polished—not studied—not smoothed and softened by education and refined by art, but flowing forth in its own native simplicity, and profusely abounding in a variety of subject and manner. He interested and edified, while, at the same time, he amused and entertained his audience; and none listened to him that were ever weary with his discourse. I have even known him to retain a congregation of willing and anxious listeners for many hours together, in the midst of cold or sunshine, rain or wind, while they were laughing at one moment and weeping the next. Even his most bitter enemies were generally overcome, if he could once get their ears.

I have known him when chained and surrounded with armed murderers and assassins who were heaping upon him every possible insult and abuse, rise up in majesty of a son of God and rebuke them, in the name of Jesus Christ, till they quailed before him, dropped their weapons, and, on their knees, begged his pardon, and ceased their abuse.

In short, in him the characters of a Daniel and a Cyrus were wonderfully blended. The gifts, wisdom, and devotion of a Daniel were united with the boldness, courage, temperance, perseverance, and generosity of a Cyrus.

—Recollection of Parley P. Pratt

SUNDAY SCHOOLS

Sunday schools were first established in England around 1780 to educate the many children employed in the mines and factories on the one day of the week they did not have to work long, grueling hours. While the primary focus was reading and writing, children also received religious training (the Bible was frequently the text) and were taught manners and morals. With the advent of universal public education, churches that sponsored Sunday schools were freed from the responsibility of teaching the "three R's," and the focus shifted from secular to spiritual learning. Sunday schools were an integral part of American culture by the early 1800s.

> *Verily, thus saith the Lord unto you, my servant Joseph Smith, I am well pleased with your offering and acknowledgments, which you have made; for unto this end I have raised you up, that I might show forth my wisdom though the weak things of the earth (D&C 124:1).*
>
> —Revelation received by Joseph Smith, 19 January 1841

family of Joseph Smith and their neighbors. This religious movement helped inspire many of the social changes taking place in America. It also stirred a young man to seek an answer to a question that many were asking and contributed to his becoming a major participant in this wonderfully dynamic era.

While the United States was born, in the immortal words of the great Ralph Waldo Emerson, of a "shot heard round the world," The Church of Jesus Christ of Latter-day Saints was born of a question heard round the world. Both were nourished by ideals that struck like lightning bolts. For America, it was found in the simple words of the Declaration of Independence—"all men are created equal." People wanted to be part of a nation where "life, liberty, and the pursuit of happiness" were viewed as God-given rights. Men, women, and children came from all over the world to swell the ranks of America's population during the early 1800s. For The Church of Jesus Christ of Latter-day Saints, the ideal is best articulated in a belief that mankind was not only created equal but also possessed a spark of the divine. Thousands of Latter-day Saints gathered to New York, Ohio, Missouri, and Illinois to learn more of their divine destiny from Joseph Smith. Today the church Joseph founded is one of the fastest-growing Christian religions in the world.

The founder of this religion, like most of Young America, was a man of the frontier. He had a personality all his own, one that frequently reflected the culture of his time. From his childhood to his death, he experienced and learned from life on the frontier. It was a life that called for physical and emotional courage, native resourcefulness, and an ability to continually adapt. Life was a constant effort to ensure survival and betterment. If ever there was an example and proof of the adage "Necessity is the mother of invention," it was surely the American frontier. Growing food, sewing clothes, building lodging, and learning to get along with neighbors, frontier folk took raw land, settled it without the benefit of immediate ordered society, and then planned and built communities. At times, differences on the frontier erupted into violence, although most people worked long and hard to bring structure and security to the wilderness.

It was not unusual for urban contemporaries, especially well-heeled Easterners, to misunderstand and underestimate people of the frontier. When wealthy Eastern elites Josiah Quincy (future Boston mayor and son of a Harvard president) and his cousin Charles Francis Adams (future minister to England) visited the Prophet in May 1844, they met a rough-hewn man of the frontier, one born and reared in poverty, wearing home-spun clothes, lacking proper pedigree, and mostly self-educated. Their two worlds could hardly have been more different.

In a 16 May 1844 letter to his wife, Mary Jane, Quincy sketched his first impression of Joseph Smith: "We . . . arrived at the seat of this 'prophet, priest, king, Mayor, Lt. General and tavern [inn] keeper' for as each and all of these is he inspired to act. The door was surrounded by dirty loafers, from among which our quixotic guide selected a man, in a checked coat, dirty pantaloons, a beard of some three day's growth

Sarah Josepha Hale, 1788–1879

THANKSGIVING

Although the Pilgrims celebrated a successful harvest in 1621 with a feast, they did not make the observance an annual event. Colonial New Englanders regularly celebrated Thanksgiving, but days of thanksgiving were not a regular part of the other colonies. The only time all thirteen colonies observed Thanksgiving together was in October 1777, when a day was appointed to commemorate America's victory over the British at the Battle of Saratoga.

Shortly after becoming president in 1789, George Washington tried to establish an annual, nationwide day of thanksgiving. He envisioned a day of prayer and giving thanks to God observed by all religious denominations. Discord, however, kept the holiday from being implemented, as many Americans, focusing only on the Pilgrims, felt that the hardships of a handful of settlers were unworthy of commemoration on a national scale. Many contended there were other, nobler events

that merited observance. Along these lines, Thomas Jefferson argued against a national Thanksgiving Day during his presidency.

While it continued to be primarily a New England feast in Young America, other states during the first half of the nineteenth century began celebrating Thanksgiving. By 1817, New York had adopted the day. In addition to previous arguments against the day, a new argument proclaimed that the country did not need another national celebration. A winter holiday (22 February, Washington's birthday) and a summer festival (4 July) were viewed as sufficient.

Much of the credit for our national Thanksgiving Day belongs to Sarah Josepha Hale of Boston. In 1827, she began crusading for such a day in the pages of her *Ladies' Magazine*. When that magazine merged with *Godey's Lady's Book* in the late 1830s, she continued her editorial campaign.

She also personally wrote each U. S. president about the issue.

Finally, in 1863, after a campaign of more than thirty years, she found an ally in President Abraham Lincoln, who established the fourth Thursday of November as a national day of Thanksgiving. This action came on the heels of the surrender of Vicksburg, Mississippi, to Union troops and the nearly simultaneous Union victory at Gettysburg, both events seemingly signaling that the tide in the American Civil War was changing in favor of the North. Three days after Lincoln proclaimed at the cemetery at Gettysburg "that from these honored dead, we take increased devotion to the cause for which they gave the last full measure of devotion; that this Nation, under God, shall have a new birth of freedom; and that government of the People by the People and for the People shall not perish from the earth," Americans started the annual tradition of celebrating Thanksgiving.

and introduced him as General Smith. He had the name but certainly but in few respects the look of a prophet."

However, much to his credit, Quincy, after a lifetime of experience and reflection, focused his attention in his 1883 *Figures of the Past* upon his discussion with Joseph, not his initial impression of the Prophet. Instead of a loafer in dirty pantaloons and rough beard, Quincy described the Mormon prophet as a hands-on frontiersman "clad in the costume of a journeyman carpenter when about his work. He was a hearty, athletic fellow . . . a fine-looking man. . . . [A] remarkable individual who had fashioned the mold which was to shape the feelings of so many thousands of his fellow mortals." The unique contribution of this frontiersman prompted Quincy to conclude, after considering the contributions of contemporaries from John Adams to Abraham Lincoln, that Joseph might later be identified as the nineteenth-century American who "exerted the most powerful influence upon the destinies of his countrymen."

Joseph remained down-to-earth while having access to the heavens. To the dismay of some, he occasionally displayed the refinement of a man of the frontier. But this frontier background was essential for the work he had to do. While reformers such as Martin Luther began with an institutional church to build on, the Lord asked Joseph to start from scratch. But as a man of the frontier, he knew what it was like to start anew, to construct something from the ground up. In that regard, his frontier background made him an excellent choice to restore the Lord's church. As was often the case on the farm, Joseph found that the initial structure he established had to be added to in order to be perfected. He had to adapt to new revelation during the course of his life until the gospel was restored in its fullness.

No person since Jesus Christ in the meridian of time had required such a complete breaking of "old vessels" as did Joseph Smith. He established not only a new way of thinking but also a new mode of being. His teachings were not a difference of degree from the other religionists but rather a complete break with the organized religions of the day. Such a revolutionary figure could not help but be noticed.

From the time of the First Vision in the spring of 1820 until his murder in 1844, Joseph Smith's life was never simple or uneventful. He was loved, hated, praised, and berated—some people denounced him as a blasphemous fraud. In fact, when he was seventeen, he was warned by the Angel Moroni that "his name should be had for good and evil among all nations, kindreds, and tongues, or that it should be good and evil spoken of among all people." Throughout a

I'M STUMPED

To create farms and roads in their young nation, Americans literally had to cut them out of dense forests. The fallen trees could be moved out of the way, but some stumps were too large for perplexed pioneers to deal with. "Stumped" at what to do, people usually left them behind to rot. While many were baffled about what to do with particularly large stumps, even small ones could present problems. Stumps were frequently left in place in the hurry to create roads but were cut to a height less than a typical wagon or stagecoach axle. Periodically a storm would soften the soil to the point where a wagon or stagecoach would sink into the mud, with the result that its progress was jarringly "stumped."

DRESS FOR SUCCESS

America's revolutionary fathers fought in knee-length breeches and debated the Declaration of Independence in them, but Americans in the first two decades of the nineteenth century increasingly viewed them as incompatible with democratic ideals. By 1820, ankle-length pants had largely replaced breeches as clothes of choice, even among America's elite and well-to-do.

As with many fashion trends, pants originated in France. French peasantry had worn rather shapeless pantaloons for centuries, but only after the French Revolution did they become popular in America. Sympathizing with the ideals of their fellow revolutionaries, but not the excesses of the French Revolution, Americans began to champion the common man with every trousered step.

James Monroe was the fifth—and last—president to lead the nation wearing knee-length breeches. In an 1823 painting of Monroe and his cabinet, he is the only one not wearing the increasingly popular symbol of democracy.

Fashion plate, ca. 1810

lifetime of constant and harsh barrages of verbal and physical harassment, the Prophet's immense love and compassion for others allowed him to stay constant in his efforts to preach and reestablish the Lord's gospel. He believed he was called of God. "I have no doubt of the truth," he proclaimed. This attitude impressed Peter Burnett, one of Joseph's attorneys in Missouri and later the first governor of California. Burnett concluded that Joseph "possessed the most indomitable perseverance" and "deemed himself born to command, and he did command."

Like a warm spring breeze after a long, cold winter, Joseph Smith brought the world renewed hope. For those who heard and understood, the message he gave soothed their souls much like the sweet warmth of the sun's loving caress. The head and heart, the finite and infinite, the earthly and heavenly were once again united. The potential for happiness and the positive divine nature of mankind was once again brought to the forefront. In the Book of Mormon—a book of scripture Joseph translated through divine inspiration—are words that denote the positive characteristic of the Lord's plan and stand in stark contrast to the ages of dark emphasis on fearing God: "Men are, that they might have joy" (2 Nephi 2:25). Given the hope Joseph brought to the world, it is hardly surprising that Brigham Young gushed, "I feel like shouting 'Hallelujah!' all the time when I think that I ever knew Joseph Smith, the Prophet."

A HOUSEWIFE'S LAMENT

Young America was uniquely optimistic, but this popular song provides a sense of how people viewed their daily grind. It also gives us a peek at specific nineteenth-century chores, worries, and needs. The song aptly expresses a timeless complaint uttered from times ancient to modern concerning the frustration of never-ending housework.

A HOUSEWIFE'S LAMENT: LIFE IS A TOIL

One day I was walking, I heard a complaining,
I saw a poor woman, the picture of gloom.
She gazed at the mud on her doorstep ('twas raining),
And this was her song as she wielded her broom:

> CHORUS:
> "O life is a toil, and love is a trouble,
> Beauty will fade and riches will flee,
> Wages will dwindle and prices will double
> And nothing is as I would wish it to be."

"There's too much of worriment goes to a bonnet,
There's too much of ironing goes to a shirt.
There's nothing that pays for the time you waste on it,
There's nothing that lasts us but trouble and dirt.

"In March it is mud, it's slush in December,
The midsummer breezes are loaded with dust.
In fall the leaves litter, in muddy September
The wallpaper rots and the candlesticks rust.

"There are worms on the cherries and slugs on the roses,
And ants in the sugar and mice in the pies.
The rubbish of spiders no mortal supposes,
And ravaging roaches and damaging flies.

"It's sweeping at six and it's dusting at seven,
It's victuals at eight and it's dishes at nine.
It's potting and panning from ten to eleven.
We scarce break our fast till we plan how to dine.

"With grease and with grime from corner to center,
Forever at war and forever alert.
No rest for a day lest the enemy enter,
I spend my whole life in the struggle with dirt.

"Last night in my dreams I was stationed forever,
On a far distant rock in the midst of the sea.
My one task of life was a ceaseless endeavor,
To brush off the waves as they swept over me.

"Alas! 'Twas no dream—ahead I behold it,
I see I am helpless my fate to avert!"
She lay down her broom, her apron she folded.
She lay down and died and was buried in dirt.

when it is considered that they were achieved by a farm boy with comparatively little formal education.

Shortly after emigrating from England to Nauvoo, Illinois, in 1840, William Clayton wrote to his former home about his impressions of Joseph:

> He is not an idiot, but a man of sound judgment, and possessed of abundance of intelligence and whilst you listen to his conversation you receive intelligence which expands your mind and causes your heart to rejoice. He is very familiar, and delights to instruct the poor saints. I can converse with him just as easy as I can with you, and with regard to being willing to communicate instruction he says "I receive it freely and I will give it freely." He is willing to answer any question I have put to him and is pleased when we ask him questions. He seems exceeding well versed in the scriptures, and whilst conversing upon any subject such light and beauty is revealed I never saw before. If I had come from England purposely to converse with him a few days I should have considered myself well paid for my trouble.

Two aspects of Joseph set him apart from his contemporaries. The first was his belief in the divinity of Jesus Christ. At a time when religionists were proclaiming Jesus to be only an important historical figure, Joseph declared that the fundamental principle of Mormonism was "the testimony of the apostles and prophets, concerning Jesus Christ, that He died, was buried, and rose again the third day, and ascended into

William Clayton (1814–1879), an English convert to Mormonism, worked as Joseph Smith's private secretary

Joseph was young, emotional, dynamic, and so loved and approachable by his people that they simply referred to him as "Brother Joseph." His was a rich and varied personality, ignited by a spark of divinity that seemed almost beyond the limits of human nature, as those limits are frequently understood. His varied accomplishments are all the more remarkable

When I first heard him preach, he brought heaven and earth together: and all the priests of the day could not tell me anything correct about heaven, hell, God, angels, or devils; they were as blind as Egyptian darkness. When I saw Joseph Smith, he took heaven, figuratively speaking, and brought it down to earth; and he took the earth, brought it up, and opened up, in plainness and simplicity, the things of God; and that is the beauty of his mission.

—Recollection of Brigham Young, 7 October 1857.

THE MAIL MUST GO THROUGH

Since letters were often the sole link to civilization in some parts of Young America, officials tried to expand the postal service as fast as the frontier grew. Although this expansion was not without its challenges, the shaky moments eventually gave way to the well-known adage that the "mail must go through."

Although Congress authorized the construction of "postal roads" to ensure that letters could be sent to all regions of the country, rain, hail, and sleet frequently turned these roads into muddy quagmires that were virtually impassable for weeks at a time. As the country grew, so did the postal roads, increasing from 5,000 miles in 1795 to nearly 105,000 in 1830. Initially, solitary postmen traveling by horseback carried the mail. In 1814, approval was given to send mail by stagecoach. Delivery continued to improve with the advent of canals and railroads, but overall mail service during the first half of the nineteenth century remained relatively expensive and haphazard.

In the more settled parts of the country, mail was frequently delivered to homes and businesses. The 1814 postal act extended mail service to frontier areas where there were no established post offices by authorizing mail delivery to any country court-houses in any state or territory. People usually learned they had mail from lists printed in news-papers and then had to pick up their letters.

Wages for mail carriers were based upon the amount of mail they handled. Letters were frequently sent C.O.D. (cash on delivery), the addressee having to pay the postage and any fees to receive his or her letter. This arrangement almost cost Zachary Taylor the United States presi-dency in 1848. He refused to pay for a number of letters sent to him, including the one informing him that he was the Whig Party's candidate for president. Only after party officials became con-cerned that their candidate had not responded did Taylor learn of his nomination by other means. Taylor's frustrations with the system were shared by others. In 1842, Joseph Smith complained that the post office at Nauvoo "is exceedingly corrupt. It is with great difficulty that we can get our letters to or from our friends." In early June 1844, a frustrated Hyrum Smith wrote in the local Nauvoo paper, "To the brethren and friends writing me on church business, I wish they would pay the postage, for no others will meet my attention, for I am not able to pay the enormous sums of postage I have heretofore paid."

In the 1830s, postal rates were set at six cents for letters going a distance up to 30 miles, twelve and a half cents for letters travel-ing between 30 and 150 miles, eighteen and three-quarter cents for letters sent 150 to 400 miles, and twenty-five cents for letters journeying over 400 miles. These amounts were about half the cost needed to mail a letter in 1815.

Legend has it that Francis Scott Key wrote the "Star Spangled Banner" on the back of an envelope, but such was not the case. Envelopes did not come into use until 1839. Prior to that time, the message was written on one side of a piece of paper, which was then folded and sealed with wax, and the address was written on the opposite side of the same paper.

THE BIG CHEESE

⁂

"The greatest cheese in America for the greatest man in America," read the sign on the side of the cart that brought a unique gift to President Thomas Jefferson on New Year's Day, 1802. Weighing more than twelve hundred pounds, this token of esteem was the brainchild of Baptist minister John Leland of Cheshire, Massachusetts. In July 1801, he and his congregation took the proceeds from one day's milking of their approximately nine hundred cows and created the mammoth cheese. The congregation dressed in their Sunday best to gather the milk, which was put to the press with prayer, hymn singing, and great solemnity. Word of the big cheese spread throughout the country. People came out to see it during its three-week journey to Washington, D.C. A lengthy and humorous poem was even written about it. The cheese was so enormous that it was still being served at presidential receptions three years later in 1805.

More than thirty years later another cheese, even bigger than the first, arrived at the President's House. This second was a gift for President Andrew Jackson from an admirer in Oswego County, New York. Weighing fourteen hundred pounds, it was decorated with Jacksonian slogans and draped in bunting. For two years it was displayed in the White House, but a month before leaving office in 1837, Jackson celebrated George Washington's birthday by inviting the public to help themselves. Business in the nation's capital came to a virtual halt as citizens mobbed the Executive Mansion one last time. Within two hours, the cheese was dismantled. What had not been eaten or carried away was ground into the carpets and floorboards. The odor of cheddar is said to have lingered in the White House for years.

heaven; and all other things which pertain to our religion are only appendages." Second, he recognized and actively acknowledged revelation to be so necessary to understanding God that he wondered why it should be "thought a thing incredible that [God] should be pleased to speak again in these last days for [our] salvation." He concluded that other churches denied and condemned latter-day revelation because of a "consequence of tradition."

Benjamin F. Johnson (1818–1915),
a friend of Joseph Smith

⁂

If I had not actually got into this work and been called of God, I would back out. But I cannot back out; I have no doubt of the truth.
—Comments by Joseph Smith, 6 April 1843.

A friend of Joseph's, Benjamin F. Johnson, summarized the prophet's life this way in 1903:

> Before 1830 the Lord began, through the Prophet Joseph, to turn the keys of knowledge, to flood the world with new light and life, or to plant in the "three measures of meal" that "leaven" through which all the world will yet become "leavened," which since its inception has been working in the world's thought to produce a great change, politically, religiously, socially, financially and scientifically—the increased light that came to the earth through the keys of knowledge turned by the Prophet Joseph, for which he was derided, hated, and killed, and toward which all searching eyes are now turning with new thoughts toward the great truths of the gospel.

This book commemorates the 200th anniversary of the Prophet Joseph Smith's birth. It is a celebration of his life, his times, and his place in America. A product of his time and place, the Prophet both influenced America and was influenced by America. However, it is the Lord's teachings that this prophet reintroduced to the earth. People seldom receive revelation unless they ask, and what was taking place around Joseph prompted him to ask many questions. But, Joseph taught, "we never inquire at the hand of God for special revelation only in case of their being no previous revelation to suit the case." Our Heavenly Father decides when, where, and through whom He will unfold His plans and reveal further knowledge.

The unique events of returning the clear light of the gospel back to an overcast world required the right person during a time and in a place that would be most accepting of His message. Such a man was Joseph Smith, and such a place and time was his America. ❧

Joseph and Hyrum Smith

HEAPING INDIGESTIONS UPON ONE ANOTHER

Although most Americans in the early part of the nineteenth century had plenty to eat, few enjoyed a balanced diet. Their daily fare was largely meat and breads and was therefore woefully vitamin deficient. The variety of food was limited since most grew their own provisions and raised or shot their own meat. Lack of year-round refrigeration, canned foods, and grocery stores meant that meat salted and smoked for preservation was the staple of most diets. Fresh fruits and vegetables were unavailable for much of the year. This fact, however, didn't bother most people, since fruits and vegetables weren't thought to contain much nutrition, and some were believed to be harmful or deadly if eaten.

Foreign visitors were shocked by the amount of greasy food consumed by Americans and the speed with which it was eaten. Constantin François de Chasseboeuf complained about the amount of lard, butter, salt pork, greasy puddings, and coffee and tea Americans consumed. Harriet Martineau noted a breakfast that consisted of "cornbread, buns, buckwheat cakes, broiled chicken, bacon, eggs, rich hominy, fish, fresh and pickled, and beef-steak." François Jean Marquis de Chastellux, in his *Travels in North America,* reported that he was made ill by a similar breakfast of fish, steak, ham, sausage, salted beef, and hot breads. "The whole day passes in heaping indigestions upon one another," he complained. In the 1840s, Charles Dickens decried the American practice of eating "unheard-of quantities of hot corn bread," which he found to be "almost as good for the digestion as a kneaded pincushion." In 1830 Frances Trollope noted that Americans "eat with the greatest possible rapidity and in total silence," no doubt just hoping to make it through another meal.

Fish and wildlife, plentiful in the early colonies and on the frontier, dwindled with the growth of civilization. The ubiquitous pig replaced these as a popular and important source of food. Requiring no special grazing lands and willing to eat whatever it was fed, or even forage for its own food, a more accommodating, cheap-to-raise animal was hard to find. Four or five pigs might produce enough meat to feed a family through the winter. In addition to meat (often generically referred to as bacon), pigs also provided tallow for candles and lard for cooking. Whether a pig was on the hoof, just slaughtered, or smoked and stored for later use, survival for a farm family might depend on whether they could "save their bacon" from scavengers and marauders, disasters such as fire, and too-quick consumption.

In addition to American eating habits, Europeans also noted that their heavy consumption of spirits completed "the ruin of the nervous system." By all accounts, the consumption of alcoholic beverages in Young America was a family affair. One estimate suggests that at the beginning of the nineteenth century, Americans over the age of fifteen annually drank forty gallons of alcoholic beverages, the vast majority of which were beer and hard cider. In 1839, Frederick Marryat summarized American's drinking habits this way: "I am sure the Americans can fix nothing without a drink. If you meet, you drink; if you part, you drink. . . . If successful in elections, they drink and rejoice; if not, they drink and swear; they begin to drink early in the morning, they leave it off late at night; they commence it early in life, and they continue it, until they soon drop into the grave." Given the American love of spiritous drinks, it usually meant something when someone was identified as a heavy drinker.

Manners at a Yankee hotel in the 1850's

As the nineteenth century progressed, American diet and health began to improve through importation of new foods, emphasis upon the benefits of fruits and vegetables, the work of reformers, the introduction of canning, and improvements in refrigeration.

Although the first recorded shipment of bananas arrived in the United States in 1804, it was not until the 1880s with the advent of refrigerated container ships that they became regular staples. The first shipment of lemons and oranges arrived from Italy in 1832, although it would be years before they were widely available. John Chapman, better known as Johnny Appleseed, began introducing apples to the masses in annual pilgrimages outside New England to plant new trees and to tend previously planted orchards. During this time, Americans learned that tomatoes were not poisonous, as had long been believed, and that a diet of fruits and vegetables could keep someone alive.

Beginning in the 1820s, temperance advocates started preaching about the harmful effects of alcohol. Their pleas to drink water instead were aided by improvements in water systems that made water supplies safer.

William Underwood of Boston and Thomas Kensett of New York began commercially canning food in 1820, two years after the process for sealing perishable foods in tin cans was introduced in the United States. By the 1840s, canned goods were being manufactured on a large scale. At the same time, improvements in the cutting and storing of ice made that precious commodity cheaper, while improvements in the designs of ice houses and iceboxes allowed for greater use of refrigeration. In 1827, only 1,900 tons of ice was shipped from Boston, a figure that climbed to more than 43,000 tons by 1848. In 1838, one newspaper proclaimed that newly improved iceboxes were as much a household necessity as a dining table. Iceboxes, however, remained a luxury out of the reach of most Americans, particularly on the frontier.

Such was also the case with a favorite—albeit expensive—treat that took Young America by storm: ice cream. Dolley Madison served it at state dinners and other social events. *Goodey's Lady's Book* proclaimed that "a party without ice cream would be like a breakfast without bread or a dinner without roast." Temperance advocates touted it as the perfect remedy for alcohol-diluted palates. Improvements in the dissemination of ice helped democratize ice cream in the first half of the nineteenth century, as did also the invention of a hand-cranked ice-cream maker in 1846. The popularity of the frozen dessert led Ralph Waldo Emerson to proclaim, "We dare not trust our wit for making our house pleasant to our friends, so we buy ice cream."

HAIL TO THE CHIEF

When Joseph Smith was born in 1805, Thomas Jefferson was in his second term as the third president of the United States. When Joseph died in 1844, John Tyler was the nation's tenth president. During this time, the chief executive was more accessible to the average American than in later generations. For instance, it was tradition for the president to personally greet anyone that showed up at the White House for the annual New Year's Day reception.

Of the eight presidents who served during Joseph's lifetime, two fought in the American Revolution. Four were widowers. Four served two terms.

Thomas Jefferson (1801–1809) was the first president to be inaugurated in Washington, D.C., which became the nation's new capital in 1800. He was the first president to shake hands rather than bow, and the first widower to serve as president, his wife Martha having died in 1782. Citing the precedent set by George Washington, Thomas Jefferson refused to run for a third term as president. James Madison, James Monroe, and Andrew Jackson also followed that example.

Although Jefferson is known for his work on the Declaration of Independence, his successor, James Madison (1809–1817), is frequently referred to as the "Father of the Constitution." Not only were Madison's theories widely embodied in the Constitution, but as a member of the House of Representatives he also introduced and steered passage of the Bill of Rights. In 1812, he persuaded Congress to declare war on Great Britain in response to British aggression on the high seas. Unpopular at home—detractors dubbed the War of 1812 "Mr. Madison's War"—it later came to be viewed as a glorious success and brought forth an upsurge in nationalism, the result of a few notable naval and military victories, climaxed by General Andrew Jackson's triumph at the Battle of New Orleans.

As an eighteen-year-old, James Monroe (1817–1825) crossed the Delaware River with General George Washington on Christmas Eve 1776 to attack Hessian troops stationed at Trenton, New Jersey. The following year, Monroe spent the terrible winter of 1777–1778 with Washington's troops at Valley Forge, Pennsylvania. Ambassador to France during the French Revolution, Monroe led the delegation that negotiated the Louisiana Purchase.

Before becoming president, John Quincy Adams (1825–1829) helped negotiate the Treaty of Ghent that ended the War of 1812. After his presidency, he became the only former president to serve in the United States Congress. Although not a candidate for the House of Representatives, he accepted the will of the people when they elected him in 1830. Nicknamed "Old Man Eloquent," he fought for what he considered to be right. Following the passage of a "gag rule" in 1836 by southern congressmen that automatically tabled slavery petitions, he tirelessly fought until it was repealed in 1844. In 1839, he led the fight to accept the donation of England's James Smithson that resulted in the establishment of

Above: President James Madison, 1751–1836
Right: President James Monroe, 1758–1831

the Smithsonian Institution. In 1841, he successfully argued before the United States Supreme Court for the freedom of slave mutineers who commandeered the Spanish ship *Amistad*. In 1848, at the age of eighty, he collapsed from a stroke on the floor of the House of Representatives and died a short time later.

At the age of thirteen, Andrew Jackson (1829–1837) joined the Continental Army. Following his capture by the British the following year, a British officer ordered Jackson to clean his boots. When the young prisoner refused, the officer struck him with his sword, leaving a permanent scar on Jackson's head. The first president elected by popular vote, Jackson considered himself a direct representative of the American people. Viewed as a man of the people, his election was seen as a triumph of the common man, many of whom gathered to the nation's capital to be part of his 1829 inaugural celebration. So many swarmed the White House that Jackson was forced to escape his new residence to keep from being crushed. A believer in a strong presidency, he vetoed more legislation than his six predecessors combined. As a result, hostile cartoonists portrayed him as "King Andrew I."

Jackson was a widower throughout his eight years in

President John Quincy Adams, 1767–1848

office. His wife, Rachel, died shortly after he was elected president. He blamed her death on the personal attacks leveled against her during the campaign. She was buried in the same white satin gown she was to have worn at his inauguration. When Jackson died eight years after leaving office, he proclaimed on his deathbed, "I expect to see you all in heaven, both white and black."

Martin Van Buren (1837–1841) was the first president born in the United States of America. Previous presidents were born in the American Colonies. Like Jefferson and Jackson, he was a widower when he took office in 1837, his wife having died in 1819.

Defeated in his 1840 reelection bid, Van Buren ran again for president in 1848 as the Free Soil Party candidate. Opposed to expansion of slavery into the western territories, the Free Soil Party was not popular in the south. When Van Buren garnered only nine votes in Virginia, party officials claimed fraud. One Virginian agreed: "Yes, fraud! And we're still looking for that son-of-a-gun who voted nine times!"

The 1840 presidential campaign was memorable for introducing both a new word and a new phrase to the American lexicon. Supporters of Van Buren, who was also known as "Old Kinderhook" or simply "O.K.," approvingly proclaimed that Van Buren was "okay." Soon the designation was being applied to all kinds of individuals and things—if they were okay! Supporters of Van Buren's opponent, William Henry Harrison, pushed a gigantic ball covered with campaign slogans from Kentucky to Baltimore while urging the locals to "keep the ball rolling."

William Henry Harrison (1841) gave the longest inaugural address in history, which likely contributed to his serving the shortest term as president. Refusing to put on a coat and hat, even though it was bitterly cold, the new president caught a cold during his nearly two-hour speech, and the cold developed into pneumonia. Thirty-one days after being sworn in as president, he died. The idea of the log cabin as home to America's heroes grew largely because of Harrison. Although born on a fine Virginia estate, Harrison campaigned for president as a man of the frontier, a "log cabin" candidate of humble origins.

With the death of Harrison, John Tyler (1841–1845) became the first vice-president to ascend to the presidency. As a result, his critics dubbed him "His Accidency." The following year, his wife died. Two years later, he became the first president to marry while in office. He had more children than any other president: fifteen. His first child was five years older than his second wife—and forty-five years older than his youngest child. A strong states' rights advocate, he was the only president to subsequently become a sworn enemy of the United States. He supported his native Virginia in its decision to secede from the Union. A member of the Provisional Congress of the Confederacy, he was elected to the Confederate States House of Representatives in November 1861 but died in January 1862 prior to taking his seat.

In a remarkable coincidence, three of the first five presidents died on the Fourth of July. John Adams, the second president, and Thomas Jefferson both died on the fiftieth anniversary of American Independence in 1826; James Monroe, the fifth president, died five years later in 1831.

President John Tyler, 1790–1862

A SURE CURE

"We were sick every fall, regular," Eliza Garfield, the mother of President James A. Garfield, recalled. Improper diet, absence of proper sanitation, and ignorance of germs contributed to the fragile existence of most Americans in the early nineteenth century. People did not know how diseases were spread, so they could not protect themselves. Tuberculosis and diphtheria were common. Devastating cholera epidemics resulting from contaminated food and water were frequent during the 1830s and 1840s. Germs and improper sanitation further led to numerous women dying in childbirth and the large number of infant deaths. Given conditions, it is not surprising that the average life expectancy of Americans in the early 1800s was less than fifty years.

Someone in Young America who heeded George Washington's advice to let a cold "go as it came" was probably as well off, or even better off, than the person who sought help from doctors or medicines. During the early nineteenth century, the odds were often against the person who sought medical help. Joseph Smith's older brother, Alvin, came down with bilious colic in 1823. The doctor prescribed a heavy dose of calomel, which, according

to Lucy Mack Smith, "lodged in his stomach, and all the powerful medicine which was afterwards prescribed by skillful physicians could not remove it." As was frequently the case, the "cure" proved fatal.

When Joseph Smith in 1841 urged "the Saints to trust in God when sick" and to "live by faith and not by medicine," he was decrying an entirely different medical profession than that of future generations. At mid-century, most states still did not license physicians. Numerous doctors were poorly educated, and a good many medical providers were "quacks," causing Joseph to plead in 1843, "All ye doctors who are fools, not well read, and do not understand the human constitution, stop your practice." Overall, the prestige of the medical profession was low; for many it was a career of last resort. Often the most respected health care provider was the village blacksmith. In addition to other vital services, he regularly pulled the never-ending stream of decayed and ulcerated teeth.

Most health-care providers learned their trade from established practitioners who were willing to mentor. The few doctors who received formal medical training generally did so in Europe. Only

one medical school, established at the University of Pennsylvania, was in existence prior to the American Revolution. By 1840, the United States had twenty-seven medical schools and one college of dentistry.

Even as the number of trained doctors grew, patients still often had more to fear from their doctors than their illnesses. Advocates of scientific medicine were often unsure of what they were doing and frequently embraced useless and dangerous treatments. Benjamin Rush, who established America's first medical school, was an advocate of bleeding and purging to treat illnesses. Doctors still subscribed to the prevailing theory that diseases were the result of an imbalance of the body's basic "humors."

Self-prescribed patent medicines were also common during this time. Among the complaints that "Hamilton's Essense and Extract of Mustard" promised to relieve were rheumatism, gout, palsy, swelling, and numbness. The recommended dose for "Robertson's Infallible Worm Destroying Lozenges" was one lozenge for humans, two for horses. In 1838, "quack remedies" dominated the advertising space of the New York *Herald* and Boston *Transcript*. Of the 130 inches of advertising in one day's *Herald,* 54 inches were devoted to these "cures," as were 134 of the 224 inches in the *Transcript.*

Most home remedies were harmless, but others were lethal. A cure for worms in children warned, "Take sage, boil it with milk to a good tea, turn it to whey with alum or vinegar, and give the whey to the child, if the worms are not knotted in the stomach, it will be a sure cure. If the worms are knotted in the stomach, it will kill the child."

Surgery, which was in its infancy during the first half of the nineteenth century, was often fatal and always painful. Performed with little regard for basic cleanliness, not to mention sterile conditions, the surgical procedure was frequently carried out with the patient tied down and plied with the standard anesthetic of the day—alcohol. Those unwilling to face both a hangover and post-operative pain, or who did not have access to this anesthetic, found other ways to make it through the operation, such as biting down on something. Soldiers frequently had no choice but to "bite the bullet" and endure the painful procedure.

Not all was negative during this time, however. Medical treatments and knowledge began to improve and progress during the first fifty years of the nineteenth century. On Christmas Day, 1809, Ephraim McDowell of Kentucky successfully saved the life of Jane Crawford when he performed the first ovariotomy and removed a twenty-two-pound ovarian tumor. The patient sang hymns during the operation to take her mind off the pain. Four years later in 1813, the leg of seven-year-old Joseph Smith became seriously infected through typhoid fever. A team of doctors from Dartmouth Medical College under the direction of the school's founder, Dr. Nathan Smith, removed the diseased bone. Hardly the inept, backwoods, "barbershop surgeon" that some have portrayed him, Dr. Smith may have been the only physician in the United States skilled in performing this operation.

Much of our knowledge about the digestive system was discovered during the 1820s by William Beaumont, a frontier army doctor. After Alexis St. Martin was accidentally shot in 1822, Beaumont treated the wound as best he could, but it never completely healed. Through the two-inch hole that remained in St. Martin's stomach, Beaumont began a ten-year study of the digestive system. Ninety percent of his observations are still valid.

Several American doctors and dentists, working independently of each other in the 1840s, successfully employed laughing gas and ether as anesthetics. Prior to this time, itinerant performers frequently toured America demonstrating the entertaining effects that "laughing gas" produced on humans. Following one such demonstration, Crawford Long, a rural Georgia physician, used ether, which produced similar results to nitrous oxide, and in March 1842 he removed a tumor from the neck of a patient in the first known surgery using modern anesthetics. That same year William E. Clarke, a medical student, administered ether so that Dr. Elijah Pope at Rochester, N.Y., could painlessly extract a tooth.

The following year, 1843, Oliver Wendell Holmes published a paper suggesting that diseases could be transmitted from one person to another. His theory was widely ridiculed by the medical profession. Four years later, Hungarian physician Philip Semmelweis concluded that puerperal fever (also known as "childbed fever") was contagious and that its occurrence could be drastically reduced by hand-washing. His further research into the matter did not produce widespread acceptance on the part of his contemporaries. Although failing to convince fellow doctors, his findings about the relationship between germs and disease were eventually vindicated and contributed to a reduction in disease and death.

23 DECEMBER 1805

On 1 December 1805, William Clark, co-leader of the Corps of Discovery, took the time to pen his thoughts about the "tempestous and horiable" sight he witnessed as he stood on the northwest coast of the American wilderness. On viewing the "great western" ocean, he was awestruck by "the emence Seas and waves.

". . . this roaring has continued ever Since our arrival in the neighborhood of the Sea Coast which has been 24 days Since we arrived in Sight of the Great Western; (for I cannot Say Pacific) Ocian as I have not Seen one pacific day Since my arrival in its vicinity, and its waters are forming and petially [perpetually] breake with emenc waves on the Sands and rockey coasts."

Two days later he recorded, "I marked my name on a large pine tree imediately on the isthmus William Clark December 3rd 1805. By Land from the U. States in 1804 & 1805."

Indeed, this was the western culmination of more than eighteen months and four thousand miles of wilderness exploration that began on 14 May 1804 as the fifty-one men of the United States Corps of Discovery started up the Missouri River in a fifty-five-foot keelboat and two dugout canoes. President Thomas Jefferson directed co-leaders Meriwether Lewis and William Clark to carefully and "with great pains and accuracy" observe, collect specimens, and record anthropological, scientific, and geological information in the territories of the acquired Louisiana Purchase.

As the month of December 1805 progressed, the Corps was a flurry of action as hunters left each day before light and men cut trees, split logs, and constructed huts that would form Fort Clatsop, their winter home. Constantly rainy, windy weather along with bad health slowed work, but by 23 December Lewis and Clark were able to move into their unfinished hut. Two days later, on Christmas day, other members moved into their huts. Corps member Patrick Gass recorded, "Another cloudy wet day.—This morning we left our camp and moved into our huts. At daybreak all the men paraded and fired a round of small arms, wishing the Commanding Officers a merry Christmas." Here they wintered until the end of March 1806, when they began their journey back east.

A continent away, on the same day that Lewis and Clark moved into their rough hut, in a log farmhouse deep within the bleak midwinter Vermont landscape, Lucy Mack Smith gave birth to a son, her fourth child. Lucy later wrote, simply and succinctly, "We had a son whom we called Joseph after the name of his father; he was born December 23, 1805." Country doctor Joseph Adam Denison is purported to have aided in the delivery. Years later, in the account book in which he recorded the birth of a son in the Smith family, Dr. Denison hatefully noted, "If I had known how he was going to turn out I'd have smothered the little cuss."

The thirty-four-year-old father and twenty-nine-year-old mother had begun their 1796 marriage in a hopeful economic condition, but financial setbacks caused the unprofitable sale of their farm in 1803. Now, on "Dairy Hill" in Sharon Vermont, the hardworking couple farmed the poor soil of land rented from Solomon Mack—Lucy's father. To bring in much-needed income, Joseph Sr. also taught school during the winter months. "In this way . . . our circumstances gradually improved," Lucy wrote.

Situated as they were on an isolated farm, it is not known how much the young couple learned of the

Midwinter Vermont, 1908

whirl of change taking place in the nation and in the world—cultural, political, religious, economic, and scientific. Thomas Jefferson, now in the second term of his presidency, was moving the United States into the future by claiming and "opening the west" through the explorations of Lewis and Clark. To further the United States' western interests, Lieutenant Zebulon M. Pike was commissioned earlier in 1805 to lead a twenty-man expedition to find the source of the Mississippi River. Prior to the 1803 Louisiana Purchase, the Mississippi was the nation's western boundary, but now it was entirely within the confines of the United States. During a two-thousand-mile round trip over land and on river from St. Louis, Pike's company mistakenly deemed Leech Lake in north central Minnesota as the source of the mighty Mississippi River. It was not until 1832 that Henry R. Schoolcraft's well-equipped party penetrated the north woods wilderness and, guided by an Ojibwa Indian, located the actual source of the Mississippi River—a lake they christened Itasca, taken from the Latin *Veritas Caput*, meaning "true source."

Young America was gaining a sense of itself in other ways, as evidenced by Mercy Otis Warren's overtly patriotic three-volume history titled *Rise, Progress, and Termination of the American Revolution*, which became an instant best-seller in 1805. Another patriotic history popular at the time showed that as the nation progressed, its heroes also grew in mythic proportions. In 1800, Mason Locke Weems, better known as Parson Weems, published a popular biography of George Washington—an account so embellished that it fell just short of being fiction.

When the fifth edition appeared in 1806, it included a new story, again the product of Weems's pen, not of Washington's life. According to Weems, six-year-old George cut down his father's cherry tree and then, when asked about it, could not tell a lie, much to his father's delight. "If the tale isn't true, it should be," one historian has proclaimed. "It is too pretty to be classified with the myths." It was not enough that Washington led the Continental army, presided over the Constitutional Convention, and served as the first president of the United States out of an overriding sacrificial sense of duty. In some ways the cherry tree story revealed more about America's view of morality than the man himself. America's heroes could not just be blessed by a divine being; they also had to possess qualities that neared divinity. Piety, truthfulness, and selflessness were traits Americans cherished in the early 1800s, and Weems's Washington embodied what people wanted to believe.

Another example of American pride evidenced in 1805 continues to shine today. American artist Charles Wilson Peale founded the still-functioning Pennsylvania Academy of Fine Art in an effort to foster and collect American art.

In Europe, the Napoleonic Wars continued as Napoleon was crowned King of Italy, overpowered Austro-Russian forces, and disrupted American commercial shipping on the high seas. The British fleet under Admiral Lord Horatio Nelson's command smashed the combined Spanish-French fleet at Trafalgar in October 1805. Nelson lost his life in the battle, but his victory stemmed the threat of a French invasion of England and ensured British supremacy on the high seas. It would be another ten years, however, until the Duke of Wellington and Prussian Marshal Gebhard von Blucher brought final defeat to Napoleon at Waterloo.

To the south of Europe in Africa, modern Egypt was established with the rise of Albanian-born Mehemet Ali to pasha (governor). To the west of Egypt, the United States was engaged in a battle against the Barbary state of Tripoli. Pirates of the Barbary states of Morocco, Algiers, Tripoli, and Tunis for years preyed upon Mediterranean Sea traffic, looting and shanghaiing the seamen of those nations who refused to pay tribute. Most countries, including the United States, found it cheaper to buy protection than go to war with the pirates. When Tripoli demanded more money in May 1801, Thomas Jefferson refused, and Tripoli declared war on the United States. In the spring of 1805, the United States achieved a major victory when U.S. Marines captured the Tripolian port city of Derna. Later that summer, a treaty was signed giving the American Navy the right to sail the Mediterranean Sea unmolested by Tripolian pirates. However, the United States continued to pay tribute to the other three

Barbary states until 1815. This victory was later immortalized in the first line of the official Marine Corps song, "From the Halls of Montezuma to the Shores of Tripoli."

Back in New England in 1805, Boston merchant Frederick Tudor began exporting what would become a lucrative trade commodity—ice. His first significant boatload of New England ice sent to the Caribbean island of Martinique was less than successful, as he lost $4,500. A later shipment was more successful, although it would take until 1820 for the ice-exporting industry to fully show its potential. Using ice as ballast on outbound trading vessels, merchants found a ready market in the Caribbean and the Far East in exchange for products to be sold in the United States.

However, deep in the New England farm country, the birth of a boy caught the attention of only a handful of people. As Lucy Smith lovingly gazed upon the newborn baby cradled in her arms, neither she nor her husband could have imagined the immense impact this innocent new arrival would have on the future of religion in America and the world. No family member could anticipate the heights of joy and the depths of tragedy the next thirty-eight years would bring as this boy grew into a man who selflessly fulfilled his prophetic mission to restore the word and will of God to His people. But on that cold, dark night of 23 December 1805, the warm glow of happiness reigned in the Smith household.

Vermont, 1907

"A REMARKABLY QUIET, WELL-DISPOSED SON"

Joseph Smith Jr. was born 23 December 1805, in a rented log farmhouse located on several acres of hardscrabble Vermont farm land owned by his maternal grandfather, Solomon Mack. He was the fourth child of Joseph and Lucy Mack Smith, who would raise nine children to adulthood.

Joseph's paternal and maternal ancestors were old New England stock, both sides having arrived in America during the seventeenth century. In 1638, the Smiths left England to settle at Topsfield, Massachusetts, eventually moving

Map of Vermont, 1795

to New Hampshire and then Vermont. The Macks, from Scotland, arrived in Lyme, Connecticut, in 1682. Like the Smith family, the Mack generations also made their way to Vermont. In Vermont, Joseph Smith Sr., son of Asael and Mary Duty Smith, met Lucy Mack, daughter of Solomon and Lydia Gate Mack. The couple married in 1796.

Born into a family of farmers, Joseph Smith Jr. learned the arduous responsibilities of farming and the tenuous nature of frontier family economics. Despite hard work and good habits, his parents were continuously in the grip of poverty. Lucy and Joseph Sr. began their life together in a relatively positive financial situation—from the Macks, a gift of $1,000 for a cash reserve; from the Smiths, part ownership of a "hand-some" farm. Unfortunately, a bad investment coupled with a dishonest partner in the speculative ginseng market forced the Smiths to sell their farm and use their cash reserve to settle the heavy debts.

Propertyless, they found themselves in circumstances typical of New England tenant farmers who were dependent on the whims of landowners as well as at the mercy of marginal soil and the predictably unreliable weather. Thus, Joseph's childhood was dominated by his family's search for financial security and prosperity—seeking to provide for their children while at the same time hoping to give their children a head start as they moved into adult years, and to prepare for the parents' senior years of infirmity and diminishing productivity. In this effort, the enterprising Joseph Sr. relocated his growing family onto and off of several tenant farms between the years 1805 and 1816. From Vermont, the Smiths moved in 1811 to Lebanon, New Hampshire, and then back to Vermont in 1814. Crop failures continued to haunt their efforts. In 1816, the Smith family moved to Palmyra, New York, relocating two years after that to nearby Manchester. The family's financial dream pointed their efforts to the goal of once again owning land and thereby creating more control over their future.

A TOKEN OF PEACE

One of the best known individuals serving with the Lewis and Clark Expedition was not an official member of the Corps of Discovery. Although seemingly an afterthought, the decision to add Sacagawea to the Corps was an important one. Without the young mother and former Indian slave, the expedition might not have reached the Pacific Ocean.

Sacagawea, a Shoshone Indian, was born in what is now Idaho. Captured in a raid on her village by the Hidatsa Indians when she was about ten years old, she was eventually sold to Toussaint Charbonneau, a French trapper and trader, who made her his wife.

When the expedition spent the winter of 1804–1805 at Fort Mandan in the Dakotas, Charbonneau was hired as an interpreter. He was encouraged to bring along his approximately sixteen-year-old wife. As William Clark noted in his journal, her inclusion was initially symbolic: "A woman with a party of men is a token of peace." Having a woman along was a sign to other Indians that this was not a war party.

In mid-February 1805, Sacagawea gave birth to her first child, Jean Baptiste Charbonneau, at Fort Mandan, with Meriwether Lewis serving as midwife. When the expedition left its winter camp in early April 1805, Sacagawea, with Jean Baptiste strapped on her back, was among its number. The following month, she earned the praise of the company's leaders. After the canoe she was in keeled over in a sudden squall, Sacagawea calmly retrieved the valuable journals, maps, medicine, and instruments that floated from the boat while the men righted the vessel. Clark, who helplessly watched the scene from shore, wrote that night, "Had the [canoe] been lost, I should have valued my life but little."

As the Corps of Discovery continued west, they had to abandon the rivers and travel overland. In August 1805, Sacagawea led the exploring party to her home village. During her reunion with her tribe, the expedition was able to obtain the horses they badly needed to continue their journey. She also helped by identifying edible plants, roots, berries, and nuts.

Her uncomplaining cheerfulness helped buoy up the company. However, she made one demand. As the company wintered in 1805 on the Columbia River, they learned that a whale was beached about thirty-five miles away. She thought it "very hard" that she had come that far and could not see the big fish. Clark arranged for a visit.

After returning to her home at Fort Mandan in the summer of 1806, she and her husband later moved near St. Louis, where Clark was serving as the Indian agent of the Louisiana Purchase. While it is known that Charbonneau returned to the Dakotas in 1811, the fate of Sacagawea is less certain. One source indicates that she died at Fort Mandan of "a putrid fever" in 1812, leaving behind both her son and "a fine infant girl." Shoshone tradition maintains that she wandered the West before returning to her village, dying on the Wind River Reservation in 1884, a venerated and influential member of the tribe.

Clark wrote of Sacagawea, "Intelligent, cheerful, resourceful, tireless, faithful, she inspired us all." He further noted that she "diserved a greater reward for her attention and services on that rout than we had in our power to give her." While the honors did not come in her life, more statues have been erected to Sacagawea than to any other woman in American history. In 2000, her contribution to the nation was further recognized by a commemorative United States coin.

Concerning young Joseph, Lucy later noted in a history of her son, "As nothing occurred during his early life except those trivial circumstances which are common to that state of human existence, I pass them in silence." That would change, however, while the family resided in New Hampshire, as young Joseph had an experience that left a permanent impression on all his family members. Lucy recalled that after arriving at Lebanon, "We settled down and began to congratulate ourselves upon our prosperity and also to renew our exertions to obtain a great abundance of the world's goods. We looked around us and said, What do we now lack? There is nothing of which we have not a sufficiency to make us and our children perfectly comfortable, both for food and raiment, as well as that which is necessary to a respectable appearance in society both at home and abroad." Disappointingly, "the scene soon changed."

During the winter of 1812–1813, a typhoid fever epidemic swept the Upper Connecticut Valley region of New Hampshire and Vermont, leaving thousands dead. Each of the Smith children suffered and recov-

Joseph Smith was born into a young, largely rural and frontier America

ered; fortunately, none died. Seven-year-old Joseph's bout was particularly harrowing, and at one time the family feared for his life. Lucy recorded her memory of those emotionally and physically exhausting days and nights: "Joseph, our third son, having recovered from the typhus fever after something like two weeks sickness, one day screamed out . . . with a pain in his shoulder, and, in a very short time he appeared to be in such agony that we feared the consequence would prove to be something very serious." Joseph later wrote, "The doctor broke the fever, after which it settled under my shoulder, and Dr. Parker called it a sprained shoulder and anointed it with bone ointment, and freely applied the hot shovel, when it proved to be a swelling under the arm, which was opened, and discharged freely; after which the disease removed and descended into my left leg and ankle and terminated in a fever sore of the worst kind." Lucy recounted that when the doctor lanced the sore, "it discharged fully a quart of matter. As soon as the sore had discharged itself the pain shot like lightning . . . down his side into the marrow of the bone of his leg. . . . My poor boy, at this, was almost in despair, and he cried out 'Oh father the pain is so severe, how can I bear it!' His leg began to swell and he continued to suffer the greatest agony for the space of two weeks longer."

New York City, 1797
Although Young America was largely rural, its urban centers were growing

Dr. Nathan Smith

Older brother Hyrum, whom Lucy described as "always remarkable for his tenderness and sympathy," sought to relieve his parents' burdens. "As he was a good, trusty boy, we let him do so," Lucy recalled. "We laid Joseph upon a low bed, and Hyrum sat beside him, almost incessantly day and night, grasping the most painful part of the affected leg between his hands and, by pressing it closely, enabled the little sufferer the better to bear the pain which otherwise seemed almost ready to take his life."

After three weeks, the Smiths called upon the services of Dr. Stone of nearby Dartmouth Medical College, who cut an eight-inch incision between the knee and ankle of the left leg. Pus was drained, relieving the swelling and pain. The infection next entered the bone, and the same procedure was repeated as the leg again swelled, and the pain became unbearable. Following this, Dr. Nathan Smith, founder of Dartmouth's Medical College, arrived with a "counsel of surgeons," no doubt students of the college. Joseph recalled, "At one time eleven doctors came from Dartmouth Medical College, at Hanover, New Hampshire, for the purpose of amputation, but, young as I was, I utterly refused to give my assent to the operation, but I consented to their trying an experiment by

1805

Joseph Smith Jr. was born at Sharon, Vermont

Thomas Jefferson began his second term as U.S. president

Sacagawea gave birth to a son prior to joining the Lewis and Clark expedition

British naval forces defeated a combined Franco-Spanish fleet in the Battle of Trafalgar

British artillery officer William Congreve invented the rocket immortalized in "The Star-Spangled Banner"

Ottoman governor Muhammad Ali seized power in Egypt; beginnings of Egypt as a modern nation

1806

William Colgate opened a candle and soap factory, the forerunner of Colgate-Palmolive

Scottish merchant Patrick Clark developed cotton thread strong enough to replace silk and linen threads

Andrew Jackson killed Charles Dickinson in a duel

Noah Webster published his *Compendious Dictionary of the English Language*

The Virginia legislature passed a law requiring free blacks to leave the state

French sculptor Claude Clodion designed the Arc de Triomphe in Paris

THE HOUSE OF THE PIONEER

In 1831 and 1832, Frenchman Alexis de Tocqueville journeyed through America, recording his observations and experiences, which he published in his masterful *Democracy in America*. The following description of a visit to a frontier New England log home, where he spent the night, is recorded in his journal:

"The bell which the pioneers hang round the necks of their cattle, in order to find them again in the woods, announced from afar our approach to a clearing; and we soon afterwards heard the stroke of the axe, hewing down the trees of the forest. As we came nearer, traces of destruction marked the presence of civilized man: the road was strewn with cut boughs; trunks of trees, half consumed by fire, or mutilated by the axe, were still standing in our way. . . .

"Beyond this field . . . we suddenly came upon the cabin of its owner, situated in the center of a plot of ground more carefully cultivated than the rest, but where man was still waging unequal warfare with the forest. There the trees were cut down, but not uprooted, and the trunks still encumbered the ground. . . . Amid this . . . stands the house of the pioneer, or, as they call it, the *log house*. . . . This rustic dwelling bore marks of recent and hasty labor; its length seemed not to exceed thirty feet, its height fifteen; the walls as well as the roof were formed of rough trunks of trees between which a little moss and clay had been inserted to keep out the cold and rain.

"As night was coming on, we determined to ask the master of the log house for a lodging. . . . We entered the log house: the inside is quite unlike that of the cottages of the peasantry of Europe; it contains more that is superfluous, less that is necessary. A single window with a muslin curtain; on a hearth of trodden

"My Early Home"

clay an immense fire, which lights the whole interior; above the hearth, a good rifle, a deerskin, and plumes of eagles' feathers; on the right hand of the chimney, a map of the United States, raised and shaken by the wind through the crannies in the wall; near the map, on a shelf formed of a roughly hewn plank, a few volumes of books: a Bible, the first six books of Milton, and two of Shakespeare's plays; along the wall, trunks instead of closets; in the center of the room, a rude table, with legs of green wood with the bark still on them, looking as if they grew out of the ground on which they stood; but on this table a teapot of British china, silver spoons, cracked teacups, and some newspapers.

"The master of this dwelling has the angular features and lank limbs peculiar to the native of New England. . . . He belongs to that restless, calculating, and adventurous race of men who . . . endure the life of savages for a time in order to conquer and civilize the backwoods. . . . By the side of the hearth sits a woman with a baby on her lap; she nods to us without disturbing herself. Like the pioneer, this woman is in the prime of life; her appearance seems superior to her condition, and her apparel even betrays a lingering taste for dress; but her delicate limbs appear shrunken, her features are drawn in, her eye is mild and melancholy; her whole physiognomy bears marks of religious resignation. . . .

"The house . . . has no internal partition or loft. In the one chamber of which it consists the whole family gathered for the night. The dwelling is itself a little world, an ark of civilization amid an ocean of foliage: a hundred steps beyond it the primeval forest spreads its shade, and solitude resumes its sway."

Lucy Mack
Smith,
ca. 1845

removing a large portion of the bone from my left leg, which they did, and fourteen additional pieces of bone afterwards worked out before my leg healed."

Dr. Smith carried out a pioneering procedure in which he cut into the bone, chipping away and removing the infected region. This operation would become standard procedure during the twentieth century but was relatively unknown at the time. Joseph endured the operation without being tied down or anesthetized. In his father's strong, loving arms, he screamed as the surgeon chipped away, blood running from the incisions. Sweating profusely, he lay exhausted on the blood-soaked bed, "pale as a corpse . . . whilst upon every feature was depicted the utmost agony." Hardly the inept, backwoods, "barbershop surgeon" that some have portrayed, Dr. Smith may have been the only physician in the United States who would operate instead of amputating.

Three months of constant pain and suffering was now near an end as Joseph's leg finally began to heal. His rehabilitation required the use of crutches for three years, from age seven until ten. The ordeal left him with a slight lifelong limp, but he retained the use of his leg.

After Joseph gained sufficient strength, he was sent to live with his uncle in Salem, Massachusetts, in 1814, in hopes that the sea air would aid his recovery.

It is not known if Joseph ever met one of Dr. Smith's Salem patients who was near him in age. Nathaniel Hawthorne, who would gain renown as an American author, was crippled for nearly a year after injuring his foot, until Dr. Smith's care eased his distress shortly after Joseph's surgery.

A year of family illness and the resulting medical bills wreaked havoc on the already weak and fragile Smith financial situation, setting them on the edge of an abyss of total privation. The family moved back to Vermont to rent, yet again, another farm. There, they made do by working the farm, hiring out to other farmers, peddling goods from door to door, working odd jobs in nearby Norwich, and selling fruit from their orchard. Two years of crop failures were followed by the "year without a summer." New Englanders planted crops twice in 1816, only to have them fail twice because of untimely frost and snow. Lucy succinctly stated that the situation prompted the family to act upon a long-discussed plan—moving to New York.

In late summer 1816, Joseph Smith Sr., continuing his herculean effort to propel his family out of poverty, moved three hundred miles from Norwich to Palmyra, New York. He went ahead to their new home while his family remained in Vermont to prepare for the move. He soon sent for them to join him.

1807

Seth Thomas and Eli Terry began producing clocks using interchangeable parts; timepieces were now available to the masses

Robert Fulton's paddle steamer Clermont successfully navigated the Hudson River from New York City to Albany

William Wordsworth's "Ode on Intimations of Immortality" was published; "Our birth is but a sleep and a forgetting," proclaimed the first line of one stanza

Robert E. Lee, confederate general, was born

1808

The Joseph Smith Sr. family was living in Tunbridge, Vermont; they moved there sometime between January 1806 and March 1808

Congress outlawed African Slave Trade at the urging of President Thomas Jefferson; later, Congress branded slave smugglers as "pirates," making them eligible for the death penalty

Ludwig van Beethoven debuted his Symphonies No. 5 and No. 6.

The French army under Napoleon occupied Madrid, Spain; Francisco Goya painted "Execution of the Third of May"

John Taylor, third president of The Church of Jesus Christ of Latter-day Saints and survivor of the martyrdom, was born

Joseph Sr. hired Caleb Howard to guide Lucy and the children on the long overland trip to Palmyra. The journey turned into a horrific experience, as Howard turned out to be, in Lucy's words, "an unprincipled and unfeeling wretch, by the way in which he handled both our goods and money, as well as by his treatment of my children, especially Joseph." Cold weather and snow made the trip particularly difficult. As the Smiths made their way westward, they joined forces with a family named Gates. What the two families hoped would be a positive joining of forces soon proved troublesome. Howard, taking a liking to the Gates's daughters, made room for the girls by physically forcing the still weak and lame Joseph out of the sleigh. Limping along, Joseph made his way on foot in a "weak state through the snow," during which time, he later recalled, "I suffered the most excruciating weariness and pain." Hyrum's and Alvin's efforts to protect Joseph were greeted with the butt of Mr. Howard's whip.

An already tempestuous situation was made worse as Howard spent the family's money on drinking and gambling. When the money ran out, some one hundred miles short of Palmyra, Howard dumped the Smith's possessions into the streets of Utica. Before he could leave with their team and wagon, the resolutely determined Lucy publicly confronted their now former guide, took the reins, and told Howard she would now take affairs into her own hands and he could make the rest of the journey as he pleased. He left them as they headed west to their future.

Frontier family on the way to church services, ca. 1820

1809

Abraham Lincoln, 16th U.S. president, was born in Hodgenville, Kentucky, the first president born outside the boundaries of the original thirteen United States

James Madison was sworn in as fourth U.S. president

Joseph Bramah patented the fountain pen using a nib of cut goose quill; previously the entire quill was used

Napoleon arrested Pope Pius VII after he issued an edict ordering "despoilers" of the Catholic Church to be excommunicated, a less-than-subtle reference to Napoleon

1810

The Joseph Smith Sr. family was residing in Royalton, Vermont; they moved there sometime between April 1808 and March 1810

The U.S. claimed possession of West Florida, the gulf-coast region of present-day Mississippi and Alabama

The U.S. population was 7,239,881, an increase of 5,297,000 from the 1800 census

King Kamehameha the Great unified the Hawaiian Islands

Frenchman Nicolas Appert published the results of his food-preservation experiments in *The Art of Preserving All Kinds of Animal and Vegetable Substances for Many Years;* in 1812 he opened the first commercial canning factory

Ornithologist Alexander Wilson estimated a flock of passenger pigeons at 2 billion birds; the passenger pigeon became extinct in 1914

Scottish physicist John Leslie created ice artificially using an air pump to freeze water

German inventor Rudolph Ackerman developed a differential gear that allowed carriages to turn sharp corners; it was later employed in "horseless carriages"

The Congregationalist Church established the American Board of Commissioners for Foreign Missions, the nation's first missionary society

ASSUMING A NATIONAL CHARACTER

"Our honor requires us to have a system of our own, in language as well as government," proclaimed Noah Webster shortly after the American Revolution. "America is an independent empire, and ought to assume a national character. Nothing can be more ridiculous, than a servile imitation of the manners, the language, and the vices of foreigners," he declared.

The creation of an American language, distinct from British English, began almost as soon as the first settlers landed in North America. Encountering new plants and animals, these settlers also came in contact with a completely foreign culture in the American Indians. Indian words such as "hickory," "moose," and "squash" soon became American English. So too

Noah Webster (1758–1843)

did words borrowed from other new-world settlers who spoke Spanish, French, Dutch, and German. Although this distinctly American lexicon became a source of national pride comparable to other unique aspects of America, borrowing from other languages turned American English into a virtual quagmire that became the subject of anti-American satires in the British press.

In 1783, Webster published the *American Spelling Book,* which attempted to remedy the situation by codifying American English. It became a bestseller second only to the Bible. Providing standardized spellings for many of the words in the American ver-nacular, it created a distinction between American and British English by offering American spellings: "Plough" became "plow"; "honour" became "honor"; "theatre" became "theater"; and "waggon" became "wagon." He also tried to simplify spellings, but not all of his suggestions caught on, as was the case with "grotesk" (grotesque), "tung" (tongue), and "laf" (laugh).

In 1806, Webster published *A Compendious Dictionary of the English Language,* which contained five thousand words not included in any British work. The volume was a compromise with his earlier calls for the creation of a unique American language and instead focused further on a standardized American English.

After more than twenty years of additional labor, Webster published his monumental two-volume *American Dictionary of the English Language* in 1828. This dictionary had seventy thousand entries, of which twelve thousand words were unique to American English.

By the time he died in 1843, Webster was synony-mous with the dictionary.

"MY BELOVED
BROTHER HYRUM"

Hyrum Smith (1800–1844) was a devoted friend and trusted counselor to his brother Joseph. He was one of the Eight Witnesses to the Book of Mormon, a founding member of the Church, a missionary, assistant president of the Church, associate president of the Church, and Church Patriarch. Speaking of their close relationship, Joseph declared, "I could pray in my heart that all my brethren were like unto my beloved brother Hyrum, for truly he possesses the mildness of a Lamb, and the integrity of a Job; and in short the meek and quiet spirit, of Jesus Christ; and I love him with that love, that is stronger than death, for I never had occasion to rebuke him, nor he me."

Hyrum, remarking on his close relationship with his brother, observed that he had been well acquainted with Joseph "ever since he was born, which was thirty seven years December last [1842], and I have not been absent from him at any one time, not even the space of six months since his birth, to my recollection, and have been intimately acquainted with all his sayings, doings, business transactions and movements, as much as any man could be acquainted with another man's business up to the present time." Sharing his testimony of Joseph's divine mission, Hyrum declared, "There were prophets before but Joseph has the spirit and power of all the prophets."

Together, brothers Joseph and Hyrum were martyred at Carthage Jail on 27 June 1844; "in life they were not divided, and in death they were not separated."

John Taylor, an associate and Apostle, wrote that if "ever there was an exemplary, honest, and virtuous man, an embodiment of all that is noble in the human form, Hyrum Smith was its representative."

Hyrum and his first wife, Jerusha, were the parents of four daughters and two sons. After her death, he married Mary Fielding in 1837, with whom he fathered a son and a daughter. His son Joseph F. Smith was the president of the Church from 1901 until his death in 1918.

"A View of the Whale Fishery"

A NANTUCKET SLEIGH RIDE

At any given time during the first half of the nineteenth century, hundreds of vessels were plying the open waters of the Atlantic and Pacific oceans hunting whales. Whale oil, a primary source of light in Young America, was in great demand. At mid-century, shortly before the demand for whale oil declined, nearly seven hundred whaling ships were in operation.

When a whale was spotted, the watchman gave the traditional cry of "Thar she blows!" A small "whale boat" holding six men was then dispatched to harpoon the prey. A rope connected the whale boat to the harpoon, and once a whale was harpooned, several potentially dangerous scenarios might follow. If the whale dove too deep, the whale boat would be capsized. If the whale turned and attacked, it could easily destroy the small craft. If the whale chose to run, it would fly over and through the water, dragging the boat behind it. The whalers described this experience as being taken on a "Nantucket Sleigh Ride," something that would make amusement-park rides seem relatively tame.

In addition to providing oil for lamps, whale oil was used as a lubricant, while the wax from the head was used for candles. Whalebones were also used to make hoopskirts, corset stays, buggy whips, and umbrella ribs. When oil was discovered in Pennsylvania in 1859, it marked the beginning of the end for the once-essential whaling industry.

1811

General William Henry Harrison defeated an Indian confederacy at Tippecanoe, Indiana; exaggerated into a "great victory," it was the basis for Harrison's military reputation and later political triumphs

The steamer *New Orleans* became the first to ply western waters; owner Nicholas Roosevelt, his wife, and a son born during the journey were the only passengers on the 700-mile voyage from Pittsburgh to New Orleans because no others would risk the trip

Work began on the Great National Road; initially connecting Cumberland, Maryland, with Wheeling, Virginia, it reached its western terminus of Vandalia, Illinois, in 1840

1812

The Joseph Smith Sr. family was residing at Lebanon, New Hampshire

Louisiana became the 18th U.S. state

Napoleon invaded Russia; although he briefly occupied Moscow, his decimated troops were forced to retreat through a Russian winter

The U.S. declared war on Great Britain after enduring years of trade restrictions growing out of the Napoleonic wars

Lucy Brewer, disguised as a man and using the name Nicolas Baker, began her three-year service on the U.S.S. *Constitution* ("Old Ironsides")

The "Clipper" ship was introduced by U.S. shipbuilders; its revolutionary design made it one of the fastest ships afloat

The waltz was introduced into English ballrooms; many considered it disgusting and immoral; by 1813 the waltz had conquered other European ballrooms

Brothers Jakob and Wilhelm Grimm published the first volume of their fairy tales

Massachusetts governor Elbridge Gerry signed a political redistricting bill, resulting in "Gerrymandering"

The President's House in "the city of Washington after the conflagration of 24 August 1814"

THE WHITE HOUSE

When the President's House was rebuilt following the burning of Washington, D.C., by the British in August 1814, the exterior was again whitewashed—this time to cover the scorch marks. After its reopening in 1818, people filled with pride at the resiliency of this symbol of the presidency increasingly referred to the building as the "White House," although it continued to be officially known as the Executive Mansion or the President's House. In 1902, President Theodore Roosevelt made the name official by having "The White House" printed on correspondence and other papers.

WHAT TIME IS IT?

When it came to setting the clock in Young America, it was every town for itself. Whether called "God's time" or "sun time," noon was the moment the sun reached its zenith. Thus, when it was noon in New York City, it was only 11:55 A.M. in Philadelphia. Although the nation's numerous "time zones" caused relatively few problems in the horse and carriage era, such was not the case with the advent of inter-city railroads. Imprecision led to chaos, even collisions. Finally, in 1883, the railroad executives persuaded government officials to synchronize the nation's watches by establishing four time zones. Dissenters vowed to continue to live on "God's time, not Vanderbilt's," but the benefits of the new system were apparent.

"When I again met my husband at Palmyra," Lucy recalled, "we were much reduced—not from indolence, but on account of many reverses of fortune, with which our lives had been singularly marked." They had two cents and only a small portion of their effects.

Palmyra was a growing frontier log-cabin village with several hundred inhabitants, all of whom hoped their town would soon be a spur of the new Erie Canal—which would bring further financial benefits. Soon after their arrival, the family "sat down, and counselled together relative to the course which was best of us to adopt in our destitute circumstances, and we came to the conclusion to unite our energies in endeavoring to obtain a piece of land." Joseph Sr., along with sons Alvin and Hyrum, hired out as laborers, farmed, dug wells, hunted, trapped, fished, tapped maple trees for syrup, and took any odd job available. Family members pitched in with a variety of endeavors—baking, making handicrafts, peddling goods and vegetables, and selling breads, cakes, eggs, and root beers out of their log home.

In a little more than "two years from the time we entered Palmyra strangers and destitute of friends, home, or employment, we were able to settle ourselves upon our own land in a snug comfortable

Evolution of a pioneer settlement

1813

Typhoid fever swept the upper Connecticut River Valley; Joseph Smith had to have portions of his leg bone removed after contracting the disease

Jane Austen published *Pride and Prejudice*

Paraguay became an independent nation

Capt. John Lawrence of the U.S.S. *Chesapeake* was killed in battle, commanding in his dying words, "Don't give up the ship!"; later adopted as the U.S. Navy motto

EIGHTEEN HUNDRED AND FROZE-TO-DEATH

Throughout New England, 1816 was the year without a summer. Popularly referred to as "eighteen hundred and froze-to-death," it was also the year Joseph Smith Sr.'s family left their Vermont home for upstate New York. Both events had their origin more than a year before in a location half a world away.

On 10 April 1815, Mount Tambora, a volcano in the Dutch East Indies (now Indonesia), erupted, sending a massive cloud of dust and ash into the upper atmosphere, affecting the climate throughout the world for some time. In New England, snow fell intermittently throughout the summer of 1816, killing crops and ushering in a season of hunger the following winter.

Following an unseasonably cold stretch in May 1816, farmers planted their fields as temperatures rose. However, in early June a bitter wind arose, and by 7 June snow was falling and ice formed on the ponds. Snow drifted to twenty inches at Danville, Vermont, less than fifty miles north of the Smith's home. During the four weeks of good weather that followed, farmers replanted. But by the Fourth of July, the region again experienced a cold wave. In spite of desperate efforts to save crops, most of the young plants froze. Preachers sermonized that the killing cold was God's punishment for sin. The return of warm weather prompted replanting, but snowfall on 21 August ushered in the long winter of 1816–1817.

Coming on the heels of two successive crop failures, Joseph Smith Sr. determined to leave New England. "This was enough," Lucy Mack Smith later recalled. "My husband was now altogether decided upon going to New York."

The Smiths were not alone in their decision to leave rural New England. Beginning in 1816 and continuing through the following year, New England farming families left their land in record numbers. Many families moved south to warmer climates. Some moved to nearby cities, where they accepted factory work and became part of the growing industrial revolution. The Smiths joined with others who now saw their future in western New York, where land was selling for two to three dollars an acre and the proposed Erie Canal promised new markets for farmers. A neighbor of the Smiths had determined to settle in the small frontier community of Palmyra, and Joseph Smith Sr. concluded to accompany him to that area to obtain land for his family. Later that year, the remainder of the family followed, traveling across the same snow that drove them to seek a new home. It would take years before rural New England recovered from the exodus spawned by the year without a summer.

LETTING THE CAT OUT OF THE BAG

Sailors who broke rules during the 1800s were commonly beaten across their bare backs with a whip made of nine cords or lines called a "cat-o'-nine tails." It was so named because the marks it left resembled cat scratches. The "cat" used to flog wayward seamen was kept in a cloth bag. If the "cat" was let out of the bag, someone was in trouble.

Actual punishments meted out to sailors in the United States Navy included six lashes "for noise at quarters" and twelve lashes "for bad cooking," "for dirty and unwashed clothes," and "for bad language."

New England schoolhouse

My Father Joseph Smith Siegnior moved to Palmyra Ontario County in the State of new York and being in indigent circumstances were obliged to labour hard for the support of a large Family having nine chilldren and as it required the exertions of all that were able to render any assistance for the support of the Family therefore we were deprived of the bennifit of an education suffice it to say I was mearly instructid in reading writing and the ground rules of Arithmatic which constuted my whole literary acquirements.

—From Joseph Smith's 1832 history, the only account written in his own hand. Other accounts were produced with the help of scribes.

though humble habitation built and neatly furnished by our own industry," Lucy recounted. They would remain in their log cabin until 1825, when they moved into a larger, frame house also built by their own labors. On their own land, consisting of one hundred acres, the dream they had so long worked for had at last become a reality.

The hard work of Joseph's youth did not allow him much formal education, but he was "instructed in reading, writing, and the ground rules of arithmetic." However, his mother remembered that her "remarkably quiet, well-disposed" son was "less inclined to the perusal of books than any of the rest of the children, but far more given to meditation and deep study."

1814

The Joseph Smith Sr. family was residing in Norwich, Vermont

Boston textile mogul Francis Cabot Lowell opened the first U.S. factory capable of manufacturing cloth from raw cotton, at Waltham, Massachusetts; the Waltham process was later used at Lowell, Massachusetts

The British burned Washington, D.C., including the Capitol, White House, and Library of Congress; later, British forces were defeated at Baltimore; in December the Treaty of Ghent ended the War of 1812

The first abdication of Napoleon; he was banished to Elba

Swedish scientist Jons Berzelius introduced modern chemical symbols

J. N. Maelzel invented the metronome at Vienna, Austria

1815

Americans under the command of Andrew Jackson defeated a superior British force at the Battle of New Orleans before word reached America that the Treaty of Ghent had ended the War of 1812

Napoleon escaped from Elba, beginning the "Hundred Days," which ended when his French forces were defeated at Waterloo; he was exiled to the island of St. Helena

The size of the full-time U.S. Army was set at 10,000 men

The Apothecaries Act forbade unqualified doctors from practicing in Britain

The Library of Congress purchased nearly 7,000 volumes from Thomas Jefferson's private library to replace books burned by the British

THE LAND OF THE FREE AND THE HOME OF THE BRAVE

The War of 1812, also known as the Second War of American Independence, grew out of the United States' desire to defend its rights as a sovereign nation. Great Britain's efforts to prevent America from trading with France during the Napoleonic Wars prompted Americans to again declare war on their mother country. For much of the war, things went badly for the Americans. Two years into the war, the British Army entered Washington, D.C., and burned many prominent buildings, including the Capitol and the President's House.

The land of the free and the home of the brave—Fort McHenry

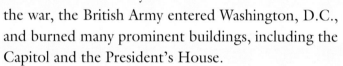

With the nation's capital smoldering behind him, British General Robert Ross turned northward toward Baltimore. On 12 September 1814 his force of some four thousand troops was within six miles of the city. Unlike the defense of Washington, D.C., the previous month, the British invaders now met heavy resistance.

The land assault was part of a two-pronged attack on the city. As Ross's troops marched toward Baltimore, British warships sailed up the Chesapeake Bay toward its harbor. Awaiting them were United States forces marshaled inside Ft. McHenry, over which flew a great symbol of American pride.

A flag measuring forty-two by thirty feet, containing more than four hundred yards of cloth and weighing more than two hundred pounds, had recently been made to fly over the fort. In 1813, Major General George Armistead, commander of the fort, had approached Mary Pickersgill about creating a flag "so large that the British will have no difficulty in seeing it at a distance." With the help of her mother, Rebecca Young; her thirteen-year-old daughter, Caroline; and two nieces, Eliza and Mary Young, ages thirteen and fifteen respectively, they created the gigantic flag. With fifteen stripes and fifteen stars, its "broad stripes" were two feet across, while its "bright stars" were of equal size.

As the British fleet sailed toward Baltimore on 13 September 1814, two Americans, Francis Scott Key and John Skinner, rowed out to meet it. They were not part of the defense of Baltimore but were on a diplomatic mission. They had been sent to negotiate the release of Dr. William Beanes, a physician, who had been accused of spying and was taken prisoner after the burning of Washington. The Americans maintained that Beanes was a noncombatant "taken from his bed, in the midst of his family and hurried off almost without clothes," a "departure from the known usages of civilized warfare."

The British received Key and Skinner courteously and agreed to release Beanes, but there was a snag. Their ships were about to begin an attack on Ft. McHenry, and they thought it best to keep the Americans on the sloop *Minden* until after the attack. Key and his comrades were, in a sense, prisoners, their fate tied to the outcome of the battle.

Late in the morning of 13 September, the British Men of War began a constant bombardment of the fort that would last until the following morning. Even after the sun had set, the Americans remained on deck, anxiously peering into the darkness, made even blacker by a late summer rainstorm and the smoke of battle. Through much of the night the object of their continued interest, the flag, could be seen by the "rockets' red glare" and "bombs bursting in air," but eventually it vanished from sight in a dense morning fog.

After the guns fell silent, the thirty-three-year-old Key saw in "the dawn's early light . . . that our flag was still there." The fort's defenders had bravely withstood the bombardment. The hoped-for surrender had not materialized. Not only had the British fleet been unsuccessful, but so also had been the land forces. Realizing they could not take Baltimore without paying a heavy price in casualties, and unwilling to pay that price, the warships sailed from the harbor on 14 September. At the same time British land forces were also in full retreat, but not before General Ross had been mortally wounded. America had achieved an important victory.

Inspired by what he had witnessed, Key began putting his thoughts on paper even before reaching shore. The first verse of his composition has Dr. Beanes asking questions. In the second, Key joyously responds to the doctor's inquiry. The third verse, which is seldom sung, contrasts the British bragging that they "a home and a country shall leave us no more" with their failure to seize the fort, while the fourth verse praises the gallantry of the brave "freemen" in the garrison who stood "between their loved homes and the war's desolation."

Key's poetic tribute to the flag appeared in a Baltimore newspaper a week later as "The Defense of Fort McHenry" and was soon printed on handbills posted throughout the nation. The tune he used was "To Anacreon in Heaven," a bawdy British drinking song that had been popular in America for years. More than eighty different poems were fitted by Americans to the tune, including one that Key himself had previously written to match the melody in 1805. Although Key's poem almost immediately became the de facto national anthem, "The Star Spangled Banner" did not officially gain that status until 1931.

For all practical purposes, the Americans' successful defense of Baltimore in September 1814, immortalized by Key, ended the War of 1812. England's precarious situation in Europe, coupled with the defeat of its forces at Baltimore, prompted the government of Lord Liverpool to agree to a peace treaty. Three months later, in December 1814, the Treaty of Ghent officially ended the conflict. As a result of this Second War of American Independence, the United States was reborn as a nation.

A MERE HALF-WAY HOUSE

In the spring of 1820, eighteen-year-old Lydia Maria Child, after having investigated several religions, wrote to her brother of her spiritual longings: "I am apt to regard a system of religion as I do any other beautiful theory. It plays round the imagination, but fails to reach the heart. I wish I could find some religion in which my heart and understanding could unite; that amidst the darkest clouds of this life I might ever be cheered with the mild halo of religious consolation."

Later in life as her religious quest continued, Maria characterized one prominent religion as "a mere half-way house, where spiritual travelers find themselves well accommodated for the night, but where they grow weary of spending the day."

> *If God preserves my life, I will cause a boy that driveth a plough to know more of the Scriptures than the pope.*
>
> —Comment attributed to reformer William Tyndale of England, who published the first English translation of the New Testament in 1525–1526 but was forced to undertake the work in exile in Germany because of opposition.

Methodist preacher

Even at an early age, Joseph was a strong force for good and endeavored to correct injustice or cruelty when he witnessed it. As a teenager, Joseph reportedly saw a man beating his wife. He lit into the man, whipped him, and then admonished the husband to treat his wife better in the future.

Joseph later wrote, "At about the age of twelve years my mind became seriously imprest with regard to all importent concerns for the welfare of my immortal Soul which led me to searching the scriptures believing as I was taught, that they contained the word of God thus applying myself to them . . . from the age of twelve years to fifteen I pondered many things in my heart concerning the sittuation of the world."

1816

Freak summer weather forced the Joseph Smith Sr. family to leave Vermont for Palmyra, New York
Indiana became the 19th state
Argentina declared its independence
Harvard College organized its Divinity School as a distinct, Christian institution
The steamboat *Washington* was launched; with a tall second deck, it became the prototype for Mississippi River steamboats
Former slave Richard Allen established the African Methodist Episcopal Church

1817

The American Colonization Society was founded to transport free black Americans to Africa
Congress divided Mississippi Territory; Alabama Territory was created and Mississippi admitted as the 20th state
U.S. educator Thomas Hopkins Gallaudet established the first U.S. public school for the deaf
Alexander Lucius Twilight, likely the first black to graduate from a U.S. college, received a B.A. degree from Middlebury College
James Monroe was inaugurated as the fifth U.S. president; Boston's *Columbian Sentinel* gave a name to Monroe's presidency: "The Era of Good Feeling"
The Staten Island ferry began operation

Camp Meeting of the Methodists in N. America

A camp meeting, ca. 1819

Frontier America baptism

1818

Mary Wollstonecraft Shelley published *Frankenstein*

Franz Gruber and Joseph Mohr composed the beloved Christmas carol "Silent Night"

Congress proclaimed that the U.S. flag would have only 13 stripes; five stars were added to the flag, and two stripes were removed

Illinois became the 21st state

Chile gained its independence

Golf was introduced to the U.S. by Scottish emigrants

Canada and the U.S. set the border between the Land of the Lakes and the crest of the Rocky Mountains as the 49th parallel; ownership of the Oregon country remained unresolved

1819

Revivals were held near Palmyra in the "burned-over district" of western New York

Alabama became the 22nd state

Colombia obtained its independence from Spain

Francois-Louis Cailler established a chocolate factory in Switzerland, the first to produce chocolate bars

The U.S. Congress separated Maine Territory from Massachusetts

The U.S. Supreme Court ruled in *McCulloch v. Maryland* that the Constitution's "necessary and proper" clause gave Congress the implied authority to charter the Second Bank of the United States

Thomas Jefferson wrote, "Advertisements contain the only truth to be relied on in a newspaper"

The first grand opera was performed in the U.S. *(The Barber of Seville)*

This concern for his spiritual welfare did not arise in a vacuum, for the Prophet readily acknowledged that his "goodly parents . . . spared no pains to instructing me in Christian religion." Also, common to most folks on the frontier, the trauma of stressful, around-the-clock survival gave need to understand the deeper meaning of life. Surely, they thought, life must be more than the constant effort to keep one's family fed and housed.

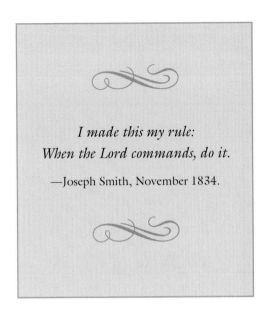

I made this my rule:
When the Lord commands, do it.

—Joseph Smith, November 1834.

In the summer of 1819, the religious revivals of the Second Great Awakening swept western New York like a firestorm. The fury of religious experiences caused the area to be dubbed the "Burned Over District." Various denominations, including Methodists, Baptists, and Presbyterians, held revivals in at least ten villages within twenty miles of the Smith home. Lucy Mack Smith recalled that "many of the world's people, becoming concerned about the salvation of their souls, came forward and presented themselves as seekers of religion." Countless Americans were asking themselves which church was right for them to join.

Joseph's mother, two brothers, and a sister joined the Presbyterians, but other family members, including Joseph and his father, were not satisfied with the available denominations. Joseph felt that the "teachers of religion of the different sects understood the same passages of scripture so differently as to destroy all confidence in settling the question by an appeal

to the Bible." Although he possessed an intense desire to "get religion," to feel the spirit and shout like others, the experience eluded him. He told his mother, "I can take my Bible and go into the woods, and learn more in two hours than you can learn at meetings in two years."

The "war of words" and "tumult of opinions" that were part of this western New York communal religious experience left young Joseph confused and seeking enlightenment. "I often said to myself: What is to be done? Who of all these parties are right?" According to Joseph's brother William, Reverend George Lane, with whom Joseph had frequently discussed religion, provided the solution when he quoted James 1:5 while preaching on "which church shall I join." Ironically, Lane would end their friendship because of what resulted from Joseph's taking his advice.

Returning home, Joseph read the New Testament scripture: "If any of you lack wisdom, let him ask of God, that giveth to all men liberally, and upbraideth not; and it shall be given him. But let him ask in faith, nothing wavering." An epiphany enlightened him: "Never did any passage of scripture come with more power to the heart of man than this did at this time to mine. . . . At length I came to the conclusion that I must either remain in darkness and confusion, or else I must do as James directs, that is, ask of God."

If any of you lack wisdom, let him ask of God.

THE JERKS

During the religious fervor of the early 1800s, it was not unusual for families to travel five, ten, or twenty or more miles (by foot, wagon, or horseback) to camp with others and listen to itinerant ordained ministers and self-appointed preachers. These revivals or camp-meetings were especially important to people of the frontier who were eager to hear the word of God. A phenomenon among early revivalists caught up in the religious frenzy was to jerk—falling, rolling, barking, laughing, jerking, twitching. In his 1804 journal, itinerant evangelist-preacher Lorenzo Dow (1777–1834) commented on observing the "jerks" while preaching and traveling in Tennessee.

I had heard about a singularity called the "jerks" or "jerking exercise," which appeared first near Knoxville in August last [1803] to the great alarm of the people, which reports at first I considered as vague and false. . . . I set out to go and see for myself. . . .

When I arrived in sight of this town, I saw hundreds of people collected in little bodies, and, observing no place appointed for meeting, before I spoke to any, I got on a log and gave out a hymn, which caused them to assemble around in solemn attentive silence. I observed several involuntary motions in the course of the meeting, which I considered as a specimen of the jerks, I rode seven miles behind a man across streams of water and held meeting in the evening, being ten miles on my way. . . .

Hence to Marysville, where I spoke to about 1500; and many appeared to feel the word, but about 50 felt the jerks. At night I lodged with one of the Nicholites, a kind of Quakers who do not feel free to wear colored clothes. I spoke to a number of people at this house that night. While at tea, I observed his daughter . . . to have the jerks, and dropped the teacup from her hand in the violent agitation. I said to her, "Young woman, what is the matter?" She replied, "I have got the jerks." I asked her how long she had it. She observed, "A few days"; and that it had been the means of the awakening and conversion of her soul by stirring her up to serious consideration about her careless state, and so forth.

Sunday, February 19, I spoke in Knoxville to hundreds more than could get into the courthouse, the governor being present. About 150 appeared to have the jerking exercise. . . .

After meeting, I rode eighteen miles to hold a meeting at night. The people of this settlement were mostly Quakers, and they had said (as I was informed): "The Methodists and Presbyterians have the jerks because they sing and pray so much; but we are a still, peaceable people, wherefore we do not have them." However, about twenty of them came to the meeting to hear one, as they said, somewhat in a Quaker line. But their usual stillness and silence was interrupted, for about a dozen of them had the jerks as keen and as powerful as any I had seen, so as to have occasioned a kind of grunt or groan when they would jerk. . . .

I have seen Presbyterians, Methodists, Quakers, Baptists, Episcopalians, and Independents exercised with the jerks—gentleman and lady, black and white, the aged and the youth, rich and poor, without exception; from which I infer, as it cannot be accounted for on natural principles, and carries such marks of involuntary motion, that it is no trifling matter. I believe that those who are most pious and given up to God are rarely touched with it, and also those naturalists who wish and try to get it to philosophize upon it are excepted. But the lukewarm, lazy, halfhearted, indolent professor is subject to it; and many of them I have seen who, when it came upon them, would be alarmed and stirred up to redouble their diligence with God; and after they would get happy, were thankful it ever came upon them.

"The Jerking Exercise"

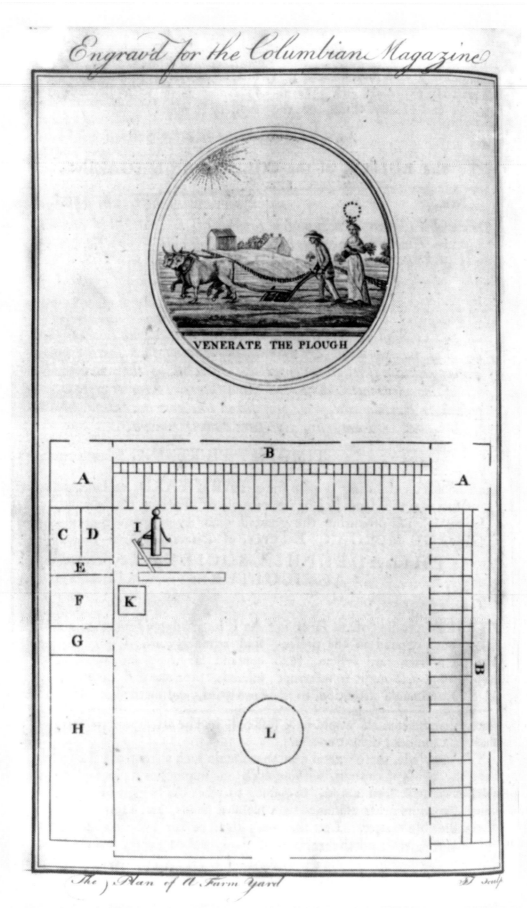

Engrav'd for the Columbian Magazine

VENERATE THE PLOUGH

The Plan of a Farm Yard

George Morgan's prizewinning "Plan for a farmyard and requisite Buildings"

A. To be filled up by young Cattle, Straw, Turnips, House Lambs or any other Purpose to which you please to appropriate them.
B. Ewes & Lambs, Fatting Weathers
C. Fat Hog Sty
D. Store Hog Sty
E. Passage
F. Breeding Sows
G. Waggon & Cart Gears
H. Waggons Carts and Farming Utensils
I. Pump
K. Hog-Wash Cistern
L. Pond

THE BEST I EVER SAW

English farmer and radical politician William Cobbett visited America, living on Long Island, from 1818 to 1819. In his book *A Year's Residence in the United States of America in Three Parts,* he shares his careful and opinionated observations on the climate, soil, landscape, farming, animal husbandry, manners, customs, laws, government, beggars, religions, tools, land prices, and housekeeping practices of America—at a time when America, and the world, was a land of farmers.

The following selection provides a positive glimpse of American farmers and the farm-life that Joseph Smith's family experienced:

It is . . . of importance to know, what sort of labourers these Americans are; for, though a labourer is a labourer, still there is some difference in them; and, these Americans are *the best that I ever saw.* They mow *four acres* of *oats, wheat, rye,* or *barley* in a day, and, with a cradle, lay it so smooth in the swarths, that it is tied up in sheaves with the greatest neatness and ease. They mow *two acres and a half of grass* in a day, and they do the work well. And the crops, upon an average, are all, except the wheat, *as heavy* as in England. The English farmer will want nothing more than these facts to convince him, that the labour, after all, is not so *very dear.*

The causes of these performances, so far beyond those in England, is first, the men are *tall* and well built; they are *bony* rather than *fleshy;* and they *live,* as to food, as well as man can live. And, secondly, they have been *educated* to do much in a day. The farmer here generally is at the *head* of his *"boys,"* as they, in the kind language of the country, are called. Here is the best of examples. My old and beloved friend, Mr James Paul, used, at the age of nearly *sixty* to go at *the head of his mowers,* though his fine farm was his own, and though he might, in other respects, be called a rich man; and, I have heard, that Mr. Elias Hicks, the famous Quaker Preacher, who lives about nine miles from this spot, has this year, at *seventy* years of age, cradled down four acres of rye in a day. I wish some of the *preachers* of other descriptions, especially our fat parsons in England, would think a little of this, and would betake themselves to "work with their hands the things which be good, that they may have to give to him who needeth," and not go on any longer gormandizing and swilling upon the labour of those who need.

Besides the great quantity of work performed by the American labourer, his *skill,* the *versatility* of his talent, is a great thing. Every man can use an *ax,* a *saw,* and a *hammer.* Scarcely one who cannot do any job at rough carpentering, and mend a plough or a waggon. Very few indeed, who cannot kill and dress pigs and sheep, and many of them Oxen and Calves. Every farmer is a *neat* butcher; a butcher for *market;* and, of course, "the boys" must learn. This is a great convenience. It makes you so independent as to a main part of the means of housekeeping. All are *ploughmen.* In short, a good labourer here, can do *anything* that is to be done upon a farm.

TEAKETTLE POWER

Robert Fulton (1765–1815)

"She'll *never* run! She'll *never* run!" naysayers yelled as Robert Fulton attempted to start the steam engines of the *Clermont.* As soon as the steamboat began moving *up* the Hudson River, the crowd on the shore began to shout, "She'll never stop! She'll never stop!" To his nervous passengers, Fulton announced, "Gentlemen, you need not be uneasy; you shall be in Albany before twelve o'clock tomorrow." And they were.

In 1807, Fulton's *Clermont* ushered in the era of steam power. Prior to "Teakettle Power," as the critics derisively called it, the time needed to travel between locations had changed little over the previous centuries. The *Clermont* made its maiden voyage from New York City to Albany in thirty-two hours, traveling at the unheard-of rate of five miles an hour. The return trip with the currents took only thirty hours.

Although not the first steamship, "Fulton's Folly" was more reliable than its predecessors and proved an economic success. Described as "a backwoods sawmill mounted on a scow and set on fire," the *Clermont* was built with the backing of Robert Livingston, who served on the committee that drafted the Declaration of Independence in 1776 and who, while U.S. minister to France in 1801, conducted negotiations that led to the Louisiana Purchase.

Because there were few good roads, river travel was important in Young America. Currents and shifting winds, however, made river navigation difficult, and most river traffic was one way—downstream. Vessels could travel upriver, against the current, but only with considerable effort, such as being pushed along by poles, being pulled by a horse or mule, or being propelled by sail if there was enough wind. Frequently the speed obtained by vessels going upstream was less than that of the average pedestrian. "Teakettle Power" overcame the currents, thus providing a reliable and relatively fast method of transportation.

Livingston's support of "Teakettle Power" helped open up the American interior he helped acquire. Boats that frequently traveled up the Mississippi River at rates less than a mile an hour would soon chug upriver in excess of ten miles an hour. By 1820, sixty steamboats sailed the Mississippi; by 1860 that number had climbed to nearly a thousand. During the 1840s, Joseph Smith owned a steamship, *The Maid of Iowa,* while residing at Nauvoo, Illinois.

In 1825, steam power was adapted to land use with the opening of the first steam-driven railroad in England. The designers of America's first passenger railroad, the Baltimore and Ohio, were warned that their route contained too many curves for a steam engine to stay on the tracks. When the B&O opened in 1830, horses initially pulled the cars. (A horse could pull a load ten times as heavy over rails as over dirt roads.) Peter Cooper, a local Baltimore inventor, undertook the challenge of converting the B&O into a steam railroad. "I had naturally a knack at contriving," he wrote, "and I told the directors that I believed I could knock together a locomotive that would get around the curve." His small train engine, christened the *Tom Thumb,* proved effective. Soon "iron horses" or "teakettles on tracks" were wending their way across many areas of America. By 1840, approximately three thousand miles of track had been laid; by 1850, more than nine thousand miles of railroads were in use.

Steamboats and steam engines were efficient and fast, but they could also be dangerous. The amount of steam produced could not be regulated, and explosions were common as pressure built inside boilers. As the death toll from boiler explosions mounted, one grim editorial cartoon portrayed Death as a train passenger. In addition to explosions, early "iron horses" often jumped the tracks, and trains occasionally crashed into each other.

The soot produced by the steam engines was both entertaining and dangerous. During an 1842 train ride, Charles Dickens "found abundance of entertainment . . . in watching the effects of the wood fire, which had been invisible in the morning but were now brought out in full relief by the darkness: for we were travelling in a whirlwind of bright sparks, which showered about us like a storm of fiery snow." Because passenger compartments were not enclosed, passengers were frequently kept busy putting out the fires on each other's clothing caused by this "fiery snow."

THE OLD OAKEN BUCKET

The sentiment captured by Samuel Woodworth's recollection of his New York boyhood in his 1818 "The Old Oaken Bucket" made it a popular song in a Young America that was overwhelmingly rural. The tune is the same one used for the Latter-day Saint hymn "Do What Is Right."

How dear to my heart are the scenes of my childhood,
When fond recollection presents them to view.
The orchard, the meadow, the deep tangled wildwood,
And ev'ry loved spot which my infancy knew.
The wide spreading pond, and the mill that stood by it,
The bridge and the rock where the cataract fell;
The cot [cottage] of my father, the dairy house nigh it,
And e'en the rude bucket that hung in the well.
The old oaken bucket, the iron bound bucket,
The moss covered bucket that hung in the well.

The moss covered bucket I hailed as a treasure,
For often at noon, when returned from the field,
I found it the source of an exquisite pleasure,
The purest and sweetest that nature can yield.
How ardent I seized it, with hands that were glowing,
And quick to the white pebbled bottom it fell.
Then soon, with the emblem of truth overflowing,
And dripping with coolness, it rose from the well.
The old oaken bucket, the iron bound bucket,
The moss covered bucket that hung in the well.

VOTE

Initially, only white male land owners could vote in America. However, prior to the War of 1812, New Jersey and Maryland abandoned property requirements. By 1824, nearly all white males over the age of twenty-one could vote, except in Rhode Island, Virginia, and Louisiana.

When New Jersey rewrote its voting law in 1807, in addition to removing the property qualification, it also failed to specify the qualifying gender of voters. One enterprising local politician took advantage of this "loophole" and stuffed the ballot box with votes from female supporters. He won his election, but women again lost the right to vote as the New Jersey legislature quickly amended the law to join other states in barring women from the polls. While women continued to be banned from voting, by 1830, the right of suffrage had been extended to free African Americans in several New England states.

Everyone knew whom you had voted for in Young America as voting was done publicly. People either announced whom they supported or voted by a show of hands. Frequently voting took place in town meetings. The secret, or Australian, ballot would not be introduced until the second half of the nineteenth century.

The 1824 presidential election was the first in which electoral votes were determined by popular vote. Prior to 1824, electoral votes were determined solely by state legislatures, but popular sentiment in the 1820s began to decry these caucuses as undemocratic. In 1824, only six states still assigned electoral votes by caucus rather than popular vote. In 1828, only two of the twenty-four states (South Carolina and Delaware) followed the old practice.

Although Americans acquired the right to vote for president in 1824, ultimately the United States House of Representatives chose the president since none of the four candidates received the requisite number of electoral votes to claim the presidency. Four years later, Andrew Jackson easily won both the popular and electoral vote.

The Constitution specifies when electoral votes are to be cast but not when elections are to be held. States were free to choose the day on which they held elections. In 1848, Congress appointed the first Tuesday after the first Monday in November as the day for presidential elections.

United States Capitol, ca. 1846

JOSEPH SMITH'S FAMILY

(Spouses listed in italics)

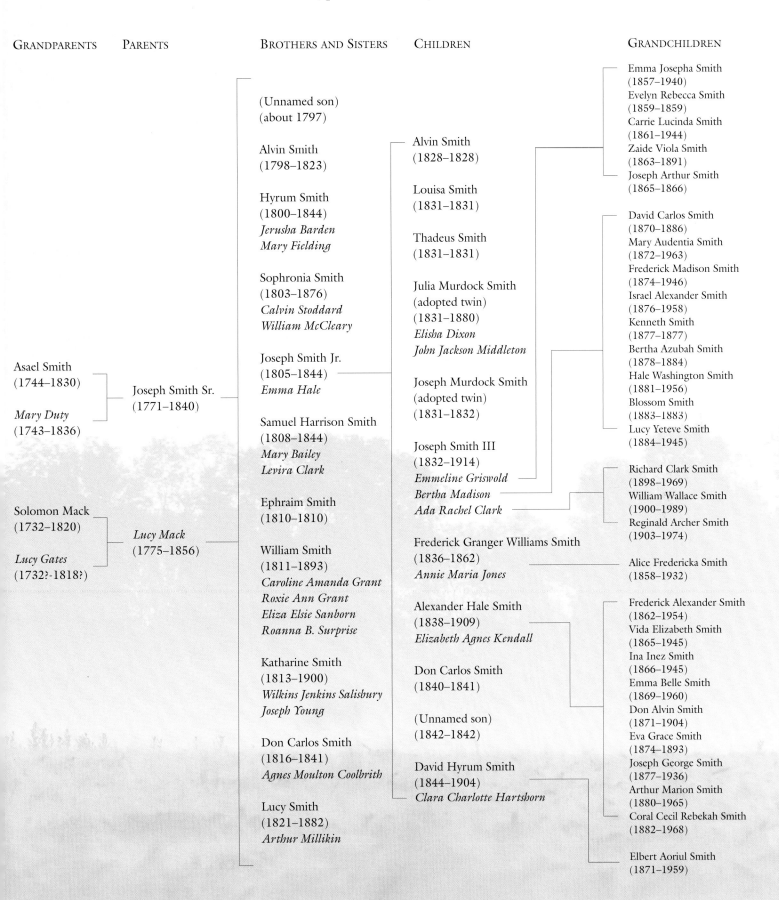

GRANDPARENTS PARENTS BROTHERS AND SISTERS CHILDREN GRANDCHILDREN

GRANDPARENTS

Asael Smith
(1744–1830)

Mary Duty
(1743–1836)

Solomon Mack
(1732–1820)

Lucy Gates
(1732?–1818?)

PARENTS

Joseph Smith Sr.
(1771–1840)

Lucy Mack
(1775–1856)

BROTHERS AND SISTERS

(Unnamed son)
(about 1797)

Alvin Smith
(1798–1823)

Hyrum Smith
(1800–1844)
Jerusha Barden
Mary Fielding

Sophronia Smith
(1803–1876)
Calvin Stoddard
William McCleary

Joseph Smith Jr.
(1805–1844)
Emma Hale

Samuel Harrison Smith
(1808–1844)
Mary Bailey
Levira Clark

Ephraim Smith
(1810–1810)

William Smith
(1811–1893)
Caroline Amanda Grant
Roxie Ann Grant
Eliza Elsie Sanborn
Roanna B. Surprise

Katharine Smith
(1813–1900)
Wilkins Jenkins Salisbury
Joseph Young

Don Carlos Smith
(1816–1841)
Agnes Moulton Coolbrith

Lucy Smith
(1821–1882)
Arthur Millikin

CHILDREN

Alvin Smith
(1828–1828)

Louisa Smith
(1831–1831)

Thadeus Smith
(1831–1831)

Julia Murdock Smith
(adopted twin)
(1831–1880)
Elisha Dixon
John Jackson Middleton

Joseph Murdock Smith
(adopted twin)
(1831–1832)

Joseph Smith III
(1832–1914)
Emmeline Griswold
Bertha Madison
Ada Rachel Clark

Frederick Granger Williams Smith
(1836–1862)
Annie Maria Jones

Alexander Hale Smith
(1838–1909)
Elizabeth Agnes Kendall

Don Carlos Smith
(1840–1841)

(Unnamed son)
(1842–1842)

David Hyrum Smith
(1844–1904)
Clara Charlotte Hartshorn

GRANDCHILDREN

Emma Josepha Smith
(1857–1940)
Evelyn Rebecca Smith
(1859–1859)
Carrie Lucinda Smith
(1861–1944)
Zaide Viola Smith
(1863–1891)
Joseph Arthur Smith
(1865–1866)

David Carlos Smith
(1870–1886)
Mary Audentia Smith
(1872–1963)
Frederick Madison Smith
(1874–1946)
Israel Alexander Smith
(1876–1958)
Kenneth Smith
(1877–1877)
Bertha Azubah Smith
(1878–1884)
Hale Washington Smith
(1881–1956)
Blossom Smith
(1883–1883)
Lucy Yeteve Smith
(1884–1945)

Richard Clark Smith
(1898–1969)
William Wallace Smith
(1900–1989)
Reginald Archer Smith
(1903–1974)

Alice Fredericka Smith
(1858–1932)

Frederick Alexander Smith
(1862–1954)
Vida Elizabeth Smith
(1865–1945)
Ina Inez Smith
(1866–1945)
Emma Belle Smith
(1869–1960)
Don Alvin Smith
(1871–1904)
Eva Grace Smith
(1874–1893)
Joseph George Smith
(1877–1936)
Arthur Marion Smith
(1880–1965)
Coral Cecil Rebekah Smith
(1882–1968)

Elbert Aoriul Smith
(1871–1959)

The Sacred Grove

N0.3A.

"THIS GENERATION SHALL HAVE MY WORD THROUGH YOU"

I t was on the morning of a beautiful clear day, early in the spring of eighteen hundred and twenty," Joseph Smith later recalled, when he experienced the vision that changed his life, the course of America, and the future of the world. Putting the Apostle James's words to the test, fourteen-year-old Joseph went to a grove of trees near his home to ask God which church he should join. The answer he received is one of the most important events in the history of the world, eclipsing all other nineteenth-century occurrences.

"I kneeled down and began to offer up the desires of my heart to God," he wrote, "but I had scarcely done so, when immediately I was seized upon by some power which entirely overcame me. . . . Thick darkness gathered around me, and it seemed to me for a time as if I were doomed to sudden destruction. But, exerting all my powers to call upon God to deliver me out of the power of this enemy which had seized upon me, and at the very moment when I was ready to sink into despair and abandon myself to destruction—not to an imaginary ruin, but to the power of some actual being from the unseen world . . . I saw a pillar of light exactly over my head, above the brightness of the sun which descended gradually until it fell upon me. It no sooner appeared than I found myself delivered from the enemy which held me bound. When the light rested upon me I saw two Personages, whose brightness and glory defy all

Inception of Mormonism— Joseph Smith's First Vision

description, standing above me in the air. One of them spake unto me, calling me by name, and said, pointing to the other—*This is My Beloved Son. Hear Him!*"

When finally able to speak again, Joseph simply asked "which of all the sects was right—and which I should join." The resurrected Christ instructed the young boy to "join none of them," for "they teach for doctrines the commandments of men, having a form of godliness, but they deny the power thereof." Joseph was further told "that the fulness of the Gospel should at some future time be made known unto" him.

Upon returning home, Joseph's concerned mother, noticing how pale he was, asked what was wrong. Joseph simply replied, "I am well enough off . . . I have learned for myself that Presbyterianism is not true."

Although physically weakened by the experience, Joseph left the grove spiritually strengthened. The reality of the Father and the Son was no longer a matter of faith to him but a personal experience. By entering the woods, falling to his knees, and praying, Joseph learned more of the character of God than could be revealed solely through the Bible. He learned firsthand how glorious the resurrection can be, and he could assuredly testify that the Father and the Son were separate and distinct individuals and that the falling away predicted by the Apostle Paul had come to pass. Only a vision such as Joseph experienced

It was nevertheless a fact that I had beheld a vision. I have thought since, that I felt much like Paul, when he made his defense before King Agrippa, and related the account of the vision he had when he saw a light, and heard a voice; but still there were few who believed him; some said he was dishonest, others said he was mad; and he was ridiculed and reviled. But all this did not destroy the reality of his vision. He had seen a vision, he knew he had, and all the persecution under heaven could not make it otherwise; and though they should persecute him unto death, yet he knew, and would know to his latest breath, that he had both seen a light and heard a voice speaking unto him, and all the world could not make him think or believe otherwise.

So it was with me. I had actually seen a light, and in the midst of that light I saw two Personages, and they did in reality speak to me; and though I was hated and persecuted for saying that I had seen a vision, yet it was true; and while they were persecuting me, reviling me, and speaking all manner of evil against me falsely for so saying, I was led to say in my heart: Why persecute me for telling the truth? I have actually seen a vision; and who am I that I can withstand God, or why does the world think to make me deny what I have actually seen? For I had seen a vision; I knew it, and I knew that God knew it, and I could not deny it, neither dared I do it; at least I knew that by so doing I would offend God, and come under condemnation.

—Joseph Smith in his 1839 history, reflecting on his 1820 First Vision.

could have penetrated the centuries-old clouds of darkness that had enveloped the Christian world. A mere impression, voice, or dream would not have accomplished the same purpose.

Joseph did not go into the grove expecting to become a prophet, and he did not come out understanding his prophetic role. But the foundation had been laid, for, as John the Revelator taught, "the testimony of Jesus is the spirit of prophecy."

The process of transforming Joseph from a typical American frontier farm boy to the "prophet, seer and revelator" "blessed to open the last dispensation" didn't happen overnight. There were missteps along the way, particularly during the early years. It would take time for him to fully comprehend what had transpired in the "sacred grove." With no contemporary role model to mentor him on how a prophet should behave, Joseph occasionally made errors in judgment that have caused some to focus more on his foibles than his prophetic work.

Nevertheless, his First Vision began a lifetime of learning no earthly institution could hope to match. It began a remarkable ten-year period of tutoring that would enable him to bring forth a new volume of scripture and reestablish the church of Jesus Christ on the earth. His training during this time included both instruction and chastisement by messengers from beyond the veil. He was taught how to receive revelation and how to translate through the revelatory process. He learned about the power and purposes of the priesthood. Eventually, his training would allow him to transcend his generation.

Joseph, showing the exuberance of youth, innocently believed that others would be excited to know what he had learned in answer to his prayer. He later recalled his utter shock when he tried to tell his neighbors what had been revealed to him. His announcement was met with contempt, doubt, and scoffing by the majority. When Joseph excitedly told Reverend George Lane of his experience, he was told that there

1820

Joseph Smith's first vision answered questions about which church he should join and the nature of God

The "Missouri Compromise" was passed; Maine became the 23rd state (a free state); Missouri was to be admitted as a slave state; slavery was prohibited in the northern portion of the Louisiana Purchase

Missouri imposed a one-dollar Bachelor Tax on unmarried men between the ages of 21 and 50

The population of the U.S. was 9.6 million; France, 30.4 (million); Prussia, Bavaria, Saxony, and the free cities of Germany, 26.1; Great Britain, 20.8; Italy, 18.0; Austria, 12.0

Scottish clergyman Sydney Smith mused, "In the four corners of the globe, who in the world reads an American book? Or goes to an American play? Or looks at an American picture or statue? What does the world yet owe to Americans?"

King George III died after 60 years as British monarch; he was king of England during the American Revolution

King Ferdinand VII of Spain abolished the Inquisition, the organization responsible for upholding Catholicism in Spain

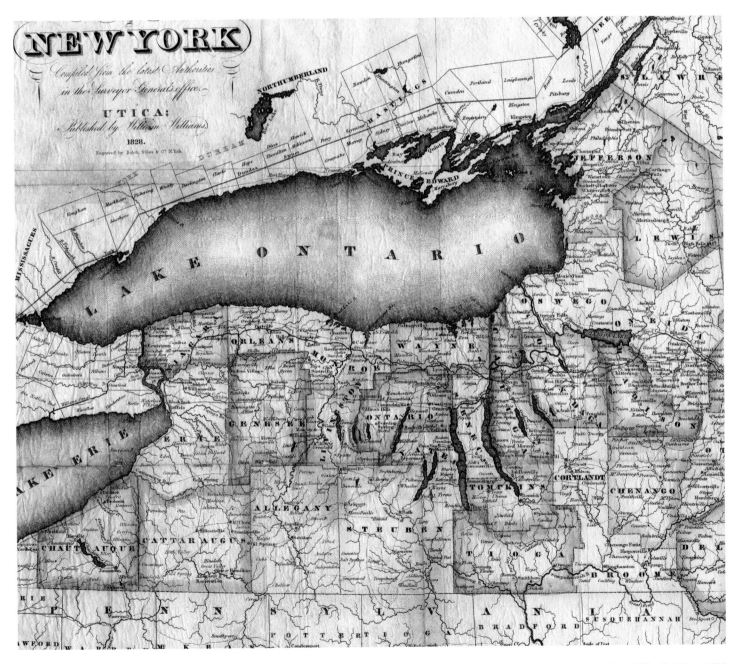

Map of New York State, 1828

"AWAKENED AND CONVERTED TO GOD": THE SECOND GREAT AWAKENING

Even though religion was important to America from its beginnings, the First and especially the Second Great Awakening intensified the religious character and identity of Young America's emerging sense of self. Whereas the revivals of the First Great Awakening (1740s) tended to take place within established congregations, the Second Great Awakening (1790s–1830s) took place in churches, frontier camp-meetings, homes, and wherever else people could come together.

The theological and doctrinal emphasis of the 1740s Awakening, in broad strokes, viewed an individual's redemption as a miraculous act of God. Preachers pushed the need for conversion by warning of the terrors of hell—one must avoid God's fearful wrath.

However, preachers during the Second Great Awakening taught that mankind's active role in drawing close to God and accepting Christ would allow one to receive salvation. In other words, one must make a personal decision to accept Christ and thereby be accepted by Him. God, although stern, was now seen as benevolent and approachable. Universal salvation was beginning to replace the fate of predestination.

Peter Cartwright, who would become a Methodist minister, recalled how an early 1800s revival meeting affected his life: "As there was a great waking up among the Churches, from the revival that had broken out at Cane Ridge [Kentucky], many flocked to sacramental meetings. . . . I went, with weeping multitudes, and bowed before the stand, and earnestly prayed for mercy. In the midst of a solemn struggle of soul, an impression was made on my mind, as though a voice said to me, 'Thy sins are all forgiven thee.' Divine light flashed all around me,

unspeakable joy sprung up in my soul. . . . I have never doubted that the Lord did, then and there, forgive my sins and give me religion."

The Second Great Awakening, although not a homogeneous development, was a time of change, innovation, and creativity affecting Christianity in America for generations. It was a populist movement, with democratic aspects, led by itinerant lay preachers who scurried through the eastern seaboard, into the frontier villages, and out to the countryside, sweeping through the Deep South and up into the northern states, all in an effort to preach the good news of Christ to (mostly) eager audiences at revival camp meetings.

Camp meetings, which were intended to "fan the flames" of evangelical emotion, ranged from simple affairs with a few people listening to a preacher for an evening, on up to large multi-week events with numerous speakers. Peter Cartwright described large gatherings where they erected "a shed, sufficiently large to protect five thousand from wind and rain, cover it with boards or shingles; build a large stand, set the shed, and here they would collect together from forty to fifty miles around. . . . Ten, twenty, and sometimes thirty ministers, of different denominations, would come together and preach night and day, four or five days . . . indeed, I have known these camp-meetings to last three or four weeks, and great good resulted from them. I have seen more than a hundred sinners fall like dead men under one powerful sermon, and I have seen and heard more than five hundred Christians all shouting aloud . . . and I will venture to assert that many happy thousands were awakened and converted to God."

The Second Great Awakening, with its emphasis on piety, active pursuit of salvation, and sense of free

Camp meeting, ca. 1829

will, helped America rise above early Calvinistic preoccupation with human depravity. Life was now beginning to be seen as a series of choices and re-directions picked from a color pallet rather than a drab existence of a black or white fate. Dramatically affecting religious thought in America, it also brought an optimism that created a surge in social action—humans could choose to effect change, not only in themselves but also in others through good works. This optimism led to the forming of missionary efforts, biblical and educational societies, and moral reform associations. Humane societies were founded; antislavery action increased; benevolent charities were founded to help the poor, to benefit children, and to aid widows; activists worked for better treatment of the mentally and emotionally handicapped; and interest in education and health rose. The Great Awakening helped move women into active public roles in effecting social change; New England women raised money for the

Society for Promoting Christian Knowledge, and in neighboring New York, the Society for the Relief of Poor Widows was founded by women.

Out of the Second Awakening came a changed religious landscape highlighted by new denominations and churches as well as shifting demographics for established churches. The Congregationalists, Presbyterians, Catholics, and Episcopalians lost members; Baptists and Methodists gained members and status. Organizations such as the Seventh-Day Adventists and The Church of Jesus Christ of Latter-day Saints were the rising newcomers. The "losers" tended to be hierarchical structures with well-educated ministers and dominated by wealthy members, whereas the "winners" fostered lay preaching, emotional worship meetings, evangelicalism rather than rationalism, piety over theology, universal salvation, and, very much fitting the times, populist, egalitarian religious cultures.

LOWELL, MASSACHUSETTS

To support his thriving textile industry, Francis Cabot Lowell established the first "factory town" in America in 1823. He envisioned that Lowell, Massachusetts, would become something better than the "dark Satanic mills" surrounded by slum towns that he encountered in the English midlands. Around his gigantic mill he built numerous boardinghouses that provided supervised dormitory living for his

factory workers, two-thirds of whom were girls and young women. For many of these fifteen hundred "mill girls," the decision to leave a rural farm life to work in a factory was born of necessity as a growing number of Yankee farm families faced economic difficulties. Because of Lowell's factory town, the parents of these "daughters of Yankee farmers" would have less concern about their children being away from home.

The company controlled nearly every aspect of a mill girl's life. The workday usually started at 5:00 A.M. with a blast from the factory whistle. The workers arrived at the factory with breakfast in one pocket and lunch in another. Fifteen minutes were allotted for breakfast, thirty for lunch. The work day ended at 7:30 P.M. On Saturdays, the girls worked half a day. On Sundays they were encouraged to attend church, and Sunday schools were available.

Lowell and other mill owners believed they were teaching children character through hard work. Children as young as seven worked the mill's long hours. Small and quick, they were prized employees because they could easily scamper around the large machines changing spindles. By 1820, an estimated half of the nation's industrial workers were children under ten. In the 1830s, Massachusetts law treated these children differently from other workers as they were allowed to work *only* nine months a year and ten hours a day.

At the age of eleven, Lucy Larcom began work as a "bobbin' girl," replacing empty bobbins of thread with full ones. "Why it is nothing but fun. It is just like play," she wrote of her first day working in the giant textile mill. "I liked it better than going to school and 'making' believe I was learning when I was not."

Lucy's excitement soon gave way to the realities of the job. "I defied the machinery to make me its slave. Its incessant discourds could not drown the music of my thoughts if I would let them fly high enough," she later wrote. Lucy tried to make the best of things, but the work remained: "When you do the same thing twenty times—a hundred times a day—it is so dull!"

Although people also worked long hours on the farm, these hours normally decreased during the cold, dark, winter months. Such was not the case with the mills, where textile workers toiled year-round for twelve to fourteen hours a day, frequently by the light of whale-oil lamps.

After Martin Van Buren approved a ten-hour workday for government workers in 1840, mill girls pressed their demands for similar hours. Two lines of a popular song sung by those striking workers vividly note the realities of factory life:

Oh, isn't it a pity such a pretty girl as I
Should be sent to the factory to pine away and die?

Visitors sometimes described Lowell as one of the wonders of the world. "Niagara [Falls] and Lowell are the two objects I will longest remember in my American journey," proclaimed one Scottish visitor, "the one the glory of American scenery, the other of American industry." Not all, however, were enamored with this company town. Renowned American artist James McNeil Whistler was born in Lowell but in later life stated, "I shall be born when and where I want, and I do not choose to be born in Lowell."

> *It seems as though the adversary was aware, at a very early period of my life, that I was destined to prove a disturber and an annoyer of his kingdom; else why should the powers of darkness combine against me? Why the opposition and persecution that arose against me, almost in my infancy?*
>
> —From Joseph Smith's 1839 history

On the evening of 21 September 1823, Joseph retired to his room "in a serious and contemplative state of mind." His prayer for forgiveness was answered by a heavenly messenger named Moroni. During three visits that occupied the entire night, the angel delivered to Joseph the same word-for-word message. He told the seventeen-year-old boy of a sacred record, hidden in a nearby hill, that contained the "fullness of the everlasting gospel." He also quoted from the biblical books of Isaiah, Joel, Malachi, and Acts regarding a latter-day work. During the last visit, Moroni warned Joseph that he "must have no other object in view in getting the plates but to glorify God." He further instructed the teenager to tell his father "all he had both seen and heard."

were no such things as visions and revelations. Even his own family initially continued to follow previously established religious patterns. As was the case with Christ's apostles of old, it would take time for them to completely understand the significance of his message.

As Reverend Lane and other ministers in the area decried the young boy, Joseph became the object of overwhelming persecution. Even his family was not spared ridicule: "We never knew we were bad folks until Joseph told his vision," William Smith later wrote. "We were considered respectable till then, but at once people began to circulate falsehoods and stories."

The intense reaction to Joseph's experience is curious since a number of other people claimed similar spiritual manifestations during this period of religious excitement. Ministers frequently touted these assertions as authentic outcomes of a personal quest for salvation. Joseph's message that the established creeds were an "abomination" before God no doubt led to the cool reception by both minister and church member.

> *He called me by name, and said unto me that he was a messenger sent from the presence of God to me, and that his name was Moroni; that God had a work for me to do; and that my name should be had for good and evil among all nations, kindreds, and tongues; or that it should be both good and evil spoken of among all people.*
>
> —Joseph Smith recounting the visit of ancient American prophet Moroni in his 1839 history

1821

The Federation of Gran Colombia, consisting of Colombia (which also included Panama), Venezuela, and Ecuador formed; disbanded in 1830

Bertel Thorvaldsen began his colossal sculpture series *Christ and the Twelve Apostles,* which includes *The Christus;* completed in 1838

French Egyptologist Jean-François Champollion deciphered Egyptian hieroglyphics using the Rosetta Stone

Missouri admitted as the 24th state

The U.S. obtained East Florida from Spain through the Adams-Onis Treaty; cost, $15 million

Mexico secured independence from Spain

Sequoyah began work on his 86-symbol Cherokee alphabet

U.S. merchant Stephen Becknell left Independence, Missouri, for Santa Fe; opening of the Santa Fe Trail

21–22 SEPTEMBER 1823

On the morning of Sunday, 21 September 1823, an armada of vessels at Montreal, Canada, hunted a whale that had somehow made its way down the St. Lawrence River. The steamboat *Laprairie* finally succeeded in harpooning the prey, which "dashed about in the breakers opposite the Town for nearly two hours" before it died. Since the whale had had little room to maneuver and was tired from having to fight river currents, crew members of the *Laprairie* had been able to "wound him with lances continually." The *Montreal Times* reported that "the movements of the boat could be plainly seen from the harbour. We seldom ever beheld a concourse of people equal to that which crowded the embankments." The crew of the *Laprairie*, described by the paper as the "favorites of fortune," stood to reap large profits from its morning's work, since whale oil was a primary source of light and in great demand.

That same day, General E. P. Gains at the frontier headquarters of the Western Department of the United States Army located at Louisville, Kentucky, wrote to his superiors at Washington, D.C., describing the "handsome and honorable result" achieved by Colonel H. Leavenworth during his "late expedition against the Ricaras Indians." While the troubles between the Native Americans and white settlers along the western Missouri border appeared at an end, Gains further reported that he had directed General Henry Atkinson "to keep an eye upon" the Ricaras and Mandans and "to make his arrangements with a view to the chastisement of the Blackfoot Indians, early in the next spring and summer, as this measure appears to be indispensably necessary to secure our citizens in that quarter."

Also that day, two ships arrived at New York City from England, both bringing the latest news from across the Atlantic. The "packet ship" *Amity*, whose regular route ran between Liverpool and New York, had crossed the ocean in thirty-four days. The "fast sailing ship" *Union* had made the same journey in a mere twenty days. Both trips were substantially less than the more than sixty days needed by the *Mayflower*. Improvements in hull design and sail layout were narrowing the distance between the old and new worlds.

By the time news of these national and world happenings reached the residents of small towns, such as Palmyra, New York, days and weeks had passed. The residents of the area, therefore, largely focused their attention on the world immediately around them. Weather continued favorable, and there was still much work to be done in the fields. They would later learn that such was not the case at Montreal, where the arrival of the autumnal equinox was accompanied by a killing frost of a "penny's depth" that destroyed what crops remained in the field.

While the subsistence of many in Ontario County, New York, depended on their labors, hard work offered another reward to the area's residents. The Ontario Agricultural Society was offering cash prizes ranging from fifteen dollars for the "best Stud Horse kept within the county" during the preceding six months to one dollar for the "4 pairs of Worsted Stockings" judged to be third best. Some of the other categories: "the best two acres of Wheat"; "the best firkin of Butter, not less than 50 lbs."; "the best twenty yards of Bleached Linen, 7.8 wide"; and "the best yoke of working Oxen." Thus, it was natural that the focus of many in the Palmyra area as they retired to their bed that Sunday evening had shifted from their spiritual to their temporal salvation and the work that lay ahead that week.

Joseph Smith's focus that night, however, continued on his spiritual status. He remained awake long after his family and the rest of Palmyra had fallen asleep. While his siblings slept near him in the loft of the Smith's lowly log cabin, Joseph prayed. The rhythmic sounds of the nearby deep breathing hung in the air as his hushed, earnest prayer ascended heavenward.

Years later Joseph recounted the events of that evening: "After I had retired to my bed for the night, I betook myself to prayer and supplication to Almighty God for forgiveness of all my sins and follies, and also for a manifestation to me, that I might know of my state and standing before him; for I had full confidence in obtaining a divine manifestation, as I previously had one." In the little more than three years since his first vision, Joseph found himself "persecuted by those who ought to have been [his] friends." A virtual outcast of organized religion, he "was left to all kinds of temptations" and "frequently fell into many foolish errors, and displayed the weakness of youth, and the foibles of human nature," although he noted that these did not include "any great or malignant sins."

What transpired that particular Sunday to cause seventeen-year-old Joseph to evaluate himself in a manner that led to such earnest prayer is not known. It may have been something that happened at one of Palmyra's churches, but those proceedings have not been preserved. It may have been the fact that the small community of Palmyra lost two of its citizens that day, for death frequently causes the living to reevaluate their lives. One of the deceased was Major Edward Durfee, age fifty-one, an "original settler of the area"; the other was thirteen-month-old Jonathan S. Hussey.

While others slept, Joseph continued calling upon God. After a time Joseph's heartfelt prayer was answered. The nighttime blackness of the cabin loft grew "lighter than at noonday" as a messenger sent from the presence of God appeared at his bedside. Identifying himself as Moroni, a prophet who had lived anciently in the Americas, he told Joseph "that God had a work for [him] to do; and that [his] name should be had for good and evil among all nations, kindreds, and tongues." He informed Joseph that "an account of the former inhabitants of this continent" containing "the fulness of the everlasting Gospel" was buried in a nearby hill. The angel told Joseph that at a future time he would be given the plates in order to publish the record. During the course of the night, the angel returned twice more to repeat his message. "Almost immediately after the heavenly messenger had ascended from me for the third time, the cock crowed," Joseph recalled. "I found that day was approaching, so that our interviews must have occupied the whole of that night."

By his own account, Joseph was little help on the family farm on Monday, 22 September. His contribution to his household would come in another form, one that would not be fully realized until years later. Joseph went to the fields as usual, but he found his "strength so exhausted" as to render him unable to continue. His father, upon learning of Moroni's visit, instructed his son to go to the hill where the plates were buried, as he had been commanded.

Situated nearly three miles southeast of the Smith home, the Hill Cumorah rises 117 feet at its highest point above the surrounding area. While residents around the area little noted what happened there that day, from near the top of the hill on the northwest side where the record was buried, Joseph could have observed some of their comings and goings. Neatly laid-out farms dotted the wooded landscape north of the hill. Beyond was Palmyra, whose northern boundary was the Erie Canal.

Still two years from completion, the Erie Canal was already reshaping life in upstate New York in September 1823. The canal had spawned a booming shipbuilding business at Albany, and barges were floating the completed portions of the canal, including the stretch near Palmyra. As horses ploddingly pulled these barges from the adjacent towpath, a debate raged as to whether steamboats could travel the waterway without damaging the canal. Shortly after Joseph visited the Hill Cumorah, a steamboat passing Palmyra seemingly ended the debate. "It was judged by those who noticed her, that the agitation of the water, caused by the wheel of the boat, would not be so injurious to the banks of the canal, as the swell which attends a boat drawn by horses, at the same speed," the Wayne *Sentinel* reported.

During the fall of 1823, a debate of a different kind was taking place at Washington, D. C. The nation's leaders were considering how best to ensure the United States' rightful place on the world stage in light of changes that had taken place in Latin America. In September 1823, Brazil celebrated the first anniversary of its independence from Portugal. Nearly all of Spain's former colonies had previously held similar celebrations. Peru, which would not officially gain its independence until the following year, had installed Simon Bolivar as its president ten days prior to the visit of Moroni to Joseph Smith. The Holy Alliance, which included Russia and France among its members, had pledged to help Spain restore its former colonies, raising fears in the United States that their promise was a ruse to conquer Latin America for themselves. These fears were heightened by Tsar Alexander I's claim that Alaska's southern boundary was now the fifty-first parallel—the current boundary between the western United States and Canada.

In his annual message to Congress in December 1823, President James Monroe articulated what became known as the Monroe Doctrine. Its principal point reiterated what Secretary of State John Quincy Adams told Russia's minister in June 1823— "The American continents are no longer subjects for any new European colonial establishments." Not only would attempts at future colonization be opposed, Monroe announced, but so would attempts to extend European customs to any part of the new world. American ways were vastly different from European ones, the president asserted. Although designed to stem European colonialism, the Monroe Doctrine received little notice across the Atlantic. It was, however, an important step in crystallizing American thinking about the Western Hemisphere and helped stimulate United States desire for territory and influence. This attitude would later be codified by the term "Manifest Destiny."

One European export, however, would soon be welcomed in the United States. In late September 1823, Scotsman Charles Macintosh was working on revolutionary waterproof rain wear. In early October 1823, he would begin selling his famous "macs."

Back at Palmyra, Joseph Smith was preparing for a deluge of a different kind. After centuries of near drought, not of "thirst for water, but of hearing the words of the Lord," as the Old Testament Prophet Amos described it, the heavens were again open.

The Angel Moroni delivering the Book of Mormon plates to Joseph Smith

Having been three years a virtual outcast after recounting his first vision, a now more-cautious Joseph failed to tell his father what had happened while they undertook their morning's work on the family farm. His strength gone, Joseph was eventually forced to leave the field where they were working. While he was returning to the house, Moroni again appeared and asked Joseph why he had not told his father. After being assured that his father would believe him, the young man returned to tell all that transpired. His father instructed Joseph to go to the Hill Cumorah as the angel commanded.

Upon seeing the gold plates, Joseph could not help but imagine how they would solve his family's financial problems. Chastised by the angel for allowing the plate's monetary value to overshadow their spiritual benefit, Joseph was then commanded to return each year to Cumorah on 22 September to be further taught. In a subsequent meeting, Moroni told Joseph he would not be allowed to obtain the plates "until he had learned to keep the commandments of God—*not only till he was willing but able to do it.*"

"Joseph, why are you so late?" . . .

Presently he smiled, and said in a calm tone, "I have taken the severest chastisement that I have ever had in my life."

My husband, supposing that it was from some of the neighbors, was quite angry and observed, "I would like to know what business anybody had to find fault with you."

"Stop, father, stop," said Joseph, "it was the angel of the Lord. As I passed by the hill of Cumorah, where the plates are, the angel met me and said that I had not been engaged enough in the work of the Lord; that the time had come for the record to be brought forth; and that I must be up and doing and set myself about the things which God had commanded me to do. But, father, give yourself no uneasiness concerning the reprimand which I have received, for I now know the course that I am to pursue, so all will be well."

—Lucy Mack Smith, describing an experience her son Joseph had shortly before receiving the plates
from which he translated the Book of Mormon.

Joseph continued to receive instructions from time to time. . . . We gathered our children together and gave our time up to the discussion of those things which he instructed to us. I presume our family presented an aspect as singular as any that ever lived upon the face of the earth—all seated in a circle, father, mother, sons and daughters, and giving the most profound attention to a boy, eighteen years of age, who had never read the Bible through in his life; he seemed much less inclined to the perusal of books than any of the rest of our children, but far more given to meditation and deep study.

—Lucy Mack Smith, describing events following the September 1823 visit of the Angel Moroni to her son Joseph.

There was much the unschooled young man needed to learn. Joseph later wrote that "many visits from the angels of God unfolded the majesty and glory of the events that should transpire in the last days." During this time, the Smith family frequently gathered to hear Joseph recount what he had learned. Lucy Mack Smith recalled Joseph sharing "some of the most amusing recitals" of the ancient inhabitants of the continent, including their dress and mode of travel.

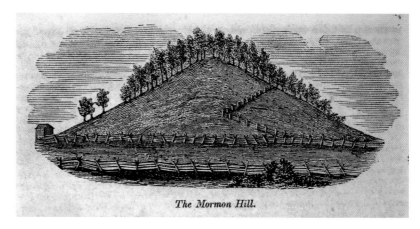

The Mormon Hill—Hill Cumorah

Two months after Moroni's visit, the Smiths suffered a devastating loss when the family's oldest son, Alvin, died. Joseph particularly felt the loss, since Alvin had shown the greatest interest of any family member in Joseph's work. Alvin's dying words to the young prophet encouraged him: "Be faithful in receiving instruction, and in keeping every commandment that is given you."

Alvin's death intensified the family's financial difficulties. In spite of their best efforts, the Smiths lost title to their newly constructed home at Manchester, New York, in December 1825 when they were unable to come up with the final house payment. They would, however, continue to live there as renters.

The family's financial problems led Joseph into money digging—a popular practice in America at the time. In 1825, a Palmyra paper proclaimed that "we could name . . . at least five hundred respectable men who . . . believe that immense treasures lie concealed upon our green mountains, many of whom have been for a number of years industriously and perseveringly engaged in digging it up." However, unlike his fellow citizens, Joseph's treasure seeking would

Eastern View in Main-street, Palmyra

View of landscape near the Joseph Smith home in Harmony, Pennsylvania

haunt him for years. Prior to the arrival of the angel Moroni, Joseph discovered a seer stone while digging a well for a neighbor. Although seer stones are intended to reveal hidden knowledge from God, Joseph tried unsuccessfully to use the stone to seek buried treasure.

In October 1825, Josiah Stowell, of Chenango County, New York, anxious to locate one of the many lost Spanish silver mines rumored to exist along the New York–Pennsylvania border, hired Joseph "on account of having heard that he possessed certain keys, by which he could discern things invisible to the natural eye." After less than a month's work, Joseph returned to his upstate New York home without having located the mine. The following year, Joseph was charged with being a "disorderly person," for reportedly using his seer stone in money digging.

While employed by Stowell, Joseph boarded at the Harmony, Pennsylvania, home of Isaac and Elizabeth Hale, whose daughter Emma caught his eye. In late 1826, Joseph again returned to Stowell's employ and renewed his acquaintance with Emma. Regarding Emma, Joseph told his parents, "She would be my choice in preference to any other woman I have ever seen." Emma later stated, "Preferring him to any other man I knew, I consented [to marry him]."

AN ELECT LADY: EMMA SMITH

Emma Hale was born 10 July 1804 in Harmony, Pennsylvania, to Isaac and Elizabeth Hale. She met Joseph Smith in October 1825 when he was working for Josiah Stoal. The Prophet wrote, "During the time that I was thus employed, I was put to board with a Mr. Isaac Hale, of that place; it was there I first saw my wife (his daughter), Emma Hale. On the 18th of January, 1827, we were married. . . . Owing to my continuing to assert that I had seen a vision, persecution still followed me, and my wife's father's family were very much opposed to our being married. I was, therefore, under the necessity of taking her elsewhere; so we went and were married at the house of Squire Tarbill, in South Bainbridge, Chenango county, New York. Immediately, after my marriage, I left Mr. Stoal's, and went to my father's and farmed with him that season."

Emma and Joseph became the parents of eleven children (two adopted), five of whom reached adulthood—Joseph III, Frederick Granger, Alexander Hale, David Hyrum, and adopted daughter Julia. The couple enjoyed a loving, close, and supportive relationship in which Emma actively participated in Joseph's divine mission. In a July 1830 revelation to Joseph Smith, Emma was told, "I speak unto you, Emma Smith, my daughter; . . . thou art an elect lady, whom I have called. . . . And the office of thy calling shall be for a comfort unto my servant, Joseph Smith, Jun., . . . in his afflictions, with consoling words, in the spirit of meekness. . . . Be unto him for a scribe, while there is no one to be a scribe for him." To help her husband with the Book of Mormon translation, she received his dictation "hour after hour; and when returning after meals, or after interruptions, he would at once begin where he had left off, without either seeing the manuscript or having any portion of it read to him." She was also called upon to select hymns for the first Church hymnal, some of which we still sing today: "Gently raise the Sacred Strain," "I Know That My Redeemer Lives," "Redeemer of Israel," "Joy to the World!" and "The Spirit of God Like a Fire Is Burning." This elect lady was a founding member and first president of Nauvoo's Female Relief Society, begun in 1842.

As the wife of a man greatly loved and hated, Emma was rarely free from anxiety and insecurity. Lucy Mack Smith empathized with her daughter-in-law and praised her, noting, "I have never seen a woman in my life who would endure every species of fatigue and hardship, from month to month, and from year to year, with that unflinching courage, zeal, and patience, which [Emma] has ever done. . . . She has breasted the storms of persecution, and [been] buffeted [by] the rage of men and devils, which would have borne down any other woman."

The Prophet often expressed the depth of his love and appreciation for Emma. After a period of forced hiding in August 1842 for his purported role in an attempted murder of former Missouri governor Lilburn W. Boggs, Joseph and Emma were reunited: "With what unspeakable delight, and what transports of joy swelled my bosom, when I took by the hand on that night, my beloved Emma, she that was my wife, even the wife of my youth; and the choice of my heart. Many were the reviberations of my mind when I contemplated for a moment the many scenes we had been called to pass through. The fatigues, and the toils, the sorrows, and sufferings, and the joys and consolations from time to time had strewed our paths and crowned our board. Oh! What a co-mingling of thought filled my mind for the moment, again she is here, even in the seventh trouble, undaunted, firm and unwavering, unchangeable, affectionate Emma."

Three and a half years after Joseph's martyrdom, Emma married Lewis Bidamon on 23 December 1847. They lived in Nauvoo, where she died 30 April 1879. She is buried alongside Joseph and his brother Hyrum.

Emma Hale Smith, ca. 1842

On 18 January 1827, the young couple wed. "I had no intention of marrying when I left home," Emma recalled of the day's events. Weddings at this time were not the elaborate productions of future generations, but since her parents disapproved of their marriage—Emma described her father as "bitterly opposed" to Joseph—the young couple eloped, a common practice. Afterward, Joseph took his new bride to the Smith farm at Manchester. In August, he returned to his in-laws to effect a reconciliation with Emma's family and to get her belongings.

"Popping the Question"—courtship in nineteenth-century America

"Was not Joseph Smith a money digger?
"Yes, but it was never a very profitable job for him,
as he only got fourteen dollars a month for it.
"Did not Joseph Smith steal his wife?
"Ask her, she was of age, she can answer for herself."

—From a self-interview Joseph Smith published in 1838 hoping to save himself having to answer the same questions "a thousand times over and over again."

In the early hours of 22 September 1827, Joseph and Emma drove to the Hill Cumorah. Leaving his new bride in a borrowed wagon, Joseph was given both the plates and the Urim and Thummim used to translate the Book of Mormon. Immediately stories circulated about Joseph's golden plates. Numerous attempts were made to steal them, forcing Joseph to devise several hiding places in and around his house. To drive away a contingent of would-be robbers, the Smiths were compelled one night to charge out into the darkness surrounding their home, shouting military orders as if leading members of the local militia.

1822

Brazil gained independence from Portugal

The first U.S. patent for artificial teeth was awarded to C. M. Graham

Charleston, South Carolina, authorities prevented a massive slave uprising led by local freeman Denmark Vessey; the treatment of slaves became harsher in its aftermath

U.S. army surgeon William Beaumont began studying the digestive system after treating a French-Canadian trapper wounded in the stomach

Franz Schubert stopped work on his Symphony No. 8 ("Unfinished")

1823

The angel Moroni first appeared to Joseph Smith; Joseph first saw the plates from which the Book of Mormon was translated

On Christmas Eve, Clement Clarke Moore first read to his children his poem "A Visit from St. Nicholas," better known as "'Twas the Night Before Christmas."

Guatemala, El Salvador, Nicaragua, Honduras, and Costa Rica formed the United Provinces of Central America; disbanded in 1838

English chemist Michael Faraday liquefied chlorine for use in bleaches and water purification

Four years after going deaf, Beethoven completed his Ninth Symphony, which includes the famous "Ode to Joy."

James Fenimore Cooper published *The Pioneers*, the first of his "Leather-Stocking" novels

Samuel F. B. Morse painted *The Old House of Representatives*

James Monroe articulated the Monroe Doctrine in his annual message to Congress

Pope Pius VII died; pope from 1800–1823, he was succeeded by Pope Leo XII

MARTIN HARRIS

Martin Harris (1783–1875) was a prosperous farmer recognized for his honesty, generosity, and industrious habits. A Christian with no denominational loyalties, he wrote, "I was inspired of the Lord and taught by the Spirit that I should not join any church." But that all began to change when Joseph Smith Sr. taught him about the visitation of Angel Moroni and the sacred golden plates. In the autumn of 1827, Harris agreed to aid Joseph Smith in publishing his translation—it was his $3,000 that financed the first 5,000 copies of the Book of Mormon.

As one of the Three Witnesses to the Book of Mormon, Martin Harris, along with Oliver Cowdery and David Whitmer, proclaimed, "We, through the grace of God the Father, and our Lord Jesus Christ, have seen the plates which contain this record, . . . and we also know that they have been translated by the gift and power of God."

Harris attended the 6 April 1830 organization of the Church, at which time he was baptized by Oliver Cowdery. In the summer of 1831, Harris traveled to Missouri with the Prophet to purchase property and designate Zion, and he was asked to live the "law of consecration." He also supervised the financing of Church publications. In 1832, he served a mission with his brother Emer. By 1834, he was back in Kirtland, just in time to march with Zion's Camp to Missouri to help the persecuted Saints. Harris attended the 1836 dedication of the Kirtland Temple, which was an intense spiritual experience for the Saints.

However, intense differences over monetary practices forced a clash with Church leaders and led to Harris's excommunication in December 1837. He was rebaptized 7 November 1842, after which he bore witness to the Book of Mormon in England and returned to Kirtland, where he preached, farmed, and served as a self-appointed tour guide of the Kirtland Temple.

In 1870, he determined to join the Saints and his family (who moved in 1856) in Utah, where he settled in Cache Valley. He died in Clarkston, Utah, on 17 July 1875.

1824

Joseph Smith returned to the Hill Cumorah to meet with the angel Moroni

South American revolutionary leader Simon Bolivar secured Peru's independence

None of four presidential candidates won an electoral majority; the House of Representatives subsequently chose John Quincy Adams as the sixth U.S. president

John Cadbury opened a tea and coffee shop in Birmingham, England, the beginnings of the Cadbury confectionery company

Jim Bridger discovered the Great Salt Lake

The Ecumenical American Sunday School Union was established as Sunday Schools proliferated

U.S. fur trader Jedediah Strong Smith opened "South Pass" as part of the Oregon Trail

English mason Joseph Aspdin patented Portland Cement

James Everett Seaver's *Life of Mary Jemison* became a best-seller, recounting her capture by the Shawnees as a teenager in 1758 and her subsequent life among the Indians (Jemison died in 1833)

LITTLE SHORT OF MADNESS

From the early days of the republic, the question of how best to link the American frontier of the Great Lakes region with the eastern seaboard was frequently and hotly debated. New York Governor DeWitt Clinton favored a canal stretching across New York linking Lake Erie with the Hudson River at Albany. No project of that size had ever been attempted. Two previous canals near Charleston, South Carolina, and Boston, Massachusetts, were only about twenty miles each. Upon learning of Clinton's proposal, Thomas Jefferson told a canal booster, "Why, sir, you talk of making a canal of 350 miles through the wilderness—it is little short of madness to talk of it at this day!" Jefferson felt that this "splendid project" might "be executed a century hence."

Nevertheless, in the spring of 1816, the New York Legislature funded what was derisively called "Clinton's Big Ditch." Because no American engineers had expertise in building such a canal, two lawyers—mockingly described by one newspaper as "a brace of country lawyers with a compass and a spirit level"—were chosen to head the project.

Work began on a middle section of the canal on 4 July 1817, the nation's forty-first birthday. The canal's engineers selected the spot as the best place to begin on-the-job training. Work was done in quarter-mile sections, usually by farmers and local contractors.

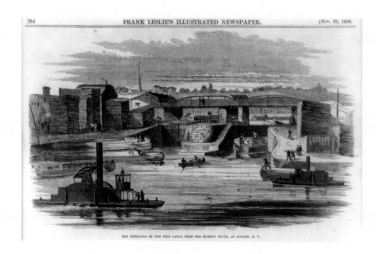

The Erie Canal at Albany, New York

1825

Joseph Smith again returned to the Hill Cumorah; he met Emma Hale while working for Josiah Stowell

Czar Alexander I of Russia died; his brother Nicholas I became czar of Russia

The first steam-powered railroad, the Stockton-Darlington, began operation in England

The canal boat *Seneca Chief* officially opened the Erie Canal

British social reformer Robert Owen established a secular utopian community at Harmony, Indiana

French physicist André Ampère published *Electrodynamics,* the foundation for electromagnetic theory

Bolivia obtained its independence from Peru

The Mexican state of Texas-Chohuila officially allowed settlers from the U.S.; in 1830 Mexico would prohibit further U.S. settlers from colonizing the area

1826

Joseph Smith was charged with disorderly conduct for his "money seeking" activities; he again returned to the Hill Cumorah

James Fenimore Cooper published *The Last of the Mohicans*

Thomas Jefferson and John Adams died on 4 July, the 50th anniversary of American Independence

English astronomer John Herschel proved conclusively that the earth revolves around the sun

Lydia Maria Child began publication of the *Juvenile Miscellany,* the nation's first children's magazine.

U.S. Secretary of State Henry Clay and Virginia Representative John Randolph fought a duel; their bad feelings arose from the outcome of the 1824 presidential election

To deal with variances in elevation, eighty-three locks and eighteen aqueducts were built. Initially only forty feet wide and four feet deep, it was later widened to seventy feet wide and seven feet deep.

Although portions were open to traffic as soon as they were completed, the Erie Canal did not officially open until November 1825 with the firing of cannon at Buffalo. Following that blast, a series of cannon salutes began, first along the canal and then down the Hudson River, with the last cannon fired in New York City an hour and twenty minutes later. Governor Clinton made the maiden voyage from Buffalo to New York City, which ended with a ceremonial pouring of a keg of Lake Erie water into the harbor in a symbolic "Wedding of the Waters."

The success of the Erie Canal inspired "the canal era" of state and federally funded waterway projects. By 1840, more than thirty-three hundred miles of inland waterways had been constructed.

Initially, horses or mules pulled the boats along the Erie Canal, but eventually steam power was also brought to play. Travelers on the canal frequently heard "Low bridge, everybody down," a phrase later immortalized in song. Even after a competing railroad was built, the canal continued to carry more freight than its competitor, before eventually falling victim to the rails in the 1880s.

The canal spawned new settlement throughout western New York and into the Great Lakes region. As well as carrying emigrants and merchandise west, it opened eastern markets to western grains and goods. Before the Erie Canal, it cost $100 to ship a ton of grain from Buffalo to New York City; by 1855 it cost $8. The time needed for the journey dropped from twenty to six days. The canal also helped establish New York City as the country's principal seaport.

The Erie Canal is also given partial credit for the diverse social reforms that originated in western New York, including numerous religious revivals and the establishment of the women's rights and temperance movements, as ideas now could spread more easily.

Joseph Smith and other Latter-day Saints took advantage of this new technology in fulfilling missions and gathering converts to Kirtland, Ohio. In 1836, Joseph traveled the canal and intersecting waterways while en route from Kirtland to Salem, Massachusetts.

1827

Joseph Smith married Emma Hale, received the ancient record from the angel Moroni, and moved to Harmony, Pennsylvania, to escape continual efforts to steal the gold plates

John Audubon published the first volume of *Birds of North America*

Joseph Dixon opened the first lead-pencil factory in the U.S.

Massachusetts adopted the nation's first compulsory education law: tax-supported schools were mandated in every community with 500 or more families; only history was a required subject

Mardi Gras was first celebrated at New Orleans

Ballet was introduced to the U.S. by famed French danseuse Mme Francisquy Hutin; many found her performance risqué

German scientist Georg Ohm published his law of electrical voltage and current

1828

Martin Harris showed examples of characters copied from the gold plates to Professor Charles Anthon, served as scribe for Joseph, and lost 116 pages of translated manuscript; Joseph Smith lost power to translate for a season

Noah Webster's monumental two-volume *American Dictionary of the English Language* was published

Andrew Jackson was elected seventh U.S. president

Sarah Josepha Hale began *Ladies' Magazine*

Uruguay obtained independence from Argentina

Amalgam, an alloy of mercury and silver, was used to fill teeth for the first time

Friedrich Wohler started the science of inorganic chemistry by synthesizing urea

As the harassment intensified, Joseph returned to Harmony, using fifty dollars Martin Harris had given him to make the trip. Although he and Emma were stopped by men attempting to obtain the plates, they successfully reached their destination. When Joseph refused to show the plates to Emma's father, the young couple was forced to move to a small house near the Hale farm.

Beginning December 1827, Joseph translated a few pages, with Emma and her brother Reuben serving as scribes. During a February 1828 visit of Martin Harris, Joseph produced a facsimile of the characters on the plates; Harris took the facsimile to New York City to discuss with scholars. Since the characters were "Reformed Egyptian," it is unlikely they could verify the translation, although they would have been able to recognize whether the characters resembled Egyptian or other ancient languages. In his meeting with Dr. Charles Anthon of Columbia College, the scholar proclaimed, "I cannot read a sealed book," fulfilling a prophecy found in Isaiah 29. Harris returned convinced of the record's authenticity and assumed the role of scribe.

Classical scholar Charles Anthon of Columbia College

Remember, remember that it is not the work of God that is frustrated, but the work of men;

For although a man may have many revelations, and have power to do many might works, yet if he boasts in his own strength, and sets at naught the counsels of God, and follows after the dictates of his own will and carnal desires, he must fall and incur the vengeance of a just God upon him. . . .

And behold, how oft you have transgressed the commandments and the laws of God, and have gone on in the persuasions of men.

For, behold, you should not have feared man more than God (D&C 3:3–4, 6–7).

—Rebuke Joseph Smith received from the Lord after Martin Harris lost the 116 pages that Joseph had translated.

KEEP YOUR NOSE TO THE GRINDSTONE

So important was the local miller to many communities in the early 1800s that he was frequently exempted from otherwise compulsory military service. Without his service, farmers would be forced to grind their harvest by hand, a process so slow, difficult, and time consuming that it was considered only for small jobs or in times of emergency.

It took skill to operate a mill. The huge grinding stones, which could weigh a ton, were four to five feet in diameter. Only certain types of stones were used, many of which were imported from Europe and could be replaced only at great cost. If the grinding stones were set too far apart, the "run of the mill," whether corn or wheat, would not be an ideal product. Set too close, the large grinding stones would rub against each other and wear out.

When the mill was operating with all the cranks and gears in motion, the noise was deafening. Given the loud noise and the fact that the miller had other duties, such as bagging flour, he couldn't constantly keep his eyes on the millstones to see that they were not wearing themselves out. The stones, however, gave off an unmistakable, pungent smell when rubbed together. So even with his back turned, the miller could get the job done if he kept his "nose to the grindstone."

By June 1828, Joseph had translated "the Book of Lehi," filling 116 manuscript pages. Harris's wife pressured her husband to let her see the manuscript. Twice Joseph went to the Lord, and twice he was told no. His third inquiry resulted in a powerful learning experience for the twenty-three-year-old prophet. Harris was permitted to take the pages on solemn oath to show them only to a specified few.

Shortly after Harris returned to Palmyra with the manuscript, Emma gave birth to the couple's first child, Alvin, who died shortly after birth. Three weeks later, Emma recovered sufficiently to allow a greatly tormented Joseph to travel to upstate New York to learn why Harris had not returned. Joseph's worst fears were realized. "Martin!" he exclaimed upon seeing his friend. "Have you broken your oath, and brought down condemnation upon my head as well as your own? . . . All is lost! All is lost! What shall I do? I have sinned—it is I who tempted the wrath of God. I should have been satisfied with the first answer which I received from the Lord; for he told me that it was not safe to let the writing go out of my possession." The Lord took away Joseph's power to translate for a season.

In September 1828, the Urim and Thummim was returned to a humbled Joseph. Back at Harmony, he again began to translate. By March 1829, however, a mere sixteen pages had been produced. At that time, Joseph received a revelation that surely inspired him. In spite of his follies and missteps, the Lord assured Joseph, "This generation shall have my word through you." The revelation, however, included an admonishment: "And now I command you, my servant Joseph, to repent and walk more uprightly before me, and to yield to the persuasions of men no more" (D&C 5:10, 21).

4 JULY 1826

With the nation's fiftieth birthday less than an hour away, Nicholas Trist faced a tough decision. Eighty-three-year-old Thomas Jefferson lay on the verge of death, valiantly hoping to live until the Fourth of July, when the nation would celebrate the fiftieth anniversary of the adoption of the Declaration of Independence. Throughout 3 July 1826, the great man faded in and out of consciousness, awaking long enough to ask, "Is it the Fourth?" Each time Trist answered no. "My eyes were constantly turning from his face to the clock in the corner," he recalled. When Jefferson again asked the question on the brink of the anniversary, Trist pretended he hadn't heard. But when Jefferson repeated the question, Trist simply nodded. "Ah," proclaimed the relieved Declaration's author, who fell back asleep. Jefferson awakened once more, on the morning of the Fourth, before finally passing away at his beloved Monticello shortly after 12:00 noon.

Far to the north at Quincy, Massachusetts, ninety-year-old John Adams, the driving force behind American Independence, was too ill to attend the local ceremonies. Previously he had provided a toast to commemorate the nation's fiftieth anniversary: "Independence now and Independence forever." In response to an effort to have him come up with something more eloquent, Adams responded that he would add "not a word." As his fellow Americans commemorated his work of a half-century earlier, Adams died shortly before 6:00 P.M. Unaware of what had transpired only hours earlier, he reportedly whispered as his dying words, "Thomas Jefferson still survives." Neither lived to see "the bonfires and the illuminations" that Adams predicted would lighten the night sky.

The odds that the two men most responsible for the events of 4 July 1776 should both die on the same glorious, significant day—the fiftieth anniversary of America's Independence—seem astronomical. As Americans learned of this remarkable occurrence, they proclaimed it was evidence of divine favor, of God's blessing on the revolution these men helped to lead and the nation that grew from their effort. These two Founding Fathers also had the distinction of being the only two signers of the Declaration who also served as president.

Thomas Jefferson, 1743–1826

While they died friends, they spent part of their life as political enemies—one a Federalist, the other a Republican—before effecting a reconciliation. "You and I ought not to die before we have explained ourselves to each other," Adams wrote in one of the many letters the two exchanged in old age. "Laboring always at the same oar," Jefferson wrote his friend, "we rode through the storm with heart and hand, and made a happy port." Such prose prompted Adams to write, "I seem to have a Bank at Monticello on which I can draw for a letter of friendship and entertainment when I please."

JOHN ADAMS,
2ᴺᴰ PRESIDENT OF THE UNITED STATES.

PHILADELPHIA.
Published by C. S. Williams, N.E. corner of Market & 7ᵗʰ St.

John Adams, 1735–1826.

Elsewhere on 4 July 1826, Americans held celebrations befitting the day. Activities at the nation's capital included a "long parade" that featured President John Quincy Adams. At the small town of Thomaston, Maine, Independence Day opened with "the roar of cannon . . . a salute of 24 guns from a brass six pounder . . . , [and] the ringing of bells." Nearly three hundred townspeople gathered to feast together, toast nation and community, and hear the Declaration of Independence read. After being entertained by "some fine patriotic songs and towards the last of it some comic songs in fine style," the residents enjoyed "a fine display of fireworks."

The Susquehanna River

After we [Joseph Smith and Oliver Cowdery] had been baptized, we experienced great and glorious blessings from our Heavenly Father. . . . We were filled with the Holy Ghost and rejoiced in the God of our salvation.

Our minds being now enlightened, we began to have the scriptures laid open to our understandings, and the true meaning and intention of their more mysterious passages revealed unto us in a manner which we never could attain to previously, nor ever before had thought of.

—From Joseph Smith's 1839 history.

Now, what do we hear in the gospel which we have received? A voice of gladness! A voice of mercy from heaven; and a voice of truth out of the earth; glad tidings for the dead; a voice of gladness for the living and the dead; glad tidings of great joy. . . .

And again, what do we hear? Glad tidings from Cumorah! Moroni, an angel from heaving declaring the fulfillment of the prophets—the book to be revealed. A voice of the Lord in the wilderness of Fayette, Seneca county, declaring the three witnesses to bear record of the book! The voice of Michael on the banks of the Susquehanna, detecting the devil when he appeared as an angel of light! The voice of Peter, James, and John in the wilderness between Harmony, Susquehanna county, and Colesville, Broome county, on the Susquehanna river, declaring themselves as possessing the keys of the kingdom, and of the dispensation of the fulness of times!

And again, the voice of God in the chamber of old Father Whitmer, in Fayette, Seneca county, and at sundry times, and in divers places through all the travels and tribulations of this Church of Jesus Christ of Latter-day Saints! And the voice of Michael, the archangel; the voice of Gabriel, and of Raphael, and of divers angels, from Michael or Adam down to the present time, all declaring their dispensation, their rights, their keys, their honors, their majesty and glory, and the power of their priesthood; giving line upon line, precept upon precept; here a little, and there a little; giving us consolation by holding forth that which is to come, confirming our hope! (D&C 128:19–21)

—Excerpt from an epistle of Joseph Smith to The Church of Jesus Christ of Latter-day Saints, 6 September 1842. Joseph B. Noble recalled Joseph stating "that the voices of the angels became so familiar that he knew their names before he saw them."

The following month, April 1829, the work of translation began in earnest, with Oliver Cowdery filling the role of scribe. After reading about the necessity of baptism while translating, Joseph and Oliver prayed near the banks of the Susquehanna River on 15 June 1829 to learn the Lord's will concerning that ordinance. Their pleas were answered by a visit from John the Baptist, who restored the Aaronic Priesthood, which includes the power to baptize. Later Joseph and Oliver received the higher, or Melchizedek, priesthood under the hands of Peter, James, and John, including the authority to confer the gift of the Holy Ghost.

Interference by residents of the Harmony area again slowed the work of translation. Consequently, Oliver wrote his friend David Whitmer, asking for assistance. Upon finding his fields miraculously plowed, David traveled to Harmony in June 1829 to help Joseph, Emma, and Oliver return to upstate New York. The translation of the Book of Mormon was then completed by 1 July 1829 at the Fayette, Seneca County, home of Peter Whitmer.

1829

Joseph Smith finished translating the Book of Mormon, with Oliver Cowdery as scribe; they received the Aaronic Priesthood from John the Baptist, and the Melchizedek Priesthood from Peter, James, and John; Joseph was allowed to show the plates to witnesses

The Age of the Common Man had a less-than-auspicious beginning as a boisterous reception at the White House followed Andrew Jackson's inauguration

A citywide police force, Scotland Yard, was formed in London to address an increase in crime

Scottish chemist James Smithson bequeathed the U.S. £100,000; used to establish the Smithsonian Institution

Slavery was abolished in Mexico, except among American settlers in Texas

Francis Lieber published the first volume of *Encyclopedia Americana*; the thirteenth and final volume was published in 1833

OLIVER COWDERY

Oliver Cowdery (1806–1850), a rural schoolteacher, was a scribe to the Prophet, one of the Three Witnesses, and associate president of the Church. In the October 1834 *Messenger and Advocate,* he expressed his feelings about witnessing and taking part in many important milestones in the restoration of the gospel: "These were days never to be forgotten—to sit under the sound of a voice dictated by the inspiration of heaven, awakened the utmost gratitude of this bosom! Day after day I continued, uninterrupted, to write from his mouth, as he translated with the Urim and Thummim, or, as the Nephites would have said, 'Interpreters,' the history or record called 'The Book of Mormon.' . . . The Lord, who is rich in mercy, and ever willing to answer the consistent prayer of the humble . . . spake peace to us, while the veil was parted and the angel of God came down . . . and delivered the anxiously looked for message, and the keys of the Gospel of repentance. What joy! what wonder! what amazement! While the world was racked and distracted—while millions were groping as the blind for the wall, and while all men were resting upon uncertainty, as a general mass, our eyes beheld, our ears heard, as in the 'blaze of day.' . . . We received under his hand the Holy Priesthood as he said, 'Upon you my fellow-servants, In the name of Messiah, I confer this Priesthood and this authority, which shall remain upon earth, that the Sons of Levi may yet offer an offering unto the Lord in righteousness!'"

Profound differences over economic and political philosophy and practice led to a deep estrangement between the Prophet and Cowdery. Excommunicated on 12 April 1838, he was rebaptized at Council Bluffs, Iowa, in November 1848. He died at Richmond, Missouri, on 3 March 1850.

After it was truly manifested unto this first elder [Joseph] that he had received a remission of his sins, he was entangled again in the vanities of the world;

But after repenting, and humbling himself sincerely, through faith, God ministered unto him by an holy angel, whose countenance was as lightning, and whose garments were pure and white above all other whiteness;

And gave unto him commandments which inspired him;

And gave him power from on high, by the means which were before prepared, to translate the Book of Mormon (D&C 20:5–8).

—From a revelation given to Joseph Smith shortly before the Church was organized on 6 April 1830.

Joseph provided only generalities about how he translated the record. "It was not intended to tell the world all the particulars of the coming forth of the Book of Mormon," he said. Because he was unacquainted with "reformed Egyptian," the translation process of necessity involved revelation. He had to study each passage in his mind and then put the idea into his own words, the language of nineteenth-century America. As with any other translated work, the Book of Mormon invariably contains expressions and characteristics consistent with its translator's background and training. Oliver Cowdery wrote of the process, "To sit under the sound of a voice directed by the inspiration of heaven awakened the utmost gratitude of this bosom." Emma noted that her husband "would dictate hour after hour, and when returning after meals, or other interruptions, he would at once begin where he left off, without either seeing the manuscript or hearing any portion read." Once the translation was completed, Joseph returned the plates to the heavenly messenger "according to arrangement."

Having read in the Book of Mormon about three witnesses who were to testify of the authenticity of the volume, Joseph inquired of the Lord in behalf of Oliver Cowdery, David Whitmer, and Martin Harris. After much fervent prayer, Joseph and the three designated witnesses were shown the plates by the angel. A relieved Joseph proclaimed, "Now they know for themselves, that I do not go about to deceive the people, and I feel as if I was relieved of a burden which was almost too heavy for me to bear, and it rejoices my soul, that I am not any longer to be entirely alone in the world." Soon afterward, Joseph was permitted to show the plates to eight additional witnesses, including members of his own family.

The Three Witnesses who saw the gold plates of the Book of Mormon

In June 1829, Joseph obtained the copyright on the Book of Mormon. Later that summer he persuaded E. B. Grandin to print 5,000 copies, a number greater than was commonly published at the time. Typesetting and printing began in August 1829, with the last pages completed seven months later in late March 1830. The process of getting the Book of Mormon into print was not without challenges. Although Martin Harris guaranteed the $3,000 cost by mortgaging his farm, concerns about payment caused Grandin to briefly suspend work. A local newspaper that shared Grandin's press obtained and briefly published sections of "Joe Smith's Gold Bible" until Joseph successfully stopped this unauthorized publication. Finally, on 26 March 1830, the Book of Mormon went on sale.

With the Book of Mormon published, Joseph began final preparations for another important step in the latter-day work. He had been directed by revelation to officially incorporate the Church of Christ on 6 April 1830. This event would serve as a commencement day following ten years of extraordinary schooling for Joseph. ✦

The E. B. Grandin bookstore (at left, in section identified by L. W. Chase sign) where the Book of Mormon was printed, in Palmyra, New York

107

Northern District
of New-York,   To wit:

Be it remembered, That on the *eleventh*
day of *June* in the *fifty third* year of
the Independence of the United States of America, A. D.
1829 *Joseph Smith Junior*
of the said District, ha*th* deposited in this Office the
title of a *Book* the right whereof *he* claim*s*
as *Author* in the words following, to wit: *The*

Book of Mormon, an account written by the hand of Mormon upon plates
taken from the plates of Nephi; Wherefore it is an abridgment of the record of the people
of Nephi and also of the Lamanites, which are a remnant of the House of Israel;
and also to Jew & Gentile written by way of commandment and also by the spirit
of Prophesy & of revelation, written & sealed & hid up unto the Lord, that they
might not be destroyed, to come forth by the gift & power of God unto the interpretation thereof — sealed up by the hand of Moroni & hid up unto the Lord, to come
forth in due time by the way of Gentile, the interpretation thereof by the gift of God, an abridgment taken from the book of Ether: Also, which is a record of the people of Jared, which
were scattered at the time the Lord confound the language of the people, when they were building
a tower to get to heaven; which is to show unto the remnant of the house of Israel how great
things the Lord hath done for their fathers; & that they may know the covenants of the Lord
that they are not cast off forever: and also to the convincing of the Jew & Gentile that
Jesus is the Christ, the eternal God, manifesting himself unto all nations. And now if there
be fault, it be the mistake of men; therefore condemn not the things of God, that
ye may be found spotless at the judgment seat of Christ. By Joseph Smith Junior, Author & proprietor.

In conformity to the act of the Congress of the United States, entitled "An act
for the encouragement of learning, by securing the copies of Maps, Charts,
and Books, to the authors and proprietors of such copies, during the times therein
mentioned;" and also, to the act entitled "An act supplementary to an act entitled 'An act for the encouragement of learning, by securing the copies of
Maps, Charts, and Books, to the authors and proprietors of such copies during
the times therein mentioned,' and extending the benefits thereof to the arts of Designing, Engraving, and Etching historical and other prints."

R R Lansing Clerk of the Dist.
Court of the United States for the Northern
District of New York

Book of Mormon copyright, 11 June 1829

The boldness of my plans and measures can readily be tested by the touchstone of all schemes, systems, projects, and adventures—truth; for truth is a matter of fact; and the fact is, that by the power of God I translated the Book of Mormon from hieroglyphics, the knowledge of which was lost to the world, in which wonderful event I stood alone, an unlearned youth, to combat the worldly wisdom and multiplied ignorance of eighteen centuries, with a new revelation, which (if they would receive the ever-lasting Gospel), would open the eyes of more than eight hundred millions of people, and make "plain the old paths," wherein if a man walk in all the ordinances of God blameless, he shall inherit eternal life.

—Joseph Smith to James
Arlington Bennett,
13 November 1843.

THE AMERICAN FRUGAL HOUSEWIFE

"The true economy of housekeeping is simply the art of gathering up all the fragments, so that nothing be lost. I mean fragments of *time,* as well as *materials,*" wrote Lydia Maria Child in her 1828 advice book, *The Frugal Housewife*. Homemakers positively responded to Mrs. Child's advice; the book became a best-seller, going through dozens of printings. It was retitled *The American Frugal Housewife* to reflect its uniquely American perspective. Child had hoped to include tid-bits from a similar book published in England, but she "found the book so little fitted to the wants of this country" that she was able to "extract but little."

Lydia Child's volume covers a wide range of sub-jects, including instructions for making calf's-foot jelly and pig's-foot jelly; remedies for health problems ("a stocking bound on warm from the foot, at night is good for the sore throat"); and counsel for raising children ("I would not cramp a boy's energies by compelling him always to cut wood, or draw water; but I would teach him not to be ashamed, should his companions happen to find him doing either one or the other.").

What follows is a sampling of advice from Mrs. Child:

> Pig's head is a profitable thing to buy. It is despised, because it is cheap; but when well cooked it is delicious. Well cleaned, the tip of the snout chopped off, and put in brine a week, it is very good for boiling; the cheeks, in particular, are very sweet; they are better than any other pieces of pork to bake with beans. The head is likewise very good baked about an hour and a half. It tastes like roast pork, and yields abun-dance of sweet fat, for shortening.
>
> A spoonful of ashes stirred in cider is good to prevent sickness of the stomach. Physicians frequently order it in cases of cholera-morbus.

In this country, we are apt to let children romp away their existence, till they get to be thir-teen or fourteen. This is not well. It is not well for the purses and patience of parents; and it has a still worse effect on the morals and habits of the children. *Begin early* is the great maxim for everything in education. A child of six years old can be made useful; and should be taught to con-sider every day lost in which some little thing has not been done to assist others.

It is a great deal better for the boys and girls on a farm to be picking blackberries at six cents a quart, than to be wearing out their clothes in useless play.

Look frequently to the pails, to see that noth-ing is thrown to the pigs which should have been in the grease-pot.

Make your own bread and cake. Some people think it is just as cheap to buy of the baker and confectioner; but it is not half as cheap. True, it is more convenient; and therefore the rich are justifiable in employing them; but those who are under the necessity of being economical, should make convenience a secondary object.

New England rum, constantly used to wash the hair, keeps it very clean, and free from dis-ease, and promotes its growth a great deal more than Macassar oil. Brandy is very strengthening to the roots of the hair; but it has a hot, drying tendency, which N.E. rum has not.

For a sudden attack of quincy or croup, bathe the neck with bear's grease, and pour it down the throat. Goose-grease, or any kind of oily grease, is as good as bear's oil.

A rind of pork bound upon a wound occa-sioned by a needle, pin, or nail, prevents the lock-jaw. Strong soft-soap, mixed with pulverized chalk, about as thick as batter, put, in a thin cloth or bag, upon the wound, is said to be a preventive to this dangerous disorder.

Blackberries are extremely useful in cases of dysentery. To eat the berries is very healthy; tea made of the roots and leaves is beneficial; and a syrup made of the berries is still better. Blackberries have sometimes effected a cure when physicians despaired.

Boiled potatoes are said to cleanse the hands as well as common soap; they prevent *chops* in the winter season, and keep the skin soft and healthy.

Let not children be dressed in tight clothes; it is necessary their limbs and muscles should have full play, if you wish for either health or beauty.

Wash the eyes thoroughly in cold water every morning. Do not read or sew at twilight, or by too dazzling a light. If far-sighted, read with rather less light, and with the book somewhat nearer to the eye, than you desire. If near-sighted, read with a book as far off as possible. Both these imperfections may be diminished in this way.

That a thorough, religious, *useful* education is the best security against misfortune, disgrace and poverty, is universally believed and acknowledged; and to this we add the firm conviction, that, when poverty comes (as it sometimes will) upon the prudent, the industrious, and the well-informed, a judicious education is all-powerful in enabling them to *endure* the evils it cannot always *prevent*. A mind full of piety and knowledge is always rich; it is a bank that never fails; it yields a perpetual dividend of happiness.

Keep children's hair cut close until ten or twelve years old; it is better for health and the beauty of the hair. Do not sleep with hair frizzled, or braided. Do not make children cross-eyed, by having hair hang about their foreheads, where they see it continually.

EAR WAX—Nothing is better than ear-wax to prevent the painful effects resulting from a wound by a nail, skewer, etc. It should be put on as soon as possible. Those who are troubled with cracked lips have found this remedy successful when others have failed.

TEETH—Honey mixed with pure pulverized charcoal is said to be excellent to cleanse the teeth and make them white.

Title page, *The American Frugal Housewife*, 1836 edition

AMERICA'S NATIONAL NOVELIST

As the story goes, in 1819 James Fennimore Cooper read a popular English novel aloud to his wife, slammed it shut, and proclaimed, "I could write you a better book myself!" Apocryphal or not, the result was the same: he began a prolific writing career that would total thirty-two novels, twelve works of nonfiction, a play, and various articles and pamphlets. It was the beginning of American novels.

Cooper was born in 1789 at Burlington, New Jersey, the son of wealthy Quakers Elizabeth Fennimore and William Cooper. His father, a political conservative, gained wealth as a land developer. A year after James's birth, the family moved to Cooperstown, New York, founded and presided over by his father. Cooper was raised in relative genteel wealth on the family estate on the shores of Otsego Lake. The high-spirited and precocious boy was allowed to roam the surrounding forests, developing a love and understanding of landscape and nature, which were distinctive features of his novels. At age thirteen he was accepted to Yale, from which he was expelled during his junior year after a series of pranks that included training a donkey to sit in a professor's chair and using gunpowder to blow down a classmate's door.

With his future now in doubt, Cooper went to sea, serving as an ordinary seaman aboard the merchant ship *Stirling,* on which he sailed to England and Spain in 1806 and 1807. When he returned to the United States, he received a warrant as a U.S. Navy midshipman. In 1811, he resigned from the navy and married Susan Augusta DeLancey, whom he met while recruiting for the navy in New York City.

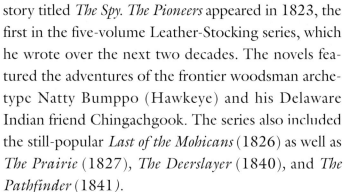

James Fennimore Cooper

Their family grew quickly—five daughters in eight years and two sons later—as Cooper farmed in various New York locations and speculated in land investments. However, by 1819 the Coopers were mired in heavy debt, having poorly managed the $50,000 inheritance he received after his father's 1809 death.

Now, at the age of thirty, with his wife's challenge to create a better story, Cooper turned to writing to assuage his family's financial misfortunes. In 1820, his first novel, *Precaution,* was published to an uninterested public. The next year he published his first of many popular novels—a patriotic Revolutionary War adventure story titled *The Spy. The Pioneers* appeared in 1823, the first in the five-volume Leather-Stocking series, which he wrote over the next two decades. The novels featured the adventures of the frontier woodsman archetype Natty Bumppo (Hawkeye) and his Delaware Indian friend Chingachgook. The series also included the still-popular *Last of the Mohicans* (1826) as well as *The Prairie* (1827), *The Deerslayer* (1840), and *The Pathfinder* (1841).

After reading Sir Walter Scott's *The Pirate,* he also began experimenting with a new literary genre—sea novels. His first was *The Pilot* (1824), an American sea adventure based on the exploits of John Paul Jones. Its best-selling success encouraged Cooper to write six more sea novels.

Although his stories followed patterns established by English writers such as Sir Walter Scott (*Ivanhoe,* for example), Cooper was the first to use American history, values, language, political conflicts, characters, and landscape in his novels. He also romanticized and humanized the American Indian. His worldwide popularity during the 1820s and 1830s allowed him to earn a considerable income as America's first professional novelist.

The Coopers lived in Europe from 1825 to 1833, where James wrote, traveled, socialized with literary figures, defended American life against European critics, and, for a time, served as U.S. consul for Lyon, France. Upon his return to the United States, Cooper bought and moved to Ostego Hall, his childhood home. He also returned to a loss in popularity and a changing America. Somewhat embittered, he became embroiled in several lawsuits against contentious reviewers and entered local and national partisan disputes.

James Fennimore Cooper's works have been criticized over the years for conventional characters, extreme plots, and stiff, unimaginative dialogue. Mark Twain's essay "Fennimore Cooper's Literary Offences" was a particularly biting review of Cooper's contributions to writing. Cooper knew how to tell a story, however, and his novels were the first successful truly American fiction. He not only set a precedent for future American literary heroes, but Cooper also helped set the tone for the treatment of wilderness and civilization in our national traditions.

Cooper died of heart failure on 14 September 1851 at his home on the shores of his beloved Lake Ostwego.

THE GIRL'S OWN BOOK

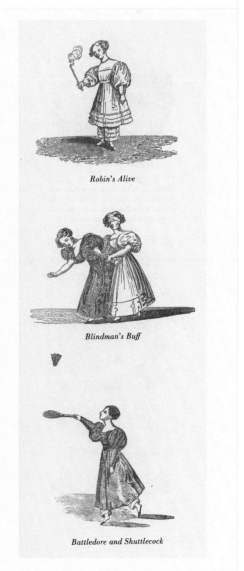

Robin's Alive

Blindman's Buff

Battledore and Shuttlecock

Lydia Maria Child's *The Girl's Own Book,* published in 1831, combined entertainment and instruction while containing "nothing to corrupt or mislead." Two of the activities Child described for her readers—"Hide and go seek!" and "Snow-balling"—are still enjoyed today.

Hide and Go Seek!

One goes out of the room, while the others hide a thimble, pocket handkerchief, or something of that sort. When they are ready, they call "Whoop!" and she enters. If she moves toward the place, they cry, "You burn!" "Now you burn more!" If she goes very near, they say, "Oh! you are almost blazing!" If she moves from the object, they say, "How cold she grows!" If the article is found, the one who hid it must take the next turn to seek for it.

Snowballing

I like this exercise, because it is played in the open air. Endurance of cold is a very good thing: it makes the constitution hardy. But rudeness and violence must never be allowed in this, or any other game: little girls should never forget that they are miniature ladies.

Games from *An American Girl's Book,* 1831

AN ECONOMY DIVIDED AGAINST ITSELF

Eli Whitney (1765–1825)

The first half of the nineteenth century has been called the age of the "common man" because a greater variety of opportunities was available to a wider spectrum of people than ever before. As a result, it was also the age of the "uncommon man," individuals who stood out from others because they contributed to the rapidly increasing pace of ideas, inventions, and discoveries that separated this period from its predecessors. It was, as John Quincy Adams proclaimed, an "era of improvement."

A number of ideas helped bring about a new, bloodless revolution—the industrial revolution. Largely a northern phenomenon, the industrial revolution contributed to the growing gap between regions that eventually resulted in the Civil War. The gap further increased because of technological improvements that made cotton more profitable and led to an increasingly agricultural southern economy.

Few individuals contributed as much to the widening regional differences that characterized American society as did Eli Whitney. Thanks in part to his famous cotton gin, the South tenaciously clung to an economy built on slave labor. The cotton gin not only made cotton more profitable, but it also turned the South into a virtual monarchy ruled by "King Cotton." U.S. cotton production, which was 171,000 bales in 1810, exploded to just under 5.4 million on the eve of the Civil War fifty years later.

Although best known for his cotton gin, Whitney demonstrated an idea in 1798 that was received with "sheer amazement." Hoping to get a contract to supply guns for the United States Army, he sorted like components for ten muskets into separate piles. Randomly taking a part from each pile, he had ten muskets assembled in ten minutes. Before this idea for interchangeable parts, every item that was produced, from guns to clocks, was built one at a time, a process that was labor intensive and extremely slow. Whitney's idea was initially ridiculed, but he ended up getting the last laugh. Not only did he get the contract, but he also changed the way items were produced and thus transformed the world. With interchangeable parts, almost anything could be built and repaired more quickly and cheaply.

Whitney's idea spread rapidly. Factories employing its principles sprang up, and productivity increased. When a clock maker promised to make 200 clocks for a local New England merchant in 1807, local villagers proclaimed it impossible, declaring that he "never would live long enough to finish them." Using interchangeable parts, the clock maker built not only the 200 but also thousands more, thus making clocks available to the masses for the first time.

Before Whitney's idea, Samuel Slater started the first factory in America in 1790. While he spun cotton into yarn in his factory, the yarn continued to be turned into cloth on hand looms in homes. Improving on Slater's idea, Francis Cabot Lowell built a factory that combined both the spinning of yarn and the weaving of cloth.

Slaves using a cotton gin

During the first half of the 1800s, northern industry grew steadily. Steam power replaced water power in the 1830s. Not only was it cheaper to run, but steam power also allowed factories to be built almost anywhere, not just alongside swift-flowing rivers. "Everywhere is heard the noise of hammers, of spindles, of bells calling the hands to their work, or dismissing them from their tasks," one person wrote. "It is the peaceful hum of an industrious population, whose movements are regulated like clockwork." Within a generation this "peaceful hum" would be drowned out by the sounds of war.

NEVER STAYING STILL

Latter-day Saints in the 1800s were not unique in the fact that they relocated more than once. They were not even unique in the experience of being forced to leave their homes at gunpoint. What made them unique was the fact that they repeatedly moved as a cohesive group. Most Americans who pulled up roots tended to move either as a "family" unit, which might consist of only one person, or by loosely aligning themselves with others traveling in the same direction.

America in the early nineteenth century was a nation in flux. The seemingly perpetual motion of its inhabitants was fueled by a growing population, the nation's expanding westward boundaries, improvements in infrastructure, and the industrial revolution.

The population of the United States, which was 5.3 million in 1800, more than quadrupled to 23.2 million at mid-century. Much of this growth was the result of European emigrants seeking to trade famine, war, and a quality of life vividly portrayed in the novels of Charles Dickens for a "land of opportunity." Land was plentiful in the new world, as was work in America's growing factories and industries, where conditions were frequently better than those in Europe.

"In America," Alexis de Tocqueville proclaimed, "men never stay still. Something is almost always provisional about their lives." Europeans tended to reside near one city their entire lives, but few Americans stayed in the same place. As America's western border extended, Americans sought new opportunities on the expanding frontier. The "grass is always greener" attitude that pervaded the country in the nineteenth century caused one foreign visitor to conclude that Americans were the only people on earth who would abandon heaven to try homesteading in hell. Acquiring new land required little cash outlay. The 1820 Land Act allowed settlers to purchase from the government eighty acres of land for $100, or $1.25 an acre.

The changing American landscape had an urban dimension as well. For every "young man" whose actions predated the advice of New York newspaperman Horace Greeley to "Go west," several others moved to a city. Tens of thousands during this time exchanged the rigors of farming for the risks and rewards of city and factory life. In 1820, five cities in the Northeast had populations above 25,000, another thirteen above 10,000. Thirty years later, that number had grown to twenty-six cities topping the 25,000 mark, and another sixty-two topping 10,000. Boston grew from 40,000 residents in 1820 to nearly 140,000 in 1850. Philadelphia grew even more rapidly, from just under 100,000 in 1820 to almost 400,000 in 1850. New York City, which had forged ahead of Philadelphia around 1810, saw its population increase from 125,000 in 1820 to more than 500,000 in 1850. In the old Northwest, Pittsburgh, St. Louis, Cincinnati, and Louisville each had populations greater than 35,000 by 1850. None of America's leading cities, however, could begin to compare with the size or sophistication of European capitals such as London and Paris.

In spite of these changes, America remained an overwhelmingly rural and agrarian nation. In 1820, more than three out of four Americans were engaged in agriculture. By 1850, the ratio had dropped to fewer than two out of three. Because of the creation of Lowell and other industrial centers, only one out of three in Massachusetts was engaged in agrarian pursuits at mid-century.

In the early days of the Republic, the Appalachian Mountains formed a formidable impediment to western expansion. Many feared that the American frontier, which was literally situated west of those mountains, might be lost to France, England, or another European power unless ways were found over or around the barrier. Three passable land routes connecting the coastal region with the interior were created. The Great Genesee Road from Massachusetts to the Mohawk River Valley (which brought the Smith family to New York in 1816); the National Road from Maryland to Ohio; and the Wilderness Road in North Carolina, Tennessee, and Kentucky unleashed a flood of westward migration.

The success of the Erie Canal ushered in an era of canal building as Americans turned their attention from building roads to digging canals. Steamboats and canals were enthusiastically embraced as a preferred alternative to having to journey over tree-stumped and pockmarked roads. Americans next turned to trains as the best way to expand their nation and connect it from east to west, north to south.

Having largely forsaken road building early in the century, pioneers going west had to blaze trails or follow along the wagon ruts created by their predecessors. Only after the invention of the automobile did Americans again turn their attention to building roads across their great nation.

WESTERN EMIGRATION.

JOURNAL

OF

DOCTOR JEREMIAH SMIPLETON'S

TOUR TO OHIO.

CONTAINING

An account of the numerous difficulties, Hair-breadth Escapes, Mortifications and Privations, which the Doctor and his family experienced on their Journey from Maine, to the 'Land of Promise,' and during a residence of three years in that highly extolled country.

BY H. TRUMBULL.

Nulli Fides Frontis.

BOSTON--PRINTED BY S. SEWALL.

Even though Young America was a frontier nation on the move, not everyone was enamored with westward migration as evidenced in this 1819 tract bemoaning "the numerous difficulties, hair-breadth escapes . . . and privations"

WHO READS AN AMERICAN BOOK?

"In the four quarters of the globe, who reads an American book? . . . What does the world yet owe to Americans?" When Scottish minister Sydney Smith raised these questions in 1820, he reflected the general views of Europeans, with their long literary tradition, about the United States' lack of literary contributions. Unfortunately, this snobbery was not without basis. As late as 1830, nearly three of every four books read in America was written and printed in England. The British Isles had produced William Shakespeare, William Wordsworth, Alexander Pope, John Milton, Jonathan Swift, John Keats, and Sir Walter Scott, to name only a few. The British had even made the Bible accessible to the masses through the King James translation. While Reverend Smith would likely have looked down his nose at her writings, the recently published works of Jane Austen, including *Sense and Sensibility* (1811), *Pride and Prejudice* (1813), and her posthumously published *Persuasion* (1818), would soon eclipse the popularity of many works by the British authors of whom the Reverend was justifiably proud.

Little could Reverend Smith realize when posing his questions that the answer would one day be found in scripture published in rural, upstate New York in 1830: The Book of Mormon. This volume recounts more than one thousand years of religious history and teachings of three groups of people (the Nephites, Lamanites, and Jaredites) who lived in the Americas between 600 B.C. and A.D. 421. It also recounts a visit of the resurrected Christ to the Americas.

The preface to the record, written by its compiler, Mormon, states that the volume was "written to the Lamanites, who are a remnant of the house of Israel . . . to show unto the remnant of the House of Israel what great things the Lord hath done for their fathers; and that they may know the covenants of the Lord, that they are not cast off forever—and also to the convincing of the Jew and Gentile that Jesus is the Christ."

Given feelings in Young America, publishing a history of the ancestors of the native inhabitants was not an obvious recipe for success. While the Book of Mormon contains elements common with other American works of the time, particularly the idea that America was a favored land, most Americans viewed the Indians as standing in the path of America's destiny.

Much of America's literature focused on the efforts of European settlers carving out a new nation from their vast wilderness. Thomas Paine's 1776 indictment of hereditary monarchy, *Common Sense,* coupled with Thomas Jefferson's *Declaration of Independence,* were embers that ignited the fire of independence. The *Autobiography of Ben Franklin* and the diary of the Lewis and Clark expedition (1814) helped provide the United States a national identity. So too did Washington Irving's "Rip Van Winkle" and "The Legend of Sleepy Hollow," both published in 1819. In the 1820s, James Fenimore Cooper began publishing his historical novels of life on the American frontier in upstate New York, including *The Last of the Mohicans* (1826).

By 1830, Edgar Allen Poe had published a few minor works, but his greatest literary contributions would come in the future. During the 1840s, Americans could begin to take pride in their own developing literary tradition that would include Herman Melville, Nathaniel Hawthorne, Henry Wadsworth Longfellow, Ralph Waldo Emerson, and Louisa May Alcott.

Among the works that appeared in print after the Book of Mormon was the first comprehensive study of the American Indians, published in the late 1830s, and the first indepth look at Meso-America, which became available in 1841.

Although some books from the time of young America receive greater attention from scholars than the Book of Mormon, none has had as lasting an impact. In 1970, Robert Downs published *Books that Changed America*, a study of the twenty-five works that "exerted the greatest impact on our national history, direct or indirect." In 2003, *Book Magazine* published a list of twenty works "that led to concrete, definable changes in the way Americans lived." The Book of Mormon made both of these lists. Of the other books mentioned in these studies, only *Common Sense* predates the Book of Mormon among the works originating in America. No other book published in Joseph's lifetime made both lists.

While these lists focus only on the United States, the influence of the Book of Mormon is felt well beyond the nation's borders. It is one of the few works from that time period still widely read. All or portions have been translated into more than one hundred languages, and today it is read in a majority of the world's nations.

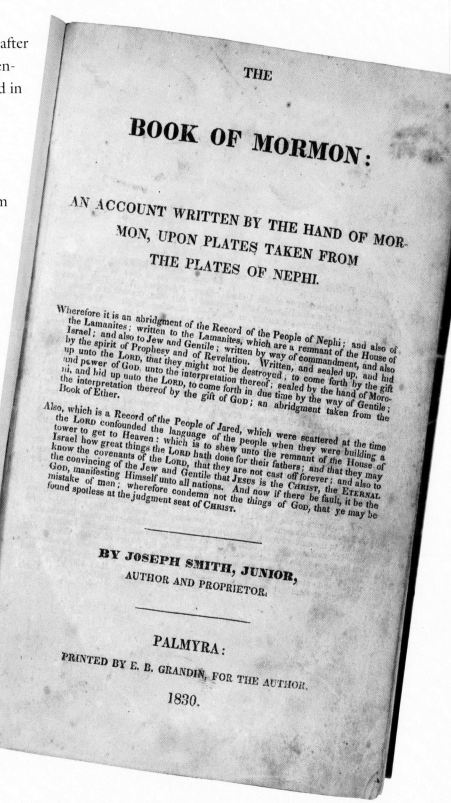

THE

BOOK OF MORMON:

AN ACCOUNT WRITTEN BY THE HAND OF MORMON, UPON PLATES TAKEN FROM THE PLATES OF NEPHI.

Wherefore it is an abridgment of the Record of the People of Nephi; and also of the Lamanites; written to the Lamanites, which are a remnant of the House of Israel; and also to Jew and Gentile; written by way of commandment, and also by the spirit of Prophesy and of Revelation. Written, and sealed up, and hid up unto the LORD, that they might not be destroyed; to come forth by the gift and power of GOD, unto the interpretation thereof; sealed by the hand of Moroni, and hid up unto the LORD, to come forth in due time by the way of Gentile; the interpretation thereof by the gift of GOD; an abridgment taken from the Book of Ether.

Also, which is a Record of the People of Jared, which were scattered at the time the LORD confounded the language of the people when they were building a tower to get to Heaven: which is to shew unto the remnant of the House of Israel how great things the LORD hath done for their fathers; and that they may know the covenants of the LORD, that they are not cast off forever; and also to the convincing of the Jew and Gentile that JESUS is the CHRIST, the ETERNAL GOD, manifesting Himself unto all nations. And now if there be fault, it be the mistake of men; wherefore condemn not the things of GOD, that ye may be found spotless at the judgment seat of CHRIST.

BY JOSEPH SMITH, JUNIOR,
AUTHOR AND PROPRIETOR.

PALMYRA:
PRINTED BY E. B. GRANDIN, FOR THE AUTHOR.
1830.

6 APRIL 1830

"TO THE POLLS—THIS DAY!" read a headline in the Rochester *Republican*. Tuesday, 6 April 1830, was election day in western upstate New York. Throughout the region, the local press implored their male readers to attend their local town meetings so they could vote for candidates whose views echoed that of the newspaper's editor.

A meeting of a different kind was taking place in the modest Peter Whitmer farmhouse at Fayette, Seneca County, New York. Joseph Smith and a small band of believers, including the six who would sign the incorporation papers, crowded into the small structure to organize the restored Church of Christ according to the laws of the land.

Even if the focus of the day had not been on the elections taking place at the town meetings, it is unlikely the local papers would have reported the organization of the Church. First, few sectarian activities made secular newspapers. Second, little attention would have been given to another new church being established in the area. Numerous religions in the "burned-over district" of New York had already formed and faded.

How much attention Joseph and the others at the farmhouse gave to what was taking place around them that day is not known. Nevertheless, some of the events that day—the elections in New York and events in Massachusetts and in the United States Senate—were foreshadowing their own later experiences, especially in Missouri, Illinois, and Utah. Other events simply reflected the unique circumstances of America at the time.

Although the 6 April elections were only for local town officials, the area's newspapers proclaimed that the outcome would determine the future of the nation. The issue upon which the course of the country was seen to rest was succinctly reported by the *Seneca Farmer* and *Waterloo Observer*: "There is only one point that divides the great mass of the people. That is, the necessity of opposing the Masonic Institution through the ballot boxes. This point once settled in the affirmative, and so settled it will be, and Freemasonry in the United States falls for ever." An opponent of this "Political Anti-Masonry," as it was called, countered: "We are confident that the democratic spirit . . . will yet preserve this country from the political ascendancy of any party whose object is to elevate one sect, society or denomination of men by the destruction of another." E. B. Grandin, shortly after completing the publication of the Book of Mormon in late March 1830, likewise addressed "Political Anti-Masonry" advocates: "Oppose masonry, if you will, but . . . march not to victory over the laws and constitution of your country. . . . [Never] will you triumph in the use of those means which you have adopted and continue to pursue—never, until you hurry in one common grave, masonry and the liberties of America."

Masonry first became an issue in the 1826 election, when the new Federalists were swept to power in upstate New York by their opposition to the secretive fraternal order. In the intervening elections Democratic-Republicans, derisively called the "Masonic Party" by Federalists, made significant inroads. As was common at the time, both sides invoked the memory of the Founding Fathers to defend their position. Following the 6 April 1830 election, ten of the fifteen villages in Wayne County, including Palmyra, Ontario, and Manchester, were declared "firm republican towns," while in neighboring Seneca County, where the Church was incorporated, six of seven villages, including Fayette, continued "Anti-Masonic."

In April 1830, Boston's *Christian Watchman* warned of a new threat to the United States—

Catholicism. Although Catholics first came to the colonies in the mid-1600s, they had primarily settled in Maryland. In 1830, recently arrived immigrants, the majority from Ireland, had swelled Boston's Catholic population to more than seven thousand. These "papists," the paper warned, had received orders from the Pope to establish the Inquisition in the United States: "That the Inquisition and the Catholic religion belong together; we concede." Before the decade was out, there were anti-Catholic riots and instances where convents and churches were destroyed by angry mobs.

To the west of Boston at Fitchburg, Massachusetts, thirty-nine-year-old Joseph Palmer was an object of contempt and ridicule. Shunned by neighbors and snubbed by local merchants, he had taunts and stones hurled at him on the village streets. He was also denounced from the pulpit and denied communion— all because he had recently chosen to grow a beard. Although many of their revered forefathers had worn beards, New Englanders had since come to view facial hair as repulsive and subversive.

Ultimately, four angry residents resorting to vigilante justice attempted to shave Palmer in the interests of community morality. After successfully fighting off his assailants, he was convicted of assault. Upon refusing to pay his fine, he was jailed. His case gained national attention, with Ralph Waldo Emerson among those supporting Palmer. Offered his freedom, Palmer refused to leave until his right to grow a beard was acknowledged. Three months in solitary confinement failed to diminish his resolve. Finally, after a year in jail, he was forcibly removed in the spring of 1831, beard and all.

Palmer subsequently left Fitchburg and joined Bronson Alcott's Fruitlands utopian community, where Bronson's daughter, Louisa May Alcott, was then a pre-teen. During Palmer's stay at Fruitlands, beards moved from unacceptability to near universality. In 1845 the *New England Farmer* conceded that "the fashion of shaving the beard" was simply a "custom of civilized life" that might be "foolish and injurious." When he returned to Fitchburg around 1850, the men who had tried to shave him now sported their own beards. By 1860, the majority of men in the United States wore beards and would continue to do so for decades to come.

In the United States Senate on 6 April 1830, the explosive issue of Indian removal was again brought up for debate. The Committee on Indian Affairs had previously recommended that the government move the Creek, Cherokee, Choctaw, and Chickasaw Indians to land "west of the territory of Arkansas." Two weeks later, on 24 April, the bill passed the Senate by a vote of twenty-seven to nineteen, with "almost every friend of Gen. Jackson voting for the Bill, and almost every member of the opposition voting against it," one paper reported. "Thus the responsibility of the act must rest upon the President and his party."

On the other side of the United States Capitol, the House of Representatives' Committee on Military Pensions addressed extending pension benefits to veterans of the Revolutionary War. One of those who would benefit was an elderly resident of upstate western New York believed "to be the only surviving revolutionary patriot who was engaged in the tea chest affair" when protestors of British policies threw tea into Boston Harbor during the 1773 Boston Tea Party.

Back in New York, a tax protest of a different kind was being reported in the newspapers on 6 April. The New York Legislature had recently implemented a steep increase in fees for users of the Erie Canal. This action was seen as a vexatious new tax that threw "an undue portion of the public burdens on western farmers." Rather than dump their flour into Lake Ontario or pay what they felt was an unfair tax, the papers reported, western New York residents chose instead to ship forty thousand barrels of flour intended for New York City from Rochester to Canada.

At the same time, the New York Legislature was debating whether to build a canal connecting the

Chenango Valley with the Erie Canal. On 6 April, "Mr. Mann spoke against it for nearly two hours, but did not finish his speech before the house adjourned." The Erie Canal was an unquestioned success, but opponents now viewed canals as yesterday's technology. One paper editorialized, "We think it well worth the consideration of the public whether a Rail road along the proposed route of the canal would not be more feasible and promote more substantially the public interests. Before the recent experiments in England as to the powers of steam locomotive carriages, it had been considered as settled that rail roads were on the whole preferable to canals; but now the question is put beyond all doubt." Additionally, calls were being made for a railroad from Albany to Buffalo that would compete with the Erie Canal: "A conveyance which would take merchandize & passengers at the rate of 15 to 20 miles an hour would be preferred to one which would transport at the rate of only three or four miles an hour even at a considerable difference in the expense."

To the south of New York, work was progressing on the nation's first passenger railroad, the Baltimore and Ohio, which would connect the Chesapeake Bay with the "vast and fertile tracts beyond the Ohio [River]." Although work had been ongoing for nearly two years, only a mile and a half of track had actually been put down by April 1830. Passengers could travel

that distance at a cost of nine cents each way. The passenger car, however, was pulled by horse, since the *Tom Thumb*, a steam engine specifically designed to travel the route, was still several months from completion.

Back at Fayette, New York, Joseph concluded an important step on his journey by organizing the Church according to previously received revelations through the ordination of "brethren to different offices of the Priesthood according as the Spirit manifested," performing baptisms, and bestowing the gift of the Holy Ghost. "After a happy time spent in witnessing and feeling for ourselves the powers and blessings of the Holy Ghost, through the grace of God bestowed upon us," Joseph later wrote, "we dismissed with the pleasing knowledge that we were now individually members of, and acknowledged of God, 'The Church of Jesus Christ,' organized in accordance with commandments and revelations given by Him to ourselves in these last days, as well as according to the order of the Church as recorded in the New Testament."

Nearby, the Rochester *Republican*, while condemning Anti-Masonry in its 6 April issue, weighed in on the recently published Book of Mormon. Its reaction was a reminder that the journey of the Latter-day Saints would not be easy:

> Blasphemy—"Book of Mormon," alias the Golden Bible
> The "Book of Mormon" has been placed in our hands. A viler imposition was never practiced. It is an evidence of fraud, blasphemy and credulity, shocking to the Christian and moralist. The "author and proprietor" is one "Joseph Smith, jr"—a fellow who, by some hocus pocus, acquired such an influence over a wealthy farmer of Wayne county, that the latter mortgaged his farm for $3000, which he paid for the printing and binding of 5000 copies of the blasphemous work.

"LIKE THE ANCIENTS"

Upwards of sixty people gathered in the Peter Whitmer Sr. farmhouse in Fayette, New York, on 6 April 1830 for the legal incorporation of the restored Church of Christ, thus marking the official beginning of The Church of Jesus Christ of Latter-day Saints. A third of those in attendance had made the nearly hundred-mile journey from southern New York to be present at the historic occasion. Twenty-four-year-old Joseph was sustained as the first elder of the Church. He also signed the incorporation papers, along with Hyrum and Samuel Smith, David and Peter Whitmer Jr., and Oliver Cowdery. Several were baptized following the organizational meeting, including Joseph's parents and Martin Harris.

Joseph later identified both Manchester and Fayette as the place where the Church was organized. Although he never addressed this apparent discrepancy, David Whitmer may have provided an insight into Joseph's thinking: "We were as fully *organized*—spiritually—before April 6th as we were on that day," Whitmer wrote. "The reason why we met on that day was this, the world had been telling us that we were not a regularly organized church, and we had no

The Temple at Kirtland, Ohio.

"Meeting in the African Church, Cincinnati, Ohio, 1830."
The great American religious revival movement of the early 1800s influenced all Americans

right to officiate in the ordinance of marriage, hold church property, etc., and that we should organize according to the laws of the land."

Manchester was where Joseph experienced his first vision and was instructed by the Angel Moroni and other heavenly messengers. It is also the place where the Hill Cumorah is located. Having obtained his "errand from the Lord" prior to 6 April 1830, the young prophet established three branches of the Church—at Fayette, Manchester, and Colesville, New York, with seventy members—prior to the incorporation of the Church.

Although the Lord prepared Joseph to lay the groundwork for the incorporation of the Church in the decade following his first vision, there was still much Joseph needed to learn and do before the fullness of the restored gospel was again on the earth. As was the case prior to the "falling away" and after Joseph's earnest prayer in 1820, the Lord continued to pour out sacred truth upon His living prophet. Through revelation He restored the complete organization established during His ministry, one "built upon the foundation of the apostles and prophets." "Line upon

MARY HAD A LITTLE LAMB

Mary had a little lamb,
Its fleece was white as snow;
And everywhere that Mary went
The lamb was sure to go.

Possibly the best-known four lines of verse in the English language, these are also the first words of recorded human speech. In 1877, Thomas Edison recited this stanza into his latest invention, the phonograph. The poem that begins with these famous lines was written in 1830 by Sarah Josepha Hale of Boston, editor of the *Ladies' Magazine,* and recounts an actual incident where a pet lamb followed its young owner to a country schoolhouse. It was first published in the September–October 1830 issue of Lydia Maria Child's *Juvenile Miscellany.* While her poem is famous, Hale is probably most closely associated with her successful one-woman crusade to create a nationwide day of Thanksgiving.

line, precept upon precept" He revealed to Joseph truths by which the plan of salvation was once again known to man.

While restoring the church that Jesus Christ established in New Testament times—the "primitive church," Joseph called it—Joseph and the Latter-day Saints faced persecution similar to that experienced by the New Testament Saints. Like the Israelites in the Old Testament, they too found their promised land already inhabited and would be forced to "wander" after failing to redeem it.

When Joseph returned to his home in Harmony, Pennsylvania, in June 1830, he found opposition to the work still strong. Later that month, he determinedly held a meeting, notwithstanding the presence of a mob, following which he baptized thirteen, including Emma. In August, the continuing persecution forced Joseph and Emma to abandon their home in Harmony and return to Fayette.

Their stay in New York would be short lived. In November 1830, Oliver Cowdery and other missionaries found a receptive audience at Kirtland, Ohio, during a brief visit to the Western Reserve of Ohio. As December 1830 dawned, the *Painesville Telegraph* reported that nearly one hundred had "embraced the ideas and assertions of Joseph Smith, Jr., many of them respectable for intelligency and piety." Among these was Sidney Rigdon, a local minister, who immediately began preaching "Mormonism" in his sermons. In a December 1830 revelation, Joseph was told, "A commandment I give unto the church, that it is expedient in me that they should assemble together at the Ohio." Joseph immediately began preparing for the gathering of the Saints.

The gathering played a major role in the development of Mormonism in the nineteenth century, but the concept was not unique to the Latter-day Saints. What was unique was both the scope and the organization employed to accomplish it. Many Americans gathered to create utopian communities such as

SIDNEY RIGDON

Soon after his November 1830 baptism, Sidney Rigdon (1793–1876), a former Baptist-Campbellite minister, began a close relationship with Joseph Smith that included serving as first counselor in the First Presidency from 1833 to 1844. As one of the Prophet's trusted advisors, Rigdon also helped with the translation of the Bible and worked with Joseph on the Book of Moses (Pearl of Great Price). He also bore hardships along with Joseph, as when they were both tarred and feathered by a mob in Ohio and, later, in Missouri, imprisoned in Liberty Jail with Hyrum Smith, Lyman Wight, Caleb Baldwin, and Alexander McRae.

However, as early as 1833, the Prophet cautioned Rigdon of his "selfishness and independence of mind, which too often manifested to destroy the confidence of those who lay down their lives for him—these are his faults. But notwithstanding these things, he is a very great and good man; a man of great power of words. . . . He is a man whom God will uphold, if he will continue faithful to his calling."

In Nauvoo, Rigdon was elected to the city council and served as postmaster and city attorney. When Joseph ran for the U.S. presidency in 1844, Rigdon was nominated and campaigned as his running mate.

However, after the martyrdom of Joseph, Rigdon's claim to Church leadership was rejected, and he refused to follow Brigham Young and the Twelve. Excommunicated in September 1844, he moved to Pennsylvania and organized a Church of Christ. He died in Friendship, New York.

1830

The Book of Mormon was published; the Church was officially incorporated; Joseph Smith began receiving the Book of Moses by revelation; Joseph left Harmony for Fayette because of persecution, sent missionaries to teach American Indians on the western frontier, and received a revelation commanding the Saints to gather to Ohio

The first U.S. passenger railroad, *Baltimore and Ohio*, began operation

The population of Great Britain was 13.9 million; of the U.S., 12.8 million; world population was 1 billion

French inventor Barthelemy Thimonnier patented the first sewing machine; a mob of tailors fearing unemployment destroyed eight machines he built to sew French army uniforms

Edward George Bulwer-Lytton published the novel *Paul Clifford*, which begins "It was a dark and stormy night . . ."

Philadelphia moralist Louis Antoine Godey began publishing *Godey's Lady's Book*

Louis Philippe, "the Citizen King," became king of France

A PRACTICING BUT INDIFFERENT POPULATION

Frenchman Alexis de Tocqueville found much to praise about the United States during his famous 1831–1832 visit, but he directed some of his harshest comments in *Democracy in America* toward America's religious institutions. Although he identified in America a "greater foundation of Christianity than in any other country in the world" that he was familiar with, he also found "a practising but indifferent population, which lives from day to day, accustoms itself to surroundings that are hardly satisfying but tranquil, and who [by all] *appearances* are satisfied. Those people live and die . . . without ever bothering to get to the bottom of things. They no longer replenish themselves." He further noted of American religious practitioners: "One follows a religion as our fathers took medicine in the month of May. If it doesn't do

*French writer and politician
Alexis de Tocqueville (1805–1859)*

any good, one seems to say, at least it can do no harm."

Raised in a nation with a dominant religion, Tocqueville partly blamed the large number of religious denominations in America for what he observed. He also censured the clergy, whom he found motivated more by expediency than by principle. Regarding the sundry churches, he wrote, "It is incredible to see the infinite number of subdivisions into which the sects in America have split. Like circles traced successively about the same point, each new one a little farther away than the next. . . . It seems clear to me that reformed religion is sort of a compromise, a kind of representative Monarchy, a kind of religion that may well fill an epoch, serve as transition from one state to another, but which could never constitute a definitive state." Concerning America's religious leaders, Tocqueville concluded, "The clergy of America freely adopt the general views of their time and country and let themselves go unresistingly with the tide of feeling and opinion which carries everything around them along with it."

1831

Joseph Smith established Kirtland, Ohio, as a gathering place; dedicated the site for the City of Zion at Independence, Missouri; began efforts to publish his revelations; instituted the Law of Consecration

Slave Nat Turner led a bloody slave rebellion; some 70 whites and 100 blacks were killed

Victor Hugo published *The Hunchback of Notre Dame*

Cyrus McCormick invented the most effective mechanical reaper for cutting wheat to date; he would not sell his first two reapers until 1841

English naturalist Charles Darwin began a five-year voyage on the H.M.S. *Beagle,* during which he developed the theory of evolution

Fruitlands, Brook Farm, and New Harmony. These groups, however, were largely short lived and seldom exceeded several hundred members. Others frequently gathered to a single location because of a common religion or nationality, but these were largely haphazard occurrences. By contrast, thousands gathered under Joseph's direction. He outlined a system to deal with the spiritual and temporal needs of his followers, even directing how communities should ideally be laid out. Additionally, Joseph ambitiously oversaw two far-spread gathering places simultaneously for much of the 1830s, one in eastern Ohio (Kirtland) and one in western Missouri (first in Jackson County, and then at Far West in an era when travel and communication between those locations took weeks. Finally, as the decade neared its close, the Latter-day Saints were forced to abandon these locations in favor of a new gathering place in Illinois. During this time, Joseph oversaw a whirlwind of activities that would take volumes to describe.

Joseph and Emma gathered to Kirtland, Ohio, "about the first of February 1830." Entering the Gilbert and Whitney Store, Joseph extended his hand to the firm's junior partner and proclaimed, "Newel K. Whitney! Thou art the man!" The startled store-keeper stammered, "You have the advantage of me. . . . I could not call you by name as you have me." "I am Joseph the Prophet. You have prayed me here, now what do you want of me?" Joseph then told Whitney that he had seen him in a vision praying for him to come to Kirtland. Whitney welcomed the young couple into his home and provided a room above the store for Joseph's use.

Joseph found "strange notions and false spirits" among the small branch at Kirtland. For example, many had come from a religious tradition where they could take what they needed from their neighbors. In response to the situation that greeted him in Ohio, Joseph inquired of the Lord and received a revelation on 9 February 1831 "embracing the law of the Church." Prior to Joseph's reaching Kirtland, the Lord had told him, "There I will give unto you my law; and there you shall be endowed with power from on high." The Lord's law included inspired teachings on how the Saints could live a more perfect way that included the consecration of their property.

Concerning the "law of consecration," Joseph taught that "for a man to consecrate his property . . . to the Lord is nothing more nor less than to feed the hungry, clothe the naked, visit the widow and father-less, the sick and afflicted, and do all he can to administer to their relief in their afflictions, and for him and his house to serve the Lord." Because many Saints were unable to live this higher law, the Lord later replaced it with a lesser law, "the tithing of my people."

A PRINCIPLE WITH PROMISE

America's quest for individual and social perfection during the first half of the nineteenth century included an emphasis upon health. Americans turned to a wide range of theories, from hydrotherapy (wherein cold baths were believed to cure numerous illnesses), to changes in diet, to the best known of America's nineteenth-century health reforms, the temperance movement.

Alcohol abuse was so widespread that even children were known to drink heavily. In the 1820s, temperance advocates began actively campaigning against "demon rum," which encompassed all alcoholic drinks. Although some advocates desired only that people drink less, others demanded the complete prohibition of alcohol. By 1836, more than five hundred temperance societies were in existence, most in upstate western New York where the movement began.

While temperance groups addressed the dangers of alcohol, other crusaders attempted to improve eating habits. In March 1830, one newspaper in upstate western New York addressed an issue familiar to later generations of Americans: "What! Another 'Temperance Society?' Why, truly, I guess you are carrying Mr. [Andrew] Jackson's reforming system to great length. Don't be alarmed, gentle reader, I am only about to warn you not to be gluttonous. . . . Let us judge how much plain food is necessary to preserve our health, and not inquire how much we may possibly eat without killing ourselves off at once."

In addition to concerns about how much food and alcohol Americans consumed, reformers also addressed what they consumed. Most Americans in the early nineteenth century believed the tomato to be poisonous. Thomas Jefferson, however, served them at presidential diners and grew them at his beloved Monticello following his presidency. Concerns about the safety of tomatoes were largely put to rest on 28 September 1820 when Colonel Robert Gibbon Johnson ate a bushel of tomatoes in front of the Salem, Massachusetts, courthouse. A crowd of more than two thousand, expecting to watch the poor man die, was shocked when he lived. Four years later, in 1824, Jefferson's son-in-law, Thomas Mann Randolph, noted that tomatoes were increasingly being eaten to ensure that one's blood remained "pure" in the summer heat. By the mid-1830s, Americans were eating tomatoes in greater numbers, although they didn't become a popular food until the following century.

In 1830, Sylvester Graham, a Connecticut-born Presbyterian minister, became a professional reformer intent on revolutionizing the nation's diet. Graham taught the gospel of temperance, vegetarianism, unbolted flour, moderate exercise, loose clothing, and hydrotherapy. An outspoken advocate of the relationship between diet and health, he warned that improper eating habits fatally weakened the ability to resist epidemics.

Graham believed that meat and white flour were particularly unhealthy. He taught that the consumption of meat led to abnormal cravings, such as sexual desires, which in turn irritated the body and caused disease. Comparing human physiology to that of orangutans, he concluded that vegetarianism was natural for both primates. Graham preached that fruits and vegetables should replace meat in the typical American diet. By practicing what he preached, he challenged accepted views that fruits and vegetables contained little nutrition.

Graham also advocated bread and crackers made from unbolted, whole-grain flour (which popularly became known as Graham flour) over commercial bread made with flour bleached white to speed baking. Although today's Graham Crackers are named for him, the sweet flour used in the modern snack food little resembles the flour used to make the original Graham crackers.

THE FRUITS OF TEMPERANCE.
"Behold the son of Temperance, with buoyant heart and step, returning to his home; the partner of his bosom looks up and smiles his welcome; his children fly to meet him, their little arms embrace him, and with lip and heart they bless him."

An ardent temperance advocate, Graham refused to drink anything stronger than water, urging the avoidance of such stimulants as tea, coffee, and tobacco. He did, however, consider it beneficial for women to drink wine or gin when pregnant or nursing.

Devoted followers of Graham—known as Grahamites—shared his religious zeal for physical and moral purity, and they practiced temperance, sexual restraint, and vegetarianism. His ideas found a home among the Shakers and in numerous utopian communities, including Bronson Alcott's Fruitlands community.

Given the widespread interest in improving health, it is not surprising that Joseph Smith also brought forth a revealed law of health known as "the Word of Wisdom." While many of the ideas of his contemporaries have been repudiated by medical science, Joseph's law of health has survived the test of time.

Received through revelation in February 1832, the Word of Wisdom (D&C 89) contained a list of do's and don'ts. It encouraged eating grains and fruits and avoiding tobacco, alcoholic drinks, and "hot drinks" (interpreted as tea and coffee). Meat was "to be used sparingly," which was a far cry from existing American eating habits.

This "principle with promise," as the Lord referred to it, tied a spiritual promise to a physical promise and was "adapted to the capacity of the weak and the weakest of all saints." Those who obeyed were promised blessings of "wisdom and . . . knowledge" as well as the ancient biblical promise of "health in their navel and marrow to their bones." The Word of Wisdom was not merely a health law but also a profound key to understanding spiritual truths.

Tobacco was still being touted as a wonder drug in the early nineteenth century, just as it had been in the seventeenth century when John Josselyn wrote that tobacco "helps digestion, the Gout, the Tooth-Ache, prevents infection . . . it heats the cold, and cools them that sweat, feedeth the hungry, spent spirits restoreth, purgeth the stomach, killeth nits and lice." Relatively little attention was given to the harmful effects of tobacco at the time, even by the most progressive reformers. Yet according to Brigham Young, concerns over tobacco brought about the Word of Wisdom. Joseph was holding what he called a "School of the Prophets" at the time, and many in attendance would

> light their pipes, and, while smoking, talk about the great things of the kingdom, and spit all over the room, and as soon as the pipe was out of their mouths a large chew of tobacco would then be taken. Often when the Prophet entered the room to give the school instructions he would find himself in a cloud of tobacco smoke. This, and the complaints of his wife at having to clean so filthy a floor, made the Prophet think upon the matter, and he inquired of the Lord relating to the conduct of the Elders in using tobacco, and the

revelation known as the Word of Wisdom was the result of his inquiry.

Years after Joseph's death, crusaders increasingly focused their attention on the dangers of tobacco. Crusading prohibitionist Carry Nation proclaimed at the end of the nineteenth century that "nicotine poisons the blood, dulls the brain, and is the cause of disease" and that "the lungs of the tobacco user are black from poison," views in harmony with scientific studies. Modern science has verified the Word of Wisdom's declaration that tobacco "is not good for man," and evidence that the tobacco industry knowingly markets an addictive and deadly poison seemingly bears out the warning that it was given "in consequence of evils and designs that do and will exist in the hearts of conspiring men."

TIME TO BREATHE AGAIN

The continued breathlessness with which novelist Charles Dickens later described an 1842 train ride through Massachusetts is not unlike how some individuals might describe a modern, high-speed roller-coaster ride. As the train hurried past clearings cut into the New England woods, Dickens was able to catch "hasty glimpses of a distant town, with its clean white houses and their cool piazzas, its prim New England church and school-house; when whir-r-r! almost before you have seen them," the town disappears again into the "same dark screen."

Even with improvements to steam engines producing faster trips, it is unlikely that the train on which Dickens rode ever reached thirty miles an hour. That speed, however, was a far cry from what the famed author would have experienced in his native England. After steam railroad engines began operating in England in 1825, a man was required to *walk* in front of the train to ensure it did not exceed the four-miles-an-hour speed limit. Against that frame of reference, Dickens wrote:

> On it whirls headlong, dives through the woods again, emerges in the light, clatters over frail arches, rumbles upon the heavy ground, shoots beneath a wooden bridge which intercepts the light for a second like a wink, suddenly awakens all the slumbering echoes in the main street of a large town, and dashes on haphazard, pell-mell, neck-or-nothing, down the middle of the road. There—with mechanics working at their trades, and people leaning from their doors and windows, and boys flying kites and playing marbles, and men smoking, and women talking, and children crawling, and pigs burrowing, and unaccustomed horses plunging and rearing, close to the very rails—there—on, on, on—tears the mad dragon of an engine with its train of cars; scattering in all directions a shower of burning sparks from its wood fire; screeching, hissing, yelling, panting; until at last the thirsty monster stops beneath a covered way to drink, the people cluster round, and you have time to breathe again.

As the Saints began gathering to Kirtland in the spring of 1831, total Church membership numbered nearly three hundred. Many came to Kirtland expecting to find a pious prophet similar to the preachers they had known. Some were troubled when they found Joseph not only to be a young man in his twenties but also a social and engaging individual. For those looking to find a flaw in Joseph, he didn't disappoint. One man, seeing the Prophet playing with children during a break from work on his inspired translation of the Bible, concluded that Joseph was not a man of God. Another apostatized when Joseph misspelled his name.

Most, however, embraced him as "Brother Joseph," a term that evinced both respect and closeness. The message of truth and love in his teaching contrasted greatly with what was being taught in other religions. Joseph lacked much of the style and eloquence of the great orators of the day, such as Daniel Webster, but the power of his message more than made up for his speaking style. "We consider that God has created man with a mind capable of instruction, and a faculty which may be enlarged in proportion to the heed and diligence given to the light communicated from heaven to the intellect," Joseph proclaimed, "and that the nearer man approaches perfection, the clearer are his views, and the greater his enjoyments, till he has overcome the evils of his life and lost every desire for sin. . . . But we consider that this is a station to which no man ever arrived in a moment."

During this time Joseph told his followers, "You know no more concerning the destinies of this Church and kingdom than a babe upon its mother's lap. You don't comprehend it. . . . It is only a little handful of Priesthood you see here tonight, but this Church will fill North and South America—it will fill the world." While not fully comprehending, most obtained enough of a glimpse through his inspired teaching that they were willing to lay the foundation for a great work. "We began to talk about the kingdom of God as if we had the whole world at our command. We talked with great confidence, and talked big things," Sidney Rigdon recalled.

Joseph continued to receive revelations outlining the proper order of the Church and the doctrines and principles essential to salvation. According to Parley P. Pratt, when Joseph received a revelation, "each sentence was uttered slowly and very distinctly, and with a pause between each, sufficiently long for it to be recorded, by an ordinary writer in long hand." Brigham Young testified that "those who were acquainted with [Joseph] knew when the Spirit of revelation was upon him, for his countenance wore an expression peculiar to himself while under the influence. He preached by the Spirit of revelation, and taught in his council by it, and those who were acquainted with him could discover it at once, for at such times there was a peculiar clearness and transparency in his face."

1832

Joseph Smith and Sidney Rigdon viewed the degrees of glory; they were subsequently tarred and feathered; Joseph made a second trip to Missouri, received a revelation on priesthood (D&C 84), and prophesied of the American Civil War and that war would be poured out on all nations (D&C 87)

U.S. artist George Catlin began studying American Indians from Oregon Territory to Florida; his more than 500 paintings are a significant record of the indigenous cultures of North America

South Carolina sparked the Nullification Crisis by nullifying federal tariffs of 1828 and 1832; President Jackson threatened force to uphold federal law; the issue was resolved by passage of a compromise tariff

The Black Hawk War was fought after Sac and Fox Indians returned to Illinois and Wisconsin from Iowa Territory hoping to reclaim tribal lands

English surgeon James Snell introduced the reclining dentist's chair

Englishwoman Frances Trollope published *The Domestic Manners of the Americans;* she went to America with high hopes, but, she wrote, "before I had half completed my tour I was quite cured. Were I an English legislator, instead of sending (a seditionist) to the Tower, I would send her to make a tour of the United States"

OF THEE I SING

The early part of the nineteenth century was a time of strong patriotism. The War of 1812 confirmed America's independence, the Monroe Doctrine validated the country's position among the world's pantheon of nations, and the beginning of expansion across the great continent seemingly signaled its manifest destiny. Numerous patriotic songs and verses appeared in print during this time, one of the most notable of which was written by Samuel Francis Smith.

A student at Andover Theological Seminary, Smith was asked to write a hymn suitable for a children's choir. Inspired by a tune from a German songbook, he set down the words to "My Country, 'Tis of Thee" (now better known as "America") within half an hour. First sung in public on 4 July 1831 at a service in the Park Street Church in Boston, it was published the following year in a collection of church music. It became an instant favorite. Oliver Wendell Holmes, a friend of Smith's, later explained its popularity this way: "If he had said 'our,' the hymn would not have been immortal, but that 'my' was a master stroke. Everyone who sings the song at once feels a personal ownership in his native land."

The tune that caught Smith's attention had previously been used for patriotic hymns by the Danish, Dutch, French, Swiss, Russian, and Austrians. Only later would Smith learn that the British had also joined the tune with a text written in the 1740s to create their national anthem, "God Save the King."

"My Country, 'Tis of Thee," with its reference to "thy woods and templed hills," speaks eloquently of the America of the early 1830s, which was situated primarily east of the Mississippi River and peopled primarily by those born within its boundaries. More than sixty years later, the words of Katherine Lee Bates in "America the Beautiful," with its references to "purple mountain majesties," "amber waves of grain," and a nation stretching from "sea to shining sea" would honor an expanded America.

Samuel Francis Smith (1808–1895)

The Lord commanded Joseph to publish these revelations. The initial effort to publish them as the Book of Commandments fell victim to Missouri mobocrats in 1833. In 1835, the revelations were published in the Doctrine and Covenants along with seven lectures on faith that Joseph and his associates had prepared. Initially ninety-nine revelations were canonized as scripture, the vast majority of which Joseph received while in Ohio. As Joseph anticipated the publication of the revealed word of God, Church leaders proclaimed:

> Search the scriptures—search the revelations which we publish, and ask your Heavenly Father, in the name of His Son Jesus Christ, to manifest the truth unto you, and if you do it with an eye single to His glory, nothing doubting, He will answer you by the power of His Holy Spirit. You will then know for yourselves and not for another. You will not then be dependent on man for the knowledge of God; nor will there be any room for speculation. No; for when men receive their instruction from Him that made them, they know how He will save them. Then again we say: Search the Scriptures, search the Prophets, and learn what portion of them belongs to you and the people of the nineteenth century. . . . If others' blessings are not your blessings, others' curses are not your curses: you stand then in these last days, as all have stood before you, agents unto yourselves.

"Sidney is not used to it as I am."

—Joseph Smith's lighthearted observation about Sidney Rigdon after they were permitted in February 1832 to glimpse the degrees of glory. One of those in the room at the time stated that during the vision, "Joseph sat firmly and calmly all the time in the midst of a magnificent glory, but Sidney sat limp and pale, apparently as limber as a rag."

In June 1831, John and Alice Johnson traveled to Kirtland from their home at Hiram, Ohio, to meet the man many proclaimed a prophet of God. During their conversation, Joseph was asked if God had given man power to heal Alice's lame arm. A few moments later, Joseph walked over to Alice, took her by the hand, and commanded her to be whole. For the first time in six years, she was able to move her arm. Later that year, after Joseph made a trip to Missouri, he and Emma accepted the Johnsons' hospitality and moved to Hiram.

While at the Johnson home, Joseph made rapid progress on his inspired translation of the Bible. In February 1832, Joseph and Sidney Rigdon, while working on the Gospel of John, were permitted to see the degrees of glory that each will inherit following this life. Although many proclaimed this teaching as pure truth, the contradiction of longstanding Christian belief of heaven and hell moved others to violence.

I have visited a grove which is Just back of the town almost every day where I can be Secluded from the eyes of any mortal and there give vent to all the feelings of my heart in meditation and prayer. I have Called to mind all the past moments of my life and am left to morn [and] shed tears of sorrow for my folly in Sufering the adversary of my Soul to have so much power over me as he has had in times past. But God is merciful and has forgiven my Sins and I rejoice that he Sendeth forth the Comferter unto as many as believe and humbleth themselves before him.

—From a June 1832 letter written by Joseph Smith at New Albany, Indiana, to Emma Smith. While returning to his home in Kirtland, Ohio, from a visit to the Saints in Missouri, the horses pulling the stagecoach bolted, and the passengers were forced to jump. Newel K. Whitney broke his leg in the process, and Joseph spent a month at New Albany while his friend convalesced.

I think that it is high time for a Christian world to awake out of sleep, and cry mightily to that God, day and night, whose anger we have justly incurred. . . . This is what has caused me to overlook my own inability, and expose my weakness to a learned world; but, trusting in that God who has said that these things are hid from the wise and prudent and revealed unto babes, I step forth into the field to tell you what the Lord is doing, and what you must do to enjoy the smiles of your Savior in these last days.

—Joseph Smith to newspaper editor N. E. Sexton, 4 January 1833. Joseph is commenting on the state of things "throughout our Christian land" that he viewed with "feelings of the most painful anxiety."

"Falling of Stars, Jackson County, Missouri." During the early morning hours of 13 November 1833, an "awful, splendid" meteor shower was witnessed across America. This phenomenon was described by numerous individuals throughout the nation, including exiled Latter-day Saints driven from their homes in Jackson County and by Joseph Smith at Kirtland, Ohio, who wrote that "the stars . . . fell like hail stones."

1833

Joseph Smith received the Word of Wisdom (D&C 89), completed his translation of the Bible, gave the first patriarchal blessings, prepared the plat for city of Zion, organized the First Presidency, and presided over cornerstone-laying services for the Kirtland Temple; the Latter-day Saints were driven from Jackson County, Missouri

The potato was brought to Idaho by Rev. Henry R. Spaulding, a Presbyterian minister and missionary to the Indians

Chicago was incorporated as a village of about 200

Great Britain outlawed slavery in all her colonies; upwards of 700,000 slaves were freed

The *New York Sun*, the first successful penny daily, was founded

The legend of Davy Crockett was augmented by the publication of his "autobiography," *A Narrative of the Life of David Crockett*

A FIREBELL IN THE NIGHT

UNITED STATES SLAVE TRADE.
1830.

Throughout the first half of the nineteenth century, the dark cloud of slavery that hung over America frequently obscured the nation's self-proclaimed role as a light to the world. Although most leading nations and the northern states outlawed this inhumanity, southerners tenaciously clung to their "peculiar institution." As a result, the United States fractured into two essentially separate nations—one modern and industrial, the other isolated and backward. While new immigrants, ideas, and inventions transformed the North, the South remained largely mired in its old way of life. Alexis de Tocqueville wrote in *Democracy in America,* "The State of Ohio is separated from that of Kentucky by a single river. On the two sides the soil is equally fertile, the position as favourable, yet everything is different." Tocqueville found it "impossible" to attribute the differences "to any other cause than slavery. It brutalizes the black population and debilitates the whites." The famous Frenchman was not alone in believing that slavery was holding back the South.

When these distinct Northern and Southern cultures collided, the outcome was often grave. Hoping to limit difficulties between free and slave interests, Congress in 1820 passed the Missouri Compromise, which allowed both Missouri and Maine to be admitted to the Union of states—one a slave state, the other a free state—in an effort to keep the balance equal. A line was also drawn across the Louisiana Purchase above which slavery was not allowed. The Missouri Compromise, however, only accentuated a growing crisis.

As the American Civil War confirmed, the establishment of a line could not easily resolve the divisiveness of slavery, since people on both sides viewed it as a moral question. Slave holders appealed to the Bible to justify their "peculiar institution," while opponents found in the same Bible a justification to end the practice. The inherent inhumanity of slavery led this latter group to go on the offensive; in response to these attacks, the former became more aggressive in their defense of the practice. Bloody slave rebellions during the 1820s and 1830s, inspired in part by abolitionist calls to end slavery, prompted slaveholders afraid of further uprisings to become even more cruel in their treatment of slaves. Laws were passed that took away the few rights of slaves. These actions in turn gave new life to the antislavery movement. The situation continued to escalate until it ended in fratricidal war.

Thomas Jefferson readily grasped the perilous situation in 1820 when asked his opinion of the Missouri Compromise:

This momentous question, like a firebell in the night, awakened and filled me with terror. I considered it at once as the knell of the Union. It is hushed, indeed, for the moment. But this is a reprieve only, not a final sentence. A geographical line, coinciding with a marked principle, moral and political, once conceived and held up to the angry passions of men, will never be obliterated; and every new irritation will make it deep and deeper. . . . I regret that I am now to die in the belief that the useless sacrifice of themselves by the generation of 1776, to acquire self-government and happiness to their country, is to be thrown away by the unwise and unworthy passions of their sons, and that my only consolation is to be that I live not to weep over it. If they would but dispassionately weigh the blessings they would throw away against an abstract principle more likely to be effected by the union than by scission, they would pause before they would perpetrate this act of suicide on themselves, and of treason against the hopes of the world.

In the early 1830s, the Latter-day Saints learned firsthand what had caused Jefferson so much concern a decade earlier. When they first settled in western Missouri, they found themselves in the middle of the sectional crisis, and then eventually burned by the firestorm of slavery.

The Latter-day Saints began gathering to western Missouri in the fall of 1831 following a revelation received by Joseph Smith proclaiming Jackson County, Missouri, as the location of the promised New Jerusalem spoken of in the Bible. By the summer of 1833, the LDS population in Jackson County reached twelve hundred. Numbers alone would have caused the "old settlers" of the area to look at the new arrivals with suspicion, but the culture shock experienced by both the Mormons and their neighbors greatly magnified the problems. Joseph's official history unabashedly proclaims with obvious hyperbole, "Our reflections were many, coming as we had from a highly cultivated state of society in the east . . . to observe the degradation . . . of a people that were nearly a century behind the times."

Differences between the two groups were magnified by the greatest difference of all—slavery. Most of the Latter-day Saints in Missouri in the early 1830s were from free states. Northerners in a slave state were often looked upon with suspicion by their slaveholding and pro-slavery neighbors as someone there to tamper with slavery. But in this battleground slave state, emotions ran even higher. Having largely been isolated from the slave culture, the Mormons failed to adequately judge the feelings of their pro-slavery neighbors, the vast majority of whom were on the defensive because of increased abolitionist activities and the bloody 1831 Nat Turner slave rebellion in Virginia. When local Latter-day Saint leaders in July 1833 published an article entitled "Free People of Color" hoping to curtail concerns about Mormon intentions regarding slavery, the article was misconstrued and only served to further fan the flames. Outraged local citizens demanded that the Mormons leave.

When the Latter-day Saints refused to negotiate away or abandon their property, mobs destroyed their press and printing house and ransacked Mormon establishments. Local Church leaders were tarred and feathered. The mob issued an ultimatum that the Mormons must leave, but before the appointed time, a new round of violence brought additional attacks, beatings, and depredations. Homes were destroyed, men whipped, and women and children terrorized. Eventually, the flame that Jefferson envisioned forced the Latter-day Saints to leave Jackson County.

Abolitionist press demolished by pro-slavery forces

THE SAGE OF CONCORD

Ralph Waldo Emerson

Ralph Waldo Emerson was born, raised, and educated in the fading twilight of New England's tainted age of conformist Puritan faith. His voice resonated with both piety and rational reason at the dawn of America's emerging industrial, scientific, artistic, intellectual, and economic populism and power. His bold, poetic, and stylistic essays and lectures were filled with original thought that embodied the ideals and spirit of his period in American history. The Sage of Concord, as he became known, was at the intellectual center of America's first influential period of national letters and was a chief spokesman for Transcendentalism. He believed and taught that within each person is an innate, optimistic spirit urging that person to discover and live the truth free from dogma, released from restrictive established authority, and unconstrained by orthodoxy. His philosophy passionately pushed self-reliance, unity with nature, integrity, and self-determination.

The fourth child born to William and Ruth Haskins Emerson, Ralph Waldo was born in Boston on Election Day, 25 May 1803. His father was the liberal-minded minister at Boston's First Church, and his mother was the daughter of a distiller. After his father's 1811 death, Emerson's childhood was notable for its "genteel poverty," which necessitated regular changes of residence.

After attending Harvard (where he began his fifty-five-year habit of journal-keeping) and a brief period of teaching, Emerson became a pastor at Boston's Second (Unitarian) Church. However, his nineteen-year-old wife Ellen's death from tuberculosis resulted in a crisis in faith that would not allow Emerson to serve communion "to an institution which . . . esteem[s] the holiest with indifference and dislike." He resigned as pastor in October 1832. From the settlement of Ellen's estate, he eventually received a $1,200 annual income.

Bereaved and adrift in the world, Emerson set sail on Christmas Day, 1832, bound for Europe, where he hoped to find inspiration and to recuperate. During his travels, he went out of his way to meet the luminaries of his time—intellectuals, writers, politicians, inventors, and military leaders. In Florence, he visited with poet Walter Savage Landor; in Paris, he saw the much-sought-after Marquis de Lafayette; in London, he conversed with philosopher, economist, and political theorist John Stuart Mill; while on the British Isle, he also shared ideas with poets Samuel Taylor Coleridge and William Wordsworth. Emerson's meeting with Thomas

Carlyle established an intellectually active, long-term friendship. However, even though he would draw inspiration from these contemporary heroes—especially Wordsworth, Coleridge, Landor, and Carlyle—Emerson felt that all were "deficient . . . in insight into religious truth. They have no idea of that species of moral truth which I call the first philosophy."

With restored health and a renewed purpose in life, Emerson returned to America in September 1833. By that November, he had embarked on his new career as a lecturer with a series on science. Subsequently, he settled in Concord and married Lydia Jackson. While continuing to lecture, he worked on his book *Nature,* which was published in 1836, the same year his son Waldo was born (he and Lydia would parent four children).

The publication of *Nature* began Emerson's three essential "questions-challenges." In *Nature,* the question-challenge dealt with philosophy; in his lecture entitled "The American Scholar," he spoke of literature and education; and in his radical "Harvard Divinity School Address," Emerson challenged orthodox views on God and criticized institutional Christianity. Emerson was now on his way to becoming one of America's most popular lecturers. He traveled throughout the United States, giving "hundreds upon hundreds" of discourses. The income from lecturing nearly doubled the annual income received from his first wife's estate.

His journals inspired many of his lectures and essays, many of which he published in book form, the most popular being *Essays* (1841 and 1844). *Essays* included contemplative writings on "Self-Reliance," "Love," "Compensation," "The Over-Soul," "Manners," "The Poet," and "Politics."

Emerson influenced a growing, gathering circle of his era's reformers, poets, artists, and thinkers—including Nathaniel Hawthorne, Margaret Fuller, Frederick Douglas, Jonas Very, Henry David Thoreau, the Alcotts, and Walt Whitman—whose own works helped forge a new artistic, intellectual, religious, and cultural identity for America. He also inspired people to link their intellectual explorations with action as he tirelessly crusaded on behalf of peace, abolition, the American Indian, and educational reform.

As Emerson grew older, his optimism was tempered, but not defeated, by experience. In later writings such as *The Conduct of Life* (1860), he acknowledged that men and women, although filled with innate potential, are limited by suffering, down-trodden circumstances, and dark realities beyond their control.

Just weeks after a rain-soaked spring walk through the woods of Concord, America's "Yankee Plato" died of pneumonia on 27 April 1882. His beloved Concord shrouded itself in black, and bells rang for each of his years. His example and teachings would ring out into the future, inspiring reformers such as Martin Luther King, Mohandas Gandhi, and Nelson Mandela.

THE GYMNASIUM

The *Journal of Health* reported in 1832 that "wealthy women in America tended to be less robust than "females in the middling classes." Oliver Wendell Holmes later lamented that America's youth were turning into "a pale, pasty-faced, narrow chested, spindle-shanked, dwarfed race." Both comments had their origin in America's growing urban population. City dwellers lived more sedentary lives than those who experienced the rigors of farm life.

Hoping to toughen flabby Americans and upgrade their physical condition, Charles Follen, an outspoken professor at Harvard College, introduced the art of gymnastics to America in 1826. Soon health enthusiasts were building gymnasiums for men and advocating various workouts involving parallel bars, ropes, wooden horses, and rings. Women were encouraged to follow a less strenuous, more private regimen, such as performing calisthenics with the aid of a suspended exercise bar wrapped in velvet to protect the hands.

In 1842, Lydia Maria Child used the new fitness craze to explain an old problem: "At present time indications are numerous that the human mind is tired out in the gymnasium of controversy, and asks earnestly for repose, protection, mystery, and undoubting faith."

> *I have thought that perhaps a few lines from me, though there may be a lack of fluency in address according to the literate of the age, may be received with a degree of satisfaction on your part, at least, when you call to mind the near relation with which we are united by the everlasting ties of the Gospel of our Lord Jesus Christ.*
>
> *. . . You know my manner of communication, how that in weakness and simplicity, I declared to you what the Lord had brought forth by the ministering of his holy angels to me for this generation. I pray that the Lord may enable you to treasure these things in your mind, for I know that his Spirit will bear testimony to all who seek diligently after knowledge from him.*
>
> —Joseph Smith to Moses C. Nickerson, 19 November 1833.

Tarring and feathering of Joseph Smith, March 1832

On 24 March 1832, an angry mob of about a dozen men broke into the Johnson house and pulled Joseph out into the cold night air. "I made a desperate struggle, as I was forced out, to extricate myself," Joseph recalled, but "they swore by G—, they would kill me if I did not be still, which quieted me." Joseph pleaded with his abductors, "You will have mercy and spare my life, I hope." They told him, "Call on yer God for help, we'll show ye no mercy." One scratched the young prophet with "his nails like a mad cat and then muttered out: 'G—d—ye, that's the way the Holy Ghost falls on folks!'" The mob tried to force Joseph to drink a bottle of acid. Joseph broke a tooth during the struggle, which caused him afterward to speak with a slight whistle. Finally, he was tarred and feathered. Friends spent the night painstakingly removing the tar so that Joseph, his "flesh all scarified and defaced," could preach the Sunday sermon as usual the next day, when he also baptized three converts.

The mobbing claimed one of Joseph's and Emma's young children. In April 1831, shortly after Joseph and Emma moved to Ohio, Emma delivered twins who lived only a few hours. All three children born to the young couple had died, and it was also common in this era of high mortality for mothers to die in childbirth. Shortly after losing their own twins, the couple adopted two newborn twins, Joseph and Julia Murdock, whose mother had died in childbirth. Eleven-month-old Joseph, sick with measles at the time his namesake father was dragged from the house, contracted a severe cold from exposure to the chilly night air and died five days later.

In 1833, the Lord commanded Joseph to build a temple, which, as in ancient times, would serve as "a house of prayer; a house of fasting, a house of faith, a house of learning, a house of glory, a house of order; a house of God." After work began in June 1833, "there was but one mainspring to all our thoughts and actions," Lucy Mack Smith wrote, "and that was the building of the Lord's house." Nothing was spared. "Shall we, brethren, build a house for our God, of logs?" Joseph asked. "No," he proclaimed. The temple's exterior reflected both the Federal and Greek Revival styles popular during this time. The temple cost between forty and sixty thousand dollars, a substantial sum for a few hundred people who frequently shared food to stay alive.

As Joseph outlined the skills needed to complete the temple, he was told of Artemus Millet, who lived in Canada but was not a member of the Church. Joseph sent Brigham Young to convert Millet and bring him to Kirtland. A substantial major portion of the money needed to complete the temple was provided by another recent convert, John Tanner, who sold his substantial property in New York and moved to Kirtland after learning in a dream that the Prophet needed his assistance. Joseph and Emma joined with others in working on the temple and providing furnishings for it.

On Sunday, 27 March 1836, Joseph dedicated the Kirtland Temple among circumstances that many compared to the New Testament day of Pentecost.

Those present testified of angels and glorious visions accompanying the dedication. "God was there, his angels were there, the Holy Ghost was in the midst of the people, the visions of the Almighty were opened to the minds of the servants of the living God," Orson Pratt wrote. Joseph noted, "The people of the neighborhood came running together (hearing an unusual sound within, and seeing a bright light like a pillar of fire resting upon the Temple), and were astonished at what was taking place." Concerning Joseph's dedicatory prayer, Daniel Tyler wrote, "Never until then had I heard a man address his Maker as though He was present listening. There was no ostentation, no raising of the voice as by enthusiasm, but a plain conversational tone."

The following Sunday, while Joseph and Oliver Cowdery were praying in the temple, Joseph later reported, "the veil was taken from our minds, and the eyes of our understanding were opened. We saw the Lord standing upon the breast work of the pulpit, before us; and under his feet was a paved work of pure gold, in color like amber. His eyes were as a flame of fire; the hair of his head was white like the pure snow; his countenance shone above the brightness of the sun; and his voice was as the sound of rushing of great waters, even the voice of Jehovah." Other heavenly messengers also appeared, including Elijah, whom the Old Testament prophet Malachi testified would return "before the great and dreadful day of the Lord."

Kirtland, Ohio

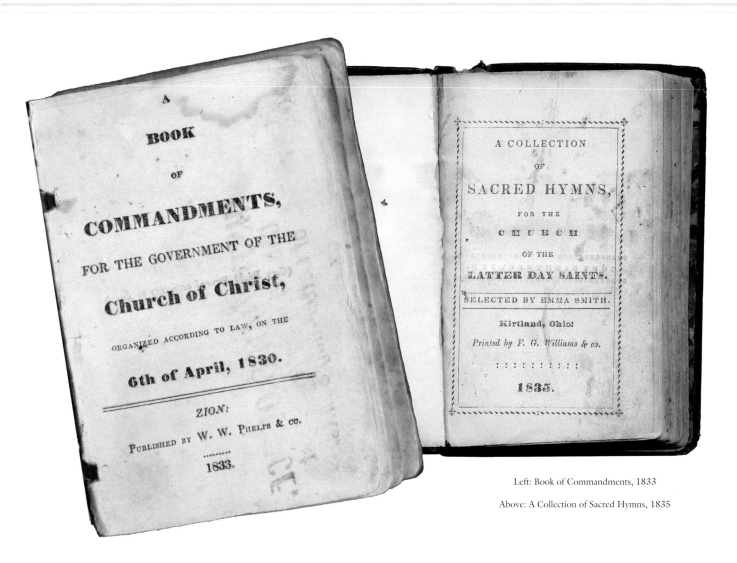

Left: Book of Commandments, 1833

Above: A Collection of Sacred Hymns, 1835

1834

Joseph Smith organized the first high council at Kirtland and organized Zion's Camp in an effort to restore Latter-day Saints to their homes in Jackson County, Missouri

A pro-slavery mob disrupted an anti-slavery meeting in New York City because blacks and whites were sitting together; riots lasted for eight days

An anti-Catholic mob destroyed the Ursuline convent in Sommerville, Massachusetts, after false reports circulated that a woman was being held there against her will

Congress created the Indian Territory (now Oklahoma) and established the Department of Indian Affairs

English mathematician Charles Babbage set forth the principles of his "analytical engine," the basis for modern computers

Swiss wax modeler Marie Tussaud opened a waxworks exhibit in London, England

1835

Joseph Smith organized the Quorum of the Twelve Apostles; received a revelation on Priesthood (D&C 107); obtained Egyptian papyrus containing the writings of Abraham; published the Doctrine and Covenants

War began with Seminole Indians after chief Osceola refused to leave Florida for Indian Territory

Hans Christian Andersen published *Tales, Told for Children*, his first collection of fairy tales

Oberlin College became the first college to admit students "without respect to color"; in 1838 it became the first co-educational college

Gold was discovered at Dahlonega, Georgia—America's first gold rush

The Liberty Bell cracked while tolling the death of Supreme Court Chief Justice John Marshall

P. T. Barnum's circus began touring the U.S.; within a year, 30 circuses were traveling the country

I was this morning introduced to a man from the east. After hearing my name, he remarked that I was nothing but a man, indicating by his expression, that he had supposed that a person to whom the Lord should see fit to reveal His will, must be something more than a man. He seemed to have forgotten the saying that fell from the lips of St. James, that Elias was a man subject to like passions as we are, yet he had such power with God, that He, in answer to his prayers, shut the heavens that they gave no rain for the space of three years and six months; and again, in answer to his prayer, the heavens gave forth rain, and the earth gave forth fruit.

—Reflections of Joseph Smith, 6 November 1835.

Young America embraced such populist frontier heroes as the much-publicized Davy Crockett, who was killed at the Battle of the Alamo in 1836

1836

The Kirtland Temple was dedicated; Jesus Christ appeared to Joseph Smith in the temple; Moses, Elias, and Elijah committed to Joseph the keys of their respective dispensations; Joseph traveled to Springfield, Massachusetts, looking for buried treasure; he helped establish the Kirtland Safety Society

After issuing 9,957 unnumbered patents, U.S. patent office issued U.S. patent number 1

Texas declared independence from Mexico; Davy Crockett was among the nearly 200 defenders killed at the Alamo; the Republic of Texas won its freedom at the Battle of San Jacinto; Sam Houston's forces were spurred on by the rallying cry "Remember the Alamo"

Arkansas became the 25th state

Martin Van Buren was elected the eighth U.S. president

The Awful Disclosures of Maria Monk, as Exhibited in a Narrative of Her Suffering During a Residence of Five Years as a Novice, and Two Years as a Black Nun, in the Hotel Dieu Nunnery at Montreal became a best-seller in an era of anti-Catholic feelings; the book was later shown to be a hoax

Ralph Waldo Emerson's "Nature" was published, one of the seminal works of Transcendentalism

U.S. educator William McGuffey published his first and second *Eclectic Readers*

I THANK GOD THAT MYSELF AND FRIENDS WERE LANDED SAFELY

THE FIRST STEAM RAILROAD TRAIN IN AMERICA.

During the summer of 1836, Joseph and Hyrum Smith, Sidney Rigdon, and Oliver Cowdery traveled from Kirtland, Ohio, to Salem, Massachusetts, where a fortune of gold and silver was reportedly buried under a house. Taking advantage of three nineteenth-century improvements in transportation—steamships, railroads, and the Erie Canal, the journey took twelve days and included time for sightseeing in New York City. A similar journey without the benefit of "teakettle power" and the Erie Canal would have taken weeks.

Catching a steamer at Fairport, Ohio, on 25 July, the group sailed on Lake Erie to Buffalo, New York. They began a three-day journey on the Erie Canal the following morning, taking a boat traveling only as far as Utica "to avoid the crowding, fisting, fighting, racing" for which the vessels that ran regular routes between Buffalo and Albany, the terminuses of the Erie Canal, were famous.

Shortly after disembarking at Utica on the morning of 29 July, they caught a train bound for Schenectady, reportedly the first passenger train to travel that railroad line. The journey of eighty miles took more than six hours at approximately thirteen miles an hour. According to Joseph's published history, "The locomotive had hardly stopped before the cry was, 'Albany baggage: the cars start in five minutes.' Amid a scene of confusion, bustle, and crowding, we succeeded, after a good share of scuffling and pulling, in getting our trunks on board the luggage car for Albany where we arrived the same evening."

The group caught a steamer bound for New York City the morning of 30 July. On this journey, however, they were unable to avoid being involved in a steamship race. When another steamer left Albany about the same time, "'Now for a race,' was the cry from different parts, and a race trial of speed it was." Joseph noted that "as fate or steam power of engine would have it," the steamship he was on "went into New York a few minutes 'ahead.'" Joseph wrote of the race, "By such undue pressure of steam the lives of thousands have been sacrificed, and I thank God that myself and friends were safely landed."

The remainder of the journey was relatively uneventful. After visiting an area of New York City that had been devastated by fire the previous year, the company traveled by steamer to Providence, Rhode Island, and then on to Boston by "steam cars" (railroad) before arriving at Salem on 6 August.

AN ANTI-BANKING SOCIETY

During an 1831 visit to Cincinnati, Ohio, Alexis de Tocqueville asked United States Supreme Court justice John McLean, "Do you know why there are so few banks in Ohio?" The esteemed jurist explained that forty banks during the previous ten years "all went bankrupt, and the people have certainly lost confidence in them. Besides, the large quantity of paper that they issued gave a distorted value to the various consumer goods. Now scarcely any notes are accepted except those of the Bank of the United States." A national bank, McLean declared, was "clearly beneficial, especially in the West where it provides a trustworthy, portable currency. Apart from its other advantages, it scores by preventing the establishment of bad banks. It refuses to accept their notes, and so discredits them on the spot."

Although McLean and others in the Western Reserve believed in a national bank, not everyone saw the institution as beneficial. Senator Thomas Hart Benton called the bank an institution "too great and powerful to be tolerated in a Government of free and equal laws." President Andrew Jackson proclaimed the Bank of the United States a "moneyed monster" that would "destroy our republican institutions." Like the legendary St. George, Jackson set forth to slay *his* dragon. "The Bank is trying to kill me," he announced, "but I will kill it." Jackson won the battle but lost the war. He successfully terminated the bank in 1836 but left the United States as the only major nation without a national bank, plunging the country into a severe, economic depression the following year. The end of the bank also contributed to the Latter-day Saints' being driven from Kirtland, Ohio, in 1838.

Thomas Jefferson, with his "strict" interpretation of the Constitution, did not believe that the United States could create a national bank. Alexander Hamilton's "loose" interpretation did not see the Constitution prohibiting such a bank. National leaders ultimately adopted Hamilton's view and established the Bank of the United States. In addition to the national bank, local "banks," which included businesses as diverse as canal companies and mercantile establishments, issued their own competing currency.

Congress refused to renew the national bank in 1811, but they chartered a second Bank of the United States in 1816, hoping to address America's continuing financial chaos, which was made worse by the growing number of "banks" lacking adequate specie reserve to redeem their own notes. When President Jackson refused in 1832 to renew the National Bank's charter, he cited the fact that the bank had "failed in the great end of establishing a uniform and sound currency." In reality, Jackson believed that the bank was a symbol of aristocratic privilege and influence and that its directors stood against the idea of democratic self-government. He helped speed the demise of the Bank of the United States by withdrawing government funds from it in 1833, thus making its notes virtually worthless.

Although Jackson succeeded in destroying the "monster," he did not kill the need for banks. The demise of the bank proved a great shock to the nation's already teetering financial structure. Because the demand for credit and money remained, the number of banks in the United States nearly doubled between 1832 and 1837. Monetary confusion and disorder reigned as banks were again free to make credit available on easy terms. Western land purchases soared from $2.6 million in 1832 to $24.9 million in 1836, most of it bought by speculators on credit. In response, Jackson issued a "specie circular" in 1836 requiring all purchases of public land to be made in hard money—gold and silver. Designed to cut down on speculators and discourage the "ruinous extension"

of bank notes and credit, Jackson's specie circular only worsened the nation's economic crisis.

While people bought less land, large sums of coinage were removed from circulation, and banks lost the gold and silver reserves needed to back up currency, thus making bank notes even more unsound. Some banks even refused to accept their own currency, knowing its value. In July 1837 Joseph Smith reported, "Almost all banks throughout the country, one after the other, have suspended specie payment, and gold and silver have risen in value in direct ratio to the depreciation of paper currency." Jackson's "specie circular" brought about a new round of bank failures, which in turn led to the devastating Panic of 1837. Hard money had brought hard times, especially in Western areas such as Ohio.

It was against this backdrop that Joseph Smith sought to address Kirtland's growing financial woes by helping organize a bank, the Kirtland Safety Society, in November 1836. As Kirtland's population tripled between 1831 and 1836, land prices skyrocketed. Outlying acreage rose from seven dollars an acre in 1832 to forty-four dollars an acre; the price of city

lots experienced an even greater jump. Many of Joseph's followers, having arrived at Kirtland impoverished by their costly migration, could barely afford food, let alone purchase land. The situation prompted Joseph to write in 1835, "The Saints have neglected the necessary preparation beforehand; . . . the rich have generally stayed back and withheld their money. . . . Under these circumstances what could be expected but the appalling scene that now presents itself?" The cash-flow problem Kirtland was experiencing, common in frontier communities, would be alleviated by a bank capable of transferring long-term assets into short-term liquidity.

Although Oliver Cowdery succeeded in getting bank notes printed, the Ohio legislature had placed a moratorium on the creation of new banks. Desperately in need of banking services in Kirtland, organizers pushed ahead with their plan by changing the name of the society to the Kirtland Safety Society Anti-Banking Company in January 1837. The word "anti" was printed before the word "bank" on their notes, and "ing" printed after it.

Given what was happening in America, the

Kirtland Safety Society was doomed before it started. Within its first month of operation, it joined a growing list of banks in Ohio that were forced to suspend specie payments. Because the notes were backed by overly inflated, nonliquid land rather than specie, they began to circulate at a heavy discount.

It was hoped that the bank would solve the financial problems of the Church and community, but it only added to them. With little demand for city lots and with their debts pressing heavily upon them, organizers of the institution were forced to invest more resources in an attempt to keep it afloat. When the Safety Society closed after a year of operation, no one had lost more than Joseph Smith, because no one had invested more. Joseph was blamed for the failure of the society, a factor that led to his having to flee Kirtland for his life.

A contemporary history of the society contained this assessment: "These things have nothing to do with the gospel, but they seem to show us the weakness of poor human nature, and how easily men can be led astray when they cease to listen to the counsel of God. . . . The fruit of such conduct is exceedingly bitter, and the results most disastrous."

The Kirtland Safety Society joined a long list of financial institutions that showed no firm grasp of banking and finance principles. Although Andrew Jackson's indictment of bank monopolies and special privilege showed a similar ignorance, his was a mixed victory. While the common people felt empowered, America's monetary system greatly suffered, and the U.S. economy remained depressed throughout Joseph's lifetime.

When Charles Dickens looked for an example of something virtually worthless in his 1843 classic, *A Christmas Carol,* he looked to Britain's former colonies in North America to make his point. Prior to the arrival of the Ghost of Christmas Past, Ebenezer Scrooge became concerned that his clock was not working. The elderly miser finally concluded that such was not the case, which "was a great relief" to him, since the contracts he signed "would have become a mere United States' security if there were no days to count by."

After a quarter-century of laissez-faire approach to banking and currency, Congress began a renewed attempt to create a uniform national currency by introducing "the greenback" dollar during the Civil War. It was not until 1914, however, with the creation of the Federal Reserve System, that America began building its modern banking and monetary system, including a standard United States currency.

Lockport, New York 1836. With its five ascending locks and five decending locks, Lockport was considered a "most stupendous" example of flourishing American industry

Many of those who gathered to Kirtland arrived with little to sustain themselves, having sold all just to make the journey. The difficult financial situation the Saints faced at Kirtland was made worse in 1836 when President Andrew Jackson issued his "specie circular," which required that land be purchased with gold and silver. These precious metals, already in short supply in the Western Reserve, became even more valuable. A solution seemed to present itself when Joseph learned of a rumored treasure trove buried under a house in Salem, Massachusetts. During the summer of 1836, Joseph and others went to Salem to claim the buried treasure. Failing to locate the money, Joseph received the following revelation: "I, the Lord your God, am not displeased with your coming this journey, notwithstanding your follies. I have much treasure in this city for you, for the benefit of Zion; and many people in this city whom I will gather out in due time for the benefit of Zion, through your instrumentality! . . . For there are more treasures than one for you in this city."

Joseph remained in Salem through early fall, "teaching the people from house to house, and preaching publicly, as opportunity presented." He also visited "sections of the surrounding country, which are rich in the history of the Pilgrim Fathers of New England, in Indian warfare, religious superstition, bigotry, persecution, and learned ignorance."

Later, the "treasure" spoken of in the revelation was found when more than one hundred people were baptized at Salem, many of whom had previously heard Joseph preach.

Back at Kirtland, Joseph joined with others in attempting to address the area's financial woes by establishing a bank, to be called the Kirtland Safety Society. Unable to obtain a bank charter, in January 1837 they established a private joint-stock company called the Kirtland Safety Society Anti-Banking Company. This financial institution was ill-fated from the start. Joseph did all he could to save the Kirtland Safety Society, but it was forced to close in late 1837. The Kirtland Safety Society failed because of poor timing, land speculation, President Jackson's "specie circular," and the panic of 1837. That same year, hundreds of banks across the nation likewise failed.

As the Saints labored on their temple, opposition at Kirtland escalated. One Presbyterian minister at Kirtland proclaimed, "It is difficult to foretell how long it will take this gust of Fanaticism to spend itself, and die away, and sink to the oblivion of the hundred others which have gone before it." By 1837, however, the Latter-day Saints in Kirtland outnumbered other residents. As the Church continued to grow, "many false reports, lies, and foolish stories, were published in the newspapers, and circulated in every direction, to prevent people from investigating the work, or embracing the faith."

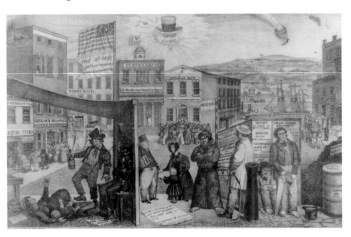

Political cartoon detailing the effects of the Financial Panic of 1837

THE ALMIGHTY DOLLAR

In November 1836, renowned American author Washington Irving added a new phrase to the American lexicon: *the almighty dollar*. Proclaiming that materialism was rampant, Irving decried the fact that Americans had turned "the almighty dollar" into a "great object of universal devotion throughout the land."

The Latter-day Saints at Kirtland, Ohio, were not immune to what was happening in the nation. Warren Cowdery observed that a large number of Saints were "guilty of wild speculation and visionary dreams of wealth and worldly grandeur, as if gold and silver were their gods." When Heber C. Kimball returned from a mission in the fall of 1836, he was amazed at the speculation: "When we left Kirtland a city lot was worth about $150; but on our return, to our astonishment, the same lot was said to be worth from $500 to $1000, according to location . . . all seemed determined to become rich."

During this time of financial trouble and growing difficulties, Joseph reported, "God revealed to me that something new must be done for the salvation of His Church." In June 1837, he directed Heber C. Kimball to organize a mission to England: "Brother Heber, the Spirit of the Lord has whispered to me: 'Let my servant Heber go to England and proclaim my Gospel, and open the door of salvation to that nation.'" This first foreign mission was indeed successful. Within eight months the Church in the British Isles had reached two thousand.

While the work was progressing in England, apostasy became widespread in Kirtland. Fueled in part by the opposition they were experiencing, people grew disenchanted with the way Joseph was unfolding the doctrines and practices of the new faith. Backbiting increased during the spring and summer of 1837, and the failure of the bank only added to a growing spirit of apostasy. Antagonistic apostates further added to the unpopular public image of the Church. By the fall of 1837, fifty leading members of the Church were excommunicated in Kirtland. Hundreds of others left the Church, approximately 10 percent of the membership in Ohio. Tensions between the "laborers on the walls" and the discontented in the area grew. "We had to guard night after night," Heber C. Kimball recalled, and "were obliged to lie with our fire locks in our arms, to preserve Brother Joseph's life." During this time, Joseph told Wilford Woodruff, "Bro. Woodruff, I am glad to see you. I hardly know when I meet those who have been my brethren in the Lord, who of them are my friends. They have become so scarce."

1837

Far West, Missouri, was surveyed and a temple site dedicated; Joseph Smith sent missionaries to England; the Kirtland Safety Society ceased operation; apostasy was widespread at Kirtland

Brothers-in-law William Procter and James Gamble set up a soap and candle business, foundation of the Procter and Gamble Company

Michigan became the 26th state

Eighteen-year-old Victoria began her sixty-four-year reign as Queen of England; the "Victorian Era" began

German educational reformer Friedrich Frobel opened the first kindergarten

The U.S. Congress increased the number of Supreme Court justices from seven to nine

Mt. Holyoke Seminary, the first in the U.S. specifically for women, began

Charles Dickens began publishing *Oliver Twist* in serial form

Nathaniel Hawthorne's *Twice-Told Tales* became a best-seller

HOW THE WEST WAS WON

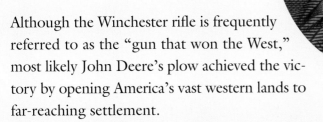

John Deere

Although the Winchester rifle is frequently referred to as the "gun that won the West," most likely John Deere's plow achieved the victory by opening America's vast western lands to far-reaching settlement.

Deere initially gained fame as a blacksmith in his native Vermont before moving to Illinois in 1836 at the age of thirty-two. His careful workmanship and ingenuity created a great demand for his services, including his highly polished hay forks and shovels. When his business fell victim to the nation's economic woes, he moved west with others from Vermont and settled at Grand Detour, Illinois, where his blacksmithing skills were again in great demand.

While shoeing horses and oxen and repairing plows and other equipment, he learned of the serious problems the local farmers faced trying to farm the fertile soil. The cast-iron plows that performed so well in New England's sandy fields were no match for the rich Midwestern soil, which clung to the plow. Farmers had to stop every few feet and scrape the dirt from the plow, making plowing a slow and laborious task. Many discouraged settlers had already returned to the East.

Deere studied the problem and became convinced that a highly polished and properly shaped moldboard (which lifted and turned the soil) on top of a highly polished share (which cut the dirt) would prevent the soil from sticking. In 1837, he built a prototype, using the steel from a broken saw blade for the share and highly polished wrought iron for the moldboard. His steel plow proved to be the solution farmers needed to conquer America's frontier, then situated largely east of the Mississippi River.

Deere faced many problems starting a manufacturing business on the frontier. Initially producing plows from whatever steel was available, he imported steel from England before turning in 1846 to the newly opened American steel mills at Pittsburgh. In 1848, he moved his factory to Moline, Illinois, to have direct access to the Mississippi River. Before opening his new factory, Deere was producing a thousand plows a year; the number had risen to thirteen thousand by 1855.

"I will never put my name on a product that does not have in it the best that is in me," Deere proclaimed. When his business partner later rebuked him for continually trying to improve the design since farmers had to buy whatever they produced, Deere replied, "They haven't got to take what we make and somebody else will beat us." Shortly after Deere died in 1868, one of the three plows he made in 1838 was sent to the Smithsonian.

THE VILLAGE BLACKSMITH

"The Village Blacksmith" was one of Henry Wadsworth Longfellow's most beloved poems. Americans positively responded to this celebration of the American worker as a hero—romantically symbolized by the ubiquitous, universally necessary, and highly respected blacksmith. The poem, with its plain diction and regular meter, extols the virtues of the simple, hands-on life that the majority of Americans understood by experience.

Unidentified blacksmith, ca. 1850

Under a spreading chestnut tree
The village smithy stands;
The smith, a mighty man is he,
With large and sinewy hands;
And the muscles of his brawny arms
Are strong as iron bands.

His hair is crisp, and black, and long,
His face is like the tan;
His brow is wet with honest sweat,
He earns whate'er he can.
And looks the whole world in the face,
For he owes not any man.

Week in, week out, from morn till night,
You can hear his bellows blow;
You can hear him swing his heavy sledge
With measured beat and slow,

Like a sexton ringing the village bell,
When the evening sun is low.
And children coming home from school
Look in at the open door;
They love to see the flaming forge,
And hear the bellows roar,
And catch the burning sparks that fly
Like chaff from a threshing floor.

He goes on Sunday to the church,
And sits among his boys;
He hears the parson pray and preach,
He hears his daughter's voice
Singing in the village choir,
And it makes his heart rejoice.

It sounds to him like her mother's voice,
Singing in Paradise!

He needs must think of her once more,
How in the grave she lies;
And with his hard, rough hand he wipes
A tear out of his eyes.

Toiling—rejoicing—sorrowing,
Onward through life he goes;
Each morning sees some task begun,
Each evening sees its close;
Something attempted, something done,
Has earned a night's repose.

Thanks, thanks to thee, my worthy friend,
For the lesson thou hast taught!
Thus at the flaming forge of life
Our fortunes must be wrought;
Thus on its sounding anvil shaped
Each burning deed and thought!

"THE VILLAGE BLACKSMITH."

LITH OF E W BOUVE

BALLAD,

By

H. W. LONGFELLOW, ESQ.

MUSIC COMPOSED AND RESPECTFULLY DEDICATED TO THE AUTHOR

By CHARLES F. HEUBERER.

62½ CTS N:

The Words of this Beautiful Ballad are founded on fact and many who now reside in Cambridge, Mass will not forget the Honest Blacksmith who lived and died in that place

BOSTON

Published by A & J. P. ORDWAY 339 Washington St

In January 1838, the situation at Kirtland deteriorated to the point that Joseph was forced to flee for his life. Warned of an impending attempt to kill him, he escaped hidden in a box and made his way to the other gathering place in Missouri.

Seven years earlier, shortly after Joseph arrived in Kirtland in February 1831, the Lord commanded him to go "to the western boundaries of the State of Missouri." At that time, Oliver Cowdery and other missionaries were near that location in Indian territory, preaching to the Native Americans, something Joseph would likewise do later that year. "The Book of Mormon has made known who Israel is," Joseph proclaimed of the work among the Native Americans. "And while we behold the government of the United States gathering the Indians, and locating them upon lands to be their own, how sweet it is to think that they may one day be gathered by the Gospel!"

Preaching the gospel was not the primary purpose for his visit to Missouri. In September 1830, Joseph received a revelation that the "city Zion shall be built, but it shall be given hereafter. Behold, I say unto you that it shall be on the borders by the Lamanites." Now the Lord had given that information to Joseph: "God . . . designated, to me and others, the very spot upon which he designed to commence the work of the gathering, and the upbuilding of an 'holy city,' which should be called Zion—Zion, because it is a place of righteousness." The "place which is now called Independence is the center place; and a spot for the temple is lying westward, upon a lot which is not far from the courthouse."

In August 1831, Joseph dedicated the temple lot and began initial preparations for the area to serve as the center of the kingdom of God on earth. As with ancient Israel, the Latter-day Saints found their promised land

Mormons fleeing Jackson County, Missouri, 1833

occupied. Although the Lord gave instructions on how Zion, the New Jerusalem, was to be established, many Saints chose not to follow His course but instead sought their own path. Ultimately, Zion was not redeemed.

By November 1832, eight hundred Latter-day Saints had gathered to Jackson County, Missouri. By their numbers, the Mormons embodied a threat to the existing economic, social, and political order of western Missouri. Their willingness to work and stick together, in the midst of a culture that stressed autonomy and individuality, set up tensions and suspicions between the Latter-day Saints and their neighbors. One Missourian characterized his new neighbors as "a tribe of locusts" that "threatens to scorch and wither the herbage of a fair and goodly portion of Missouri." Other Missourians characterized the Mormons as "deluded fanatics" and "the very dregs" of society.

"The Lord's Army marching to the deliverance of Zion." Zion's Camp, May 1834

The Mormons set to work redeeming their Zion: "It was a strange sight indeed to see four or five yoke of oxen turning up the rich soil. Fencing and other improvements went on in rapid succession. Cabins were built and prepared for families as fast as time, money and labor could accomplish the work; and our homes in the new country presented a prosperous appearance—almost equal to Paradise itself—and our peace and happiness, as we flattered ourselves, were not in a great degree deficient to that of our first parents in the garden of Eden." Newel K. Whitney noted, "We were not accustomed to a frontier life, so things around us seemed new and strange and the work we had to do was of a different nature to that which had been done in the East. Yet we took hold with cheerful hearts, and a determination to do our best."

"Mormon troubles in Missouri begin." Election-day fights at Gallatin, Missouri, August 1838

1838

Joseph Smith and other Latter-day Saints left Kirtland for Missouri; Joseph received a revelation giving the official name of the Church (The Church of Jesus Christ of Latter-day Saints, D&C 115), identifying Adam-ondi-Ahman (D&C 116), and outlining the law of tithing (D&C 119); renewed difficulties between the Latter-day Saints and their Missouri neighbors resulted in Governor Lilburn Boggs's extermination order and the imprisonment of Joseph Smith and others in the Liberty Jail

Iowa Territory was created (comprising present-day Iowa, Minnesota, and North and South Dakota)

The Trail of Tears began as 15,000 Cherokees were forced from their homes in Georgia; as many as one-quarter died during the march to Indian Teritory

The *Great Western* and *Sirius* became the first steamships to cross the Atlantic entirely using steam; they crossed in half the time (15 days) sailing ships normally took

Edward Hoyle published *Rules for the Playing of Fashionable Games;* "According to Hoyle . . ." later became a popular phrase

>
>
> *In Missouri, when mob forces oppressed the Saints, we were encamped in Adam-ondi-Ahman, mostly around campfires without tents. One night the snow fell four or five inches. The Prophet, seeing our forlorn condition, called on us to form into two parties—Lyman Wight at the head of one line and he (Joseph) heading the other line—to have a sham battle. The weapons were snowballs. We set to with a will full of glee and fun.*
>
> —Recollection of Edward Stevenson.

Additionally, while the Lord had cautioned them to be careful in what they said, some Mormons were not always wise in their comments. Particularly galling to Missourians was the Mormons' claim of a true religion, their belief that God had given the land to them, and their references to unbelievers as sinners.

Because Mormons were largely from the northern states, they were viewed with suspicion by their largely southern neighbor. Eventually accused of tampering with slavery, a strong issue in this battleground slave state, the Mormons were driven from their homes by enraged mobs in July 1833. Upon learning what had happened, Joseph wrote to the Missouri Saints, "We know not what we shall be called to pass through before Zion is delivered and established; therefore, we have great need to live near to God, and always be in strict obedience to all His commandments, that we may have a conscience void of offense toward God and man. . . . I have always expected that Zion would suffer some affliction, from what I could learn from the commandments which have been given. But I would remind you of a certain clause in one which says, that after much tribulation cometh the blessing." He subsequently led Zion's Camp from Kirtland to Missouri in an unsuccessful effort to restore the embattled Saints to their homes in Jackson County.

In 1835, Missouri officials created Caldwell County as a refuge for the Latter-day Saints. Removed from the state's population center situated largely along the Missouri River, their western frontier location was reflected in the name of their settlement, "Far West."

Upon reaching Far West in early 1838, Joseph learned that he had not left his problems behind him. Several former stalwarts, including Oliver Cowdery and David Whitmer, were soon excommunicated, and a former friend, William W. Phelps, later sided with the Missouri antagonists.

Later that year, the faithful followed Joseph from Kirtland to Far West in a wagon train reportedly one mile long. Joseph's uncle John Smith lamented, "We are like the ancients wandering from place to place in the wilderness." The new arrivals expanded the Latter-day Saint population in Caldwell County to nearly five thousand.

As Mormon numbers increased during the hot summer of 1838, relations between Latter-day Saints and their neighbors deteriorated. Joseph tried his best

1839

The Latter-day Saints were forced to leave Missouri in the dead of winter; they found refuge at Quincy, Illinois; Joseph Smith was eventually allowed to escape from Liberty Jail; he selected Commerce, Illinois, as a new gathering place for the Saints; healed a large number of sick during a "Day of God's Power"; appointed members of the Quorum of the Twelve to missions to England; and traveled to Washington, D.C., to lay grievances before U.S. president Martin Van Buren

Louis-Jacques-Mande Daguerre's process for making "daguerreotypes," the first successful form of photography, was disclosed; Samuel F. B. Morse took the first daguerreotype in the U.S. shortly after the process was announced

Charles Goodyear accidentally discovered the "vulcanization" process, allowing for the commercial use of rubber

The U.S. Navy seized the Spanish vessel *Amistead*, provoking international controversy; John Quincy Adams secured the mutinous slaves' freedom in 1841

U.S. Congress outlawed duels within the District of Columbia

VOX POPULI VOX DEI

America in the nineteenth century was a violent society. From the halls of Congress to the expanding American frontier, the sound of violence rang out across the land. Mobs often ruled, and differences were regularly settled with pistols at twenty paces.

After mobs drove the Latter-day Saints from their Jackson County homes, the displaced refugees turned to Missouri Governor Dunklin for help. His response reflected the prevailing attitude in America during the first half of the nineteenth century that might made right:

The time was when the people (except those in Jackson county) were divided, and the major part in your favor; that does not now seem to be the case. Why is this so? Does your conduct merit such censures as exist against you? It is not necessary for me to give my opinion. Your neighbors accuse your people of holding illicit communication with the Indians, and of being opposed to slavery. . . . Whether true or false, the consequences will be the same (if your opponents are not merely gasconading [boasting]), unless you can, by your conduct and arguments convince them of your innocence. If you cannot do this, all I can say to you is that in this Republic the *vox populi* is the *vox dei* [The voice of the people is the voice of God].

The voice of the people frequently proclaimed that physical force and resorts to violence were acceptable ways of settling differences, dealing with those who were disliked or dissimilar, and obtaining desired ends. Those who made threats of violence, destroyed property, carried out physical assaults such as tarring and feathering, and even murdered could find ready approval if their victims were out of favor. After the speaker of the Arkansas House of Representatives killed a fellow House member during an 1838 debate, a jury declared him "guilty of excusable homicide and not guilty in any manner or form as charged in the indictment." In reporting a shocking knife attack on an abolitionist delivering an antislavery speech, the local newspaper editor decried only the fact that the victim lived.

By the mid-1830s, vigilante justice had acquired a new name, "lynching," named after Virginia justice of the peace John Lynch, who actively promoted extra-legal acts. The prevailing attitude in Young America prompted Joseph Smith to proclaim that the United States Constitution "has but this one fault. Under its provision, a man or a people who are able to protect themselves can get along well enough; but those who have the misfortune to be weak or unpopular are left to the merciless rage of popular fury."

Joseph Smith spoke with the voice of experience. He and his followers were no strangers to mob action, experiencing persecution wherever they went. Joseph was regularly hounded in New York and Pennsylvania as he tried to translate the Book of Mormon and lay the foundation for the restored gospel. After moving to Ohio, both he and Sidney Rigdon were pulled from their beds in the middle of the night and tarred and feathered. The following year, two other Church leaders in Missouri suffered the same indignity before the Saints were driven from their homes in Jackson County. When Missouri mobs again formed in 1838 to drive the Latter-day Saints from the state, some Mormons fought back by organizing their own vigilante justice committee, popularly known as the Danites. Having endured mob threats in Ohio and Missouri, eventually Joseph and Hyrum Smith would die at the hands of an Illinois mob. Shortly afterward, the Latter-day Saints were once again forced from their homes, this time to seek refuge in the West. The Mormon experience was only a microcosm of the contentious nature of American society during the first half of the nineteenth century.

Although outlawed, dueling remained a national pastime in Young America. The most famous duel took place in 1804, when Vice President Aaron Burr fatally wounded former Secretary of the Treasury Alexander Hamilton at Weehawken, New Jersey. Even though an arrest warrant was issued for him, Burr returned to Washington, D.C., and completed his term as vice president. Andrew Jackson reportedly participated in dozens of duels before becoming president. Even mild-mannered Abraham Lincoln was challenged to a duel in 1842 but successfully averted it by using his wits.

Few places were as contentious as Congress. In addition to traditional party differences, the United States Capitol was one place where those on opposite sides of the increasingly bitter sectional divide regularly faced each other. Debates were known to end in duels. Wars of words between elected officials escalated into physical attacks. Bad feelings over the outcome of the 1824 presidential election propelled Speaker of the House Henry Clay and U.S. Senator John Randolph of Virginia into a duel in 1826. A running feud between two United States senators resulted in one leveling a cocked revolver at the other on the Senate floor. Frequent altercations prompted Vice President Martin Van Buren to wear a pair of pistols when presiding over the Senate during the early 1830s.

Slavery, by its very nature, depended upon force and coercion to survive. Whipping and beating of slaves were common. This frequently unmerciful treatment contributed to several slave uprisings, such as the brutal 1831 slave rebellion in Virginia led by Nat Turner in which nearly seventy whites were killed and upwards of a hundred slaves were summarily executed in response.

Corporal punishment was also practiced in school and on the high seas. The "cane" was viewed as acceptable for controlling unruly children and sometimes as proper punishment for students who failed to learn. One man who believed that beatings aided learning was Charles Anthon, the man to whom Martin Harris took the characters Joseph Smith copied from the gold plates to translate. One of Anthon's former students, George Templeton Strong, attended the funeral of his old teacher. As Strong gazed upon his deceased mentor, he momentarily thought he heard the corpse ask him to recite a Latin phrase, thus once again subjecting him to the cane. Misbehavior by sailors was usually met by lashes across the back from a "cat-o-nine-tails."

While the "Wild West" has been a favorite subject of Hollywood, the early nineteenth-century American frontier was in many ways more wild and turbulent than the post–Civil War creations of filmmakers. Life on the frontier could be both frightening and dangerous, especially when competing cultures clashed over issues such as land and resources. The fact is that brute strength was needed to expand America's frontiers. These conditions frequently led to a "survival of the fittest" mentality that carried over to other aspects of life. Even recreation had a violent side. Many men on the frontier had only one eye, having lost the other in wrestling matches fought by combatants with long thumbnails grown for the express purpose of blinding their opponents.

Violence was also part of urban life. Food and election riots occurred in cities such as New York. Beginning in the 1830s, anti-Catholic mobs burned monasteries and churches. Conflicts between native-born American Protestants and Catholic immigrants at Philadelphia in May and July 1844 left twenty dead.

A long history of violent clashes characterized the relationship between Anglo-Americans and Native Americans as settlers spread across the continent. Whites frequently took what they wanted at the point of a gun, which in turn caused Native Americans to fight back. As the population of the nation grew, many whites increasingly believed that all Indians should live west of the Mississippi. Although some Americans believed that Native Americans could preserve their cultures in the wide-open West, most people agreed with Henry Clay that Indians were "essentially inferior to the Anglo-Saxon race . . . and their disappearance from the human family will be no great loss to the world."

In 1830, Congress passed the Indian Removal Act, authorizing the forced removal of Indian tribes in the eastern United States to newly created Indian territory, largely located in what are now the states of Oklahoma, Kansas, and Iowa. During the summer of 1832, the Black Hawk War rocked Illinois and Wisconsin as the local tribes resisted eviction. Among those marshaled against these Native Americans were Lieutenant Jefferson Davis, a United States Army regular, and Abraham Lincoln, a local militia captain. Thirty years later, these two individuals would prominently figure in an even bloodier conflict, the Civil War.

Florida's Seminole Indians retreated into the Everglades rather than submit to relocation. From there they waged a bitter guerilla war from 1835 to 1842. More than fifteen hundred United States soldiers were killed trying to remove the tribe. (By comparison, fewer than three hundred soldiers of Custer's Seventh Cavalry died at the Little Bighorn in 1876. During this prolonged conflict, U.S. soldiers treacherously seized and imprisoned Osceola, leader of the tribe, after he agreed to a peace conference.

After the Supreme Court ruled that the federal government could not force the Cherokee Nation from its land, President Jackson tersely responded, "John Marshall has made his decision, now let him enforce it!" He couldn't, and in the fall of 1838 more than fifteen thousand Cherokees were forcibly removed from their ancestral homelands in southwestern United States to the "Indian Territory" of present-day Oklahoma. Freezing weather and inadequate food supplies led to great suffering as escorting troops refused to slow the march so the ill could recover. Some four thousand Cherokees died during the 116-day journey known as the "Trail of Tears."

At the same time the Cherokees were being driven west during the fall and winter of 1838–1839, to the north in Missouri, Mormons were being forced from their homes eastward toward Illinois.

THE SALE.

SOLD!

Stop the Runaway!!! $25 Reward. Ran away from the Eagle Tave[r]
a Negro fellow named Nat. He is no doubt attempting to follow his
wife, who was lately sold to a speculator named Redmond. The abov[e]
reward will be paid by Mrs. Lucy M. Downman, of Sussex County, V[a.]

—Notice in the Richmond (VA.) *Enquirer*, 20 February 1838.

Moses Grandy also experienced the devastation of having his wife
sold to a new master. Later he vividly recalled his reaction upon seein[g]
her pass by in company with other slaves who had just been sold:

> Mr. Rogerson was with them on his horse, armed with pistols.
> I said to him, "Have you bought my wife?" He said he had; when I
> asked him what she had done, he said she had done nothing, but
> that her master wanted more money. He drew a pistol out and said
> that if I went near the wagon on which she was, he would shoot
> me. I asked for leave to shake hands with her, but he refused, but
> said I might stand a distance and talk with her. My heart was so full
> that I could say very little. . . . I have never seen or heard from her
> from that day to this. I loved her as I love my life.

AM I NOT A WOMAN AND A SISTER?

Pity the negro, lady! Hers is not,
Like thine, a blessed and most happy lot.

So began Elizabeth Margaret Chandler's anti-slavery
poem, "The Kneeling Slave." As was the case with her
other abolitionist writings, she directed her comments to
a largely female audience who she believed as wives, sisters, and mothers would "give the first bent to the minds
of those, who at some future day are to be the country's
counselors." After recounting the "servile bondage" that
characterized slavery, Chandler asked:

She is thy sister, woman! Shall her cry,
Uncared for, and unheeded, pass thee by?

The Kneeling Slave: "Am I not a woman and a sister?" she pleads

RAFFLE

Mr. Joseph Jennings respectfully informs his friends and the public that, at the request of many acquaintances, he has been induced to purchase from Mr. Osborne, of Missouri, the celebrated

DARK BAY HORSE, "STAR,"

Aged five years, square trotter and warranted sound; with a new light Trotting Buggy and Harness; also, the dark, stout

MULATTO GIRL, "SARAH,"

Aged about twenty years, general house servant, valued at *nine hundred dollars*, and guaranteed, and

Will be Raffled for

At 4 o'clock P. M., February first, at the selection hotel of the subscribers. The above is as represented, and those persons who may wish to engage in the usual practice of raffling, will, I assure them, be perfectly satisfied with their destiny in this affair.

The whole is valued at its just worth, fifteen hundred dollars; fifteen hundred

CHANCES AT ONE DOLLAR EACH.

The Raffle will be conducted by gentlemen selected by the interested subscribers present. Five nights will be allowed to complete the Raffle. BOTH OF THE ABOVE DESCRIBED CAN BE SEEN AT MY STORE, No. 78 Common St., second door from Camp, at from 9 o'clock A. M. to 2 P. M.

Highest throw to take the first choice; the lowest throw the remaining prize, and the fortunate winners will pay twenty dollars each for the refreshments furnished on the occasion.

N. B. No chances recognized unless paid for previous to the commencement.

JOSEPH JENNINGS.

The winner of this raffle had the choice of either a horse or a "mulatto" slave girl; the runner-up received "the remaining prize"

READY TO DIE FOR A PRINCIPLE AND STARVE FOR AN IDEA

It is *my* mission to help in the breaking down of classes, and to make *all* men feel as if they were brethren of the same family, sharing the same rights, the same capabilities, and the same responsibilities. While my hand can hold a pen, I will use it to this end; and while my brain can earn a dollar, I will devote it to this end.

Thus wrote Lydia Maria Francis Child, one of nineteenth-century America's most prolific and influential writers and activists. Totaling nearly fifty books and pamphlets, her work, although little known today, is remarkable for its intellect, originality, and diversity.

Lydia Maria Child

Her works range from historical novels to short stories and poetry, from advice and self-help books to histories of women and world religions, from appeals on behalf of Native Americans to condemnations of slavery. Much of her work was inspired by a strong sense of justice, even though her beliefs cost her an even more promising literary career.

Maria—she disliked the name Lydia—was born in 1802, the youngest child of a Medford, Massachusetts, baker who created the Medford cracker, a staple of sailor diets. Following her mother's death, her father became "alarmed at her increasing fondness for books" and sent her to live with an older sister where she could be schooled in the domestic arts befitting a woman.

In 1824, she published her first novel, *Hobomak: A Tale of Early Time,* which gave an unusually sympathetic portrait to its title character, an American Indian, who was portrayed as heroic and noble rather than as a savage. The following year she published her second novel, *The Rebels, or Boston before the Revolution.* The words she put into the mouth of her characters were so stirring and sounded so authentic that one oration she had real-life patriot James Otis deliver was included in many nineteenth-century schoolbooks as a standard memorization piece.

She helped inaugurate American juvenile literature in 1826 with the publication of the *Juvenile Miscellany,* the nation's first children's magazine. A regular theme in the *Miscellany* was the mistreatment of Native Americans by European settlers.

In 1828, she married idealistic but imprudent lawyer and newspaper editor David Child. He shared her crusader's instinct—they used his paper, the *Massachusetts Journal,* to denounce Georgia's attempt to remove the Cherokee Indians from their lands—but his enthusiasm for good causes led him into financial difficulties. Having lost two libel suits, he went into debt to keep his paper going. His financial problems became hers.

To help meet their monetary crisis, she published what would become the first of three best-selling advice manuals. Borrowing an idea from England, in 1829 she published *The Frugal Housewife,* which provided ingenious ideas for making do with little means. Previous domestic-advice manuals in America had been aimed at the upper-middle class, but her audience was the many who could not afford servants.

Drawing in part from her own experiences, this volume was "dedicated to those who are not ashamed of economy." It became an instant success.

In 1831 her life changed upon reading William Lloyd Garrison's abolitionist newspaper *The Liberator.* Garrison "got hold of the strings of my conscience, and pulled me into Reforms," she later wrote. "Old dreams vanished, old associates departed, and all things became new." She joined forces in raising her voice against slavery in 1833 by publishing the groundbreaking *An Appeal in Favor of That Class of Americans Called Africans.* It placed slavery in an international historical context, denounced all forms of racial discrimination, and refuted theories of African inferiority. She pointed out contradictions between slavery and Christian teachings and described the moral and physical degradation it brought upon slave and owners alike. She did not exempt the North from its share of responsibility for the system. "I am fully aware of the unpopularity of the task I have undertaken, but though I expect ridicule and censure, it is not in my nature to fear them," she wrote in the introduction.

This work attracted new abolitionists and provided a serious, informed look at slavery, but indeed the general public was not ready to accept her views. As a result of her antislavery stand, sales of her books plummeted. The following year she was forced to fold the *Juvenile Miscellany.* A new advice book, *The Family Nurse,* published in 1837, sold only a small fraction of her previous works.

Nevertheless, she went on to write more than a dozen books and many articles and short stories for the abolitionist cause, including *The Evils of Slavery, and the Cure of Slavery. The First Provided by the Opinions of Southerners Themselves, the Last Shown by Historical Evidence* (1839).

During this time she also turned her attention to women's rights. Between 1832 and 1835, she wrote a five-volume *Ladies Family Library.* Largely containing short biographies exemplifying feminine virtues, the *Library* also included a *History and Condition of Women, in Various Ages and Nations* (1835), which greatly influenced such future women's rights advocates as Sarah Grimke, Susan B. Anthony, and Elizabeth Cady Stanton.

From 1841 to 1843 she served as editor of the *National Anti-Slavery Standard.* She resigned her position, however, when disagreements over how best to advance the abolitionist cause split the movement. She also cut her ties to organized antislavery moments.

In 1843, she published some of her columns from the *National Anti-Slavery Standard* focusing on the plight of New York City's poor as *Letters from New York.* The following year, 1844, she published two volumes of poetry for children.

An almost lifelong search for spiritual fulfillment led her to become a student of world religions. In 1855, she published *Progress of Religious Ideas, through Successive Ages,* a three-volume work designed to combat bigotry and dogmatism by highlighting the commonalities between Christianity and other faiths.

The death of John Brown in 1859 renewed her "youth and strength" in the abolitionist movement. "Men, however great they may be, are of small consequence in comparison with principles," she wrote at the time, praising his heroism while condemning his method. She again took up her abolitionist pen.

Following the Civil War she published the *Freeman's Book,* a reading primer for former slaves, and turned her attention to the plight of Native Americans in *An Appeal for the Indians.* She also returned to the domestic advice genre with *Looking toward Sunset,* a positive portrayal of old age.

At her 1880 funeral, Wendell Phillips proclaimed that Maria "was ready to die for a principle and starve for an idea. We felt that neither fame, nor gain, nor danger, nor calumny had any weight with her."

Myself and fellow prisoners were taken to the town, into the public square, and before our departure we, after much entreaty, were suffered to see our families, being attended all the while by a strong guard. I found my wife and children in tears, who feared we had been shot by those who had sworn to take our lives, and that they would see me no more. When I entered my house, they clung to my garments, their eyes streaming with tears, while mingled emotions of joy and sorrow were manifested in their countenances. I requested to have a private interview with them a few minutes, but this privilege was denied me by the guard. I was then obliged to take my departure. Who can realize the feelings which I experienced at that time, to be thus torn from my companion, and leave her surrounded with monsters in the shape of men, and my children, too, not knowing how their wants would be supplied; while I was to be taken far from them in order that my enemies might destroy me when they thought proper to do so. My partner wept, my children clung to me, until they were thrust from me by the swords of the guards. I felt overwhelmed while I witnessed the scene, and could only recommend them to the care of that God whose kindness had followed me to the present time, and who alone could protect them, and deliver me from the hands of my enemies, and restore me to my family.

—Joseph Smith's account of events following his arrest at Far West, Missouri.

to calm fears and even arranged for a "covenant of peace" between the Mormons and non-Mormons. But the goodwill was short lived. Exaggerated stories of Mormon aggression circulated throughout Missouri, prompting the *Jefferson Republic* to write, "Our ploughshares have been turned into swords." In spite of the growing excitement among the Missourians, Joseph proclaimed, "We do not fear them, for the Lord God, the Eternal Father is our God and Jesus . . . is our strength and confidence."

The situation worsened as Joseph's followers ignored his counsel. Although Joseph proclaimed that the Saints would "not act on the offensive, but always on the defensive," once again some of his followers ignored his counsel. Following the Battle of Crooked River, which claimed lives on both sides, a mob attacked the Mormon settlement at Haun's Mill, whose residents had ignored Joseph's counsel to gather to Far West.

By the end of October, Far West was under siege. "We had now, no hopes whatever, of successfully resisting the mob, who kept constantly increasing,"

Joseph recalled. "Our provisions were entirely exhausted and we being wearied out, by continually standing on guard, and watching the movements of our enemies; who, during the time I was there, fired at us a great many times." During this time, Governor Lilburn Boggs issued his infamous extermination order, proclaiming the Mormons "enemies" who "must be exterminated or driven from the state."

As the situation deteriorated, Joseph agreed to another peace conference. Instead of a discussion, however, Joseph found it was a trick, and he and other Mormon leaders, including his brother Hyrum, were taken prisoner and ordered to be shot the following day, 1 November, on the Far West public square. General Alexander Doniphan, however, refused to carry out the order, telling his superiors, "It is cold-blooded murder. If you execute these men, I will hold you responsible before an earthly tribunal, so help me God." Joseph's life was spared. He and the other prisoners were taken briefly to the jail at Richmond and then at Liberty.

"Massacre of Mormons at Haun's Mill," 30 October 1838

"He was a very remarkable man. I carried him to my house, a prisoner in chains, and in less than two hours my wife loved him better than she did me."

—Recollection of a Missouri militiaman who had charge of Joseph Smith following his arrest.

ADVICE FOR MOTHERS

In her 1831 *Mother's Book,* Lydia Maria Child gave advice on raising children that still rings true today:

The period from twelve to sixteen years of age is extremely critical in the formation of character, particularly with regard to daughters. The imagination is then all alive, and the affections are in full vigor, while the judgment is unstrengthened by observation, and enthusiasm has never learned moderation of experience. During this important period, a mother cannot be too watchful. As much as possible, she should keep a daughter under her own eye; and above all things she should encourage entire confidence towards herself. This can be done by a ready sympathy with youthful feelings, and by avoiding all unnecessary restraint and harshness. I believe it is extremely natural to choose a mother in preference to all other friends and confidants; but if a daughter, by harshness, indifference, or an unwillingness to make allowance for youthful feelings, is driven from the holy resting place, which nature has provided for her security, the greatest danger is to be apprehended. Nevertheless, I would not have mothers too indulgent, for fear of weaning the affections of children. This is not the way to gain the perfect love of young people; a judicious parent is always better beloved, and more respected, than a foolishly indulgent one. The real secret is, for a mother never to sanction the slightest error, or imprudence, but at the same time to keep her heart warm and fresh, ready to sympathize with all the innocent gayety and enthusiasm of youth. Salutary restraint, but not unnecessary restraint, is desirable.

It is a great mistake to think that education is finished when young people leave school. Education is never finished. Half the character is formed after we cease to learn lessons from books; and at that active and eager age it is formed with a rapidity and strength absolutely startling to think of. Do you ask what forms it? I answer the every-day conversation they hear, the habits they witness, and the people they are taught to respect. Sentiments thrown out in jest, or carelessness, and perhaps forgotten by the speaker, as soon as uttered, often sink deeply into the youthful mind, and have a powerful influence on future character. This is true in very early childhood; and it is peculiarly true of the period when youth is just ripening into manhood. Employ what teachers we may, the influences at home will have the mightiest influences in education. School-masters may cultivate the intellect; but the things said and done at home are busy agents in forming the affections; and the last have infinitely more important consequences than the first.

I WILL BE HEARD

William Lloyd Garrison (1805-1879)

Starting in the 1820s, a spirit of reform swept America that was only momentarily slowed by the Civil War. Nearly every aspect of society was affected as crusaders campaigned for basic rights and suffrage for women; changes in diet; prison, educational, and labor reforms; and the end of slavery, to name a few. "We are all a little wild here with numberless projects for social reform," Ralph Waldo Emerson noted in 1840. "But," he continued, "what is man born for but to be a Reformer, a Re-maker of what man has made . . . a restorer of truth and good?" Charles Dana was more succinct: "Our ultimate aim is nothing less than Heaven on Earth." American efforts to recreate the garden of Eden were sparked by the feelings of hope that accompanied the Second Great Awakening, the rational spirit of the Enlightenment imported

from Europe, and the homegrown idealism of American Romanticism.

Although most reformers desired to change only one aspect of society, abolitionists advocated what amounted to a complete overhaul of the United States, something that neither the North nor South was ready to face. As calls to end slavery increased, Southerners tenaciously clung to a way of life built largely on the backs of slaves. At the same time, Northerners, who increasingly condemned the South's "peculiar institution," did little to address the problem, largely because of racial prejudice. Thomas Jefferson proclaimed, "We have the wolf by the ears, and we can neither hold him, nor safely let him go." Abolitionists, however, did not see a dilemma. By the 1830s, they were proclaiming slavery to be a moral evil that needed to be immediately abolished.

Abolitionist sentiments were stirring during the Revolution, especially among Quakers. In 1775, Benjamin Franklin established the first abolitionist society in America. Many early abolitionists favored transporting freed blacks to Africa. The Republic of Liberia was established in 1820 as a home for former slaves; its capital, Monrovia, was named for President James Monroe. Inasmuch as the African slave trade had previously been outlawed, most slaves who gained their freedom were African-Americans, not Africans, and the plan generated little interest.

Abolitionism took on the energy of a crusade in the 1830s. Among its leaders was William Lloyd Garrison, who fired a shattering blast in 1831 when he started the militantly antislavery newspaper, *The Liberator,* which undertook an unrelenting thirty-year campaign against slavery. "I will be as harsh as truth, and as uncompromising as justice," Garrison wrote in the first edition. "I am in earnest—I will not equivocate—I will not excuse—I will not retreat a single inch—AND I WILL BE HEARD."

Unfortunately, strident tactics sometimes made abolitionists their own worst enemy. Garrison's critics, including some former friends, charged that he cruelly probed what was a festering wound on America's underbelly without offering an acceptable balm to ease the pain. His intemperate language and uncompromising stance antagonized both sections. While the Georgia senate offered a $5,000 reward for Garrison's apprehension and subsequent conviction in a Georgia court, the abolitionist narrowly escaped with his life from an 1835 Boston mob. Enraged by his preaching that all men were created equal, the mob, estimated at two thousand, paraded Garrison through Boston streets with a rope around his neck before police rescued him. For his own safety, the police lodged him that night in jail. On 4 July 1854, Garrison further incited nationwide feelings when he called for the "virtuous" North to secede from the "wicked" South and burned a copy of the Constitution, calling it a "covenant with death and an agreement with hell."

Other abolitionists were also the target of violence. Mobs disrupted antislavery meetings held in New York City and Utica, New York. Mobs also burned the Philadelphia Female Anti-Slavery Society meetinghouse and destroyed or burned a number of abolitionist presses. In 1837, abolitionist Elijah Lovejoy was murdered at Alton, Illinois, while attempting to protect his press from being destroyed for the fourth time.

During the 1830s, the American Anti-Slavery Society began flooding slave states with abolitionist literature. While proclaiming that he could not officially ban abolitionist publications from the mails, the United States postmaster general advised Southern postmasters to intercept such material. "We owe an obligation to the laws, but a higher one to the communities in which we live," he proclaimed. After abolitionist literature was publicly burned in Charleston, South Carolina, Governor George McDuffie told the South Carolina legislature that "the laws of every community should punish this species of interference by death without benefit of society." As tensions grew, President Andrew Jackson unsuccessfully proposed a law prohibiting the circulation of antislavery publications through the mail.

Northerners also found political avenues for addressing slavery concerns blocked by southerners. In 1831, former president John Quincy Adams, who was antislavery but not sympathetic to the abolitionist cause, presented to Congress fifteen petitions from Pennsylvania calling for the abolition of slavery in the District of Columbia. Congress was subsequently bombarded with other petitions demanding the abolishment of slavery. Southerners, outraged by this new attack, were able to institute what Adams called a "gag rule," which required all such petitions to be tabled without discussion. Instead of burying the issue, the "gag rule" served to sharpen the differences between the two sides and helped win new converts to abolitionism.

Many found that the best way to deal with slavery was to take the matter into their own hands. Among the most successful attempts was the Underground Railroad, which helped slaves escape northward to freedom. Many people risked their lives working on the Underground Railroad, including "station masters" who sheltered fugitive slaves on the journey and "conductors" who led them to freedom. Harriet Tubman, herself an escaped slave, made repeated trips to lead slaves to the freedom she enjoyed. Between 1830 and 1860, an estimated forty thousand former slaves passed through Ohio alone.

Many escaped slaves distinguished themselves as living monuments to the abolitionist cause. The most prominent was Frederick Douglass, who escaped from slavery in 1838 at the age of twenty-one.

I recieved your letter which I read over and over again, it was a sweet morsal to me. Oh God grant that I may have the privaliege of seeing once more my lovely Family, in the injoyment, of the sweets of liberty, and sotiaial life, to press them to my bosam and kissng their lovely cheeks would fill my heart with unspeakable great grattitude, tell the chilldren that I am alive and trust I shall come and see them before long, comfort their hearts all you can, and try to be comforted yourself. . . . tell little Joseph, he must be a good boy, Father loves him <with> a perfect llove, he is the Eldest must not hurt those that <are> smaller then him, but cumfor<t> them tell little Frederick, Father, loves him, with all his heart, he is a lovely boy. Julia is a lovely little girl, I love hir also She is a promising child, tell her Father wants her to remember him and be a good girl, tell all the rest that I think of them and pray for them all, Br Babbit is waiting to carry our letters for us the colonal <price> is wa inspecting them therefore my time is short <the> little baby Elexander is on my mind continuly Oh my affectionate Emma, I want you to remember that I am <a> true and faithful friend, to you and the chilldren, forever, my heart is intwined around you[r]s forever and ever, oh may God bless you all

—Letter from Joseph Smith to Emma Smith written from Richmond Jail, 12 November 1838.

Liberty Jail

For more than five months, Joseph would be forced to view the world "through the grates of this lonesome prison." During this time, the Latter-day Saints at Far West were driven from their homes, most in the dead of winter. In early February, Emma and her four young children—Julia, Joseph, Frederick, and Alexander—left Far West. Eventually these exiles would find a place of refuge among the citizens of Quincy, Illinois. Separated from all but a few of the Latter-day Saints, Joseph wrote near the end of his imprisonment, "I feel like Joseph in Egypt doth my friends yet live if they live do they remember me?"

Following an extended season of whirlwind activities, Liberty Jail became a bittersweet sanctuary for Joseph. Biblical prophets frequently went into the wilderness for periods of meditation and communion, and Joseph's imprisonment provided him uninterrupted time to ponder "the peaceable things of the kingdom" and communicate with God. His time before this had largely been spent traveling, meeting converts and curious visitors, teaching, translating, working on a temple, planning cities, dealing with financial shortages and other temporal affairs of the Saints, trying to defuse growing hostilities, and directing the daily affairs of a growing Church. Now far removed from the day-to-day operation of the Church, Joseph experienced a season of contemplation, reflection, and learning. As with the other

In one of those tedious nights we had lain as if in sleep till the hour of midnight had passed, and our ears and hearts had been pained, while we had listened for hours to the obscene jests, the horrid oaths, the dreadful blasphemies and filthy language of our guards, Colonel Price at their head, as they recounted to each other their deeds of rapine, murder, robbery, etc., which they had committed among the "Mormons" while at Far West and vicinity. They even boasted of defiling by force wives, daughters and virgins, and of shooting or dashing out the brains of men, women and children.

I had listened till I became so disgusted, shocked, horrified, and so filled with the spirit of indignant justice that I could scarcely refrain from rising upon my feet and rebuking the guards; but had said nothing to Joseph, or any one else, although I lay next to him and knew he was awake. On a sudden he arose to his feet, and spoke in a voice of thunder, or as the roaring lion, uttering, as near as I can recollect, the following words:

"SILENCE, ye fiends of the infernal pit. In the name of Jesus Christ I rebuke you, and command you to be still; I will not live another minute and bear such language. Cease such talk, or you or I die THIS INSTANT!"

He ceased to speak. He stood erect in terrible majesty. Chained, and without a weapon; calm, unruffled and dignified as an angel, he looked upon the quailing guards, whose weapons were lowered or dropped to the ground; whose knees smote together, and who, shrinking into a corner, or crouching at his feet, begged his pardon, and remained quiet till a change of guards.

I have seen the ministers of justice, clothed in magisterial robes, and criminals arraigned before them, while life was suspended on a breath, in the Courts of England; I have witnessed a Congress in solemn session to give laws to nations; I have tried to conceive of kings, of royal courts, of thrones and crowns; and of emperors assembled to decide the fate of kingdoms; but dignity and majesty have I seen but once, as it stood in chains, at midnight, in a dungeon in an obscure village of Missouri.

—Parley P. Pratt recounting an experience during his November 1838
incarceration with Joseph Smith in the jail at Richmond, Missouri.

> *I very well know your toils and simpathise with you if God will spare my life once more to have the privelege of takeing care of you I will ease your care and indeavour to cumfort your heart . . . write to me a long letter and tell me all you can . . . and what those little pratlers say that cling around you[r] neck do you tell them I am in prison that their lives might be saved?*
>
> —Joseph Smith, Liberty Jail, Missouri, to Emma Smith, Quincy, Illinois, 21 March 1839.

prisoners, his principal avenue of escape was in his own mind; his source of solace was communion with God. The thick walls that held him in could not keep revelation out. Joseph provided a glimpse of what he had learned in a lengthy letter he composed in late March 1839; portions of this inspired writing were later canonized as scripture.

Having obtained a clearer sense of his mission, of God's love and mercy, and of the mysteries of God from which he never wavered, he wrote in his confinement, "It seems to me that my heart will always be more tender after this than ever it was before. . . . I think I never could have felt as I now do if I had not suffered."

After more than five months in his "prison temple," Joseph and the other prisoners were granted a change of venue in early April 1839. Lax conditions during the transfer—perhaps purposely so—allowed the prisoners to flee. "We thought it a favorable opportunity to make our escape," Joseph said of their flight. After ten days traveling across Missouri, they experienced a joyous reunion with the Saints at Quincy. "I cried to the Lord what will you have me to do?" Joseph recounted of his new-found freedom. "The answer was build up a city and call my saints to this place!" he wrote shortly after establishing a new gathering place for the Saints in Illinois. ⌘

BY EXPERIENCE AND OBSERVATION

Using an oven in Young America was both a science and an art. Lydia Maria Child offered the following advice in her *American Frugal Housewife:*

Heating ovens must be regulated by experience and observation. There is a difference in wood in giving out heat; there is a great difference in the construction of ovens; and when an oven is extremely cold, either on account of the weather, or want of use, it must be heated more. Economical people heat ovens with pine wood, fagots, brush, and such light stuff. If you have none but hard wood, you must remember that it makes very hot coals, and therefore less of it will answer. A smart fire for an hour and a half is a general rule for common sized family ovens, provided brown bread and beans are to be baked. An hour is long enough to heat an oven for flour bread. Pies bear about as much heat as flour bread; pumpkin pies will bear more. If you are afraid your oven is too hot, throw in a little flour, and shut it up for a minute. If it scorches black immediately, the heat is too furious; if it merely browns, it is right. Some people wet an old broom two or three times, and turn it round near the top of the oven till it dries; this prevents pies and cake from scorching on the top.

Joseph rebuking the guards

O God, where art thou? And where is the pavilion that covereth thy hiding place?

How long shall thy hand be stayed, and thine eye, yea thy pure eye, behold from the eternal heavens the wrongs of thy people and of thy servants, and thine ear be penetrated with their cries?

Yea, O Lord, how long shall they suffer these wrongs and unlawful oppressions, before thine heart shall be softened toward them, and thy bowels be moved with compassion toward them? . . .

Let thine anger be kindled against our enemies; and, in the fury of thine heart, with thy sword avenge us of our wrongs.

Remember thy suffering saints, O our God; and thy servants will rejoice in thy name forever.

My son, peace be unto thy soul; thine adversity and thine afflictions shall be but a small moment;

And then, if thou endure it well, God shall exalt thee on high; thou shall triumph over all thy foes. . . .

The Son of Man hath descended below them all. Art thou greater than he?

Therefore, hold on thy way, and the priesthood shall remain with thee; for their bounds are set, they cannot pass. Thy days are known, and thy years shall not be numbered less; therefore, fear not what man can do, for God shall be with you forever and ever (D&C 121:1–3, 5–8; 122:8–9).

—Joseph Smith in a 25 March 1839 letter from Liberty Jail to the Saints in Illinois recounting the assurance he had received from the Lord.

AN AMERICAN SLAVE

I never saw my mother . . . more than four or five times in my life. . . . She made her journeys to see me in the night, travelling the whole distance on foot [twelve miles], after the performance of her day's work. She was a field hand, and a whipping was the penalty of not being in the field at sunrise. . . . I do not recollect of ever seeing my mother by the light of day. She was with me in the night. She would lie down with me, and get me to sleep, but long before I waked she was gone. . . . She died when I was about seven years old. . . . I was not allowed to be present during her illness, at her death, or burial.

This account, from *Narrative of the Life of Frederick Douglass, an American Slave,* introduced much of America to the lonely, harsh realities of southern slavery. It was written by ardent abolitionist and runaway slave Frederick Douglass.

Douglass, son of a black slave and an unknown white father, was born Frederick Augustus Washington Bailey in 1818 on Maryland's eastern shore. As a youth, his work included household servitude in Baltimore and field work in the Maryland countryside, where he witnessed and experienced whippings and forced hunger. In Baltimore, his master's wife taught him to read, which was against the law. Douglass later wrote that "going to live at Baltimore laid the foundation, and opened the gateway, to all my subsequent prosperity."

After seven straight years in the Baltimore household, Douglass was again hired out as a field worker, and brutal treatment left him "broken in body, soul, and spirit." By the beginning of 1836 he vowed to flee slavery by year's end. He was caught attempting to escape and was jailed. It would be nearly two more years until he tried to escape again.

On 3 September 1838, dressed in a sailor's uniform and carrying sailor's identification papers, Douglass boarded a train in Baltimore bound for Wilmington, Delaware; made his way to Philadelphia and then New York; and finally traveled to New Bedford, Massachusetts. His effort was aided by a free African-American woman named Anna Murray who sold her bed to buy the identification papers used in Douglass's escape. They were married in New York.

With a bride and a new name, Douglass found work on the New Bedford docks. He also set himself on a course of vigorous self-education, joined a black church, and attended abolitionist meetings. In 1841, he attended the Bristol Anti-Slavery Society's annual meeting, where he was newly inspired by the speaker, William Lloyd Garrison, who became Douglass's mentor. Of the meeting Douglass later wrote, "No face and form ever impressed me with such sentiments [against slavery] as did those of William Lloyd Garrison."

Several days later, Douglass was invited to speak at a meeting of the Massachusetts Anti-Slavery Society. The tall, handsome twenty-three-year-old was hesitant to speak, even though he "felt strongly moved to speak. . . . The truth was, I felt myself a slave, and the idea of speaking to white people weighed me down." The audience was spellbound as he described his experiences, one listener reporting that "flinty hearts were pierced, and cold ones melted by his eloquence." This speech launched his lifelong career fighting slavery and the oppression of former slaves.

After the 1845 publication of his *Narrative,* he was advised to go to the British Isles to avoid capture by his owner. There he lectured and toured for two years. To enable his safe return to America, two English women purchased his freedom from his owner—for $710.96.

At the beginning of the Civil War, Frederick Douglass was the most celebrated black in the country. His eloquent speeches against slavery, on the condition of African-Americans generally, and in favor of women's rights were renowned. During the Civil War, through his writings and his role in the formation of black Union regiments, he sought to transform a war of states' rights into a war to abolish slavery.

In 1872, he moved to Washington, D.C., where, for a time, he published the *National New Era,* which eventually lost its financial backing. He served variously as president of the Freedman's Savings Bank; U.S. marshal in the District of Columbia; recorder of deeds in Washington, D.C.; and diplomat to Haiti.

Although generally respected at the time of his death in 1895, he had also received a great deal of criticism for his advocacy of racial assimilation, his renunciation of black nationalism, and his support of women's rights. Throughout his life, he held fast to his belief in the equality of races, an individual's capacity for self-renewal, and the belief that moral virtue ultimately triumphs over institutional degradation.

Frederick Douglass

HARVARD DIVINITY SCHOOL ADDRESS

In 1838 the incomparable Ralph Waldo Emerson was invited to speak at the Harvard Divinity School to the "newborn bards of the Holy Ghost," as he described them. In his address, which was quite controversial, Emerson, a former Unitarian minister, criticized institutional religion and "Historical Christianity," proclaiming that established religions had strayed from Christ's teachings and that new revelation was needed to understand the mind of God. In addition to calling for changes to make religion more meaningful, he challenged his audience to recognize the good and beautiful in themselves and act accordingly: "Truth is beautiful within and without for evermore; virtue, I am thine; save me; use me." He also emphaized the importance of mankind's inherent good over their potential for evil: "Good is positive. Evil is merely privation, not absolute: it is like cold, which is the privation of heat." This concept was clearly contrary to the New England religious tradition, which tended to stress the overcoming of one's inherent evil rather than primarily maximizing the natural good within an individual.

His comments were not readily embraced by his audience and were generally ignored by the established ministers. Not finding what he sought in traditional religions, Emerson turned to Transcendentalism in his personal effort to find meaning in life.

His address to the Harvard Divinity School is a beautiful illustration of what Joseph Smith wrote the following year: "There are many yet on the earth among all sects, parties and denominations, who are only kept from the truth because they know not where to find it" (D&C 123:12).

Emerson began his address with a lyrical recounting of the beauty of the world, noting how "one is constrained to respect the perfection of the world." He

Ralph Waldo Emerson

then proceeded to contrast the feelings he experienced with what he found largely lacking in religion:

What am I? and What is? asks the human spirit with a curiosity new-kindled, but never to be quenched. . . .

A more secret, sweet, and overpowering beauty appears to man when his heart and mind open to the sentiment of virtue. Then he is instructed in what is above him. He learns that his being is without bound; that, to the good, to the perfect, he is born, low as he now lies in evil and weakness. . . .

The sentiment of virtue is a reverence and delight in the presence of certain divine laws. . . . As this sentiment is the essence of all religion, let me guide your eye to . . . some of those classes of facts in which this element is conspicuous.

The intuition of the moral sentiment is an insight of the perfection of the laws of the soul. These laws execute themselves. . . . Thus; in the soul of man there is a justice whose retributions are instant and entire. He who does a good deed, is instantly ennobled. He who does a mean deed, is by the action itself contracted. . . . Thus of their own volition, souls proceed into heaven, into hell.

These facts have always suggested to man the sublime creed, that the world is not the product of manifold power, but of one will, of one mind. . . . Whatever opposes that will, is everywhere balked and baffled, because things are made so, and not otherwise. . . .

The perception of this law of laws awakens in the mind a sentiment which we call the religious sentiment. . . . Wonderful is its power to charm and to command. It is a mountain air. It is the embalmer of the world. It is myrrh and storax, and chlorine and rosemary. It makes the sky and hills sublime, and the silent song of the stars is it. By it, is the universe made safe and habitable, not by science and power. . . .

This sentiment is divine and deifying. . . . It corrects the capital mistake of the infant man, who seeks to be great by following the great, and hopes to derive advantages *from another*. . . .

Meantime, whilst the doors of the temple stand open, night and day, before every man, and the oracles of this truth cease never, it is guarded by one stern condition; this, namely; it is an intuition. It cannot be received at second hand. Truly speaking, it is not instruction, but provocation, that I can receive from another soul. . . . Let this faith depart, and the very words it spake, and the things it made, become false and hurtful. Then falls the church, the state, art, letters, life. The doctrine of the divine nature being forgotten, a sickness infects and dwarfs the constitution. Once man was all; now he is an appendage, a nuisance. And because the indwelling Supreme Spirit cannot wholly be got rid of, the doctrine of it suffers this perversion, that the divine nature is attributed to one or two persons, and denied to all the rest. . . . The doctrine of inspiration is lost; the base doctrine of the majority of voices, usurps the place of the doctrine of the soul. Miracles, prophecy, poetry; the ideal life, the holy life, exist as ancient history merely; they are not in the belief, nor in the inspiration of society; but, when suggested, seem ridiculous. . . . And man becomes near-sighted, and can only attend to what addresses the senses.

Jesus Christ . . . saw with open eye the mystery of the soul. . . . But what a distortion did his doctrine and memory suffer in the same, in the next, and the following ages! . . .

In this point of view we become very sensible of the first defect of historical Christianity. Historical Christianity has fallen into the error that corrupts all attempts to communicate religion. As it appears to us, and as it has appeared for ages, it is not the doctrine of the soul, but an exaggeration of the personal, the positive, the ritual. . . . All who hear me, feel that the language that describes Christ to

Europe and America is not the style of friendship and enthusiasm to a good and noble heart, but is appropriated and formal. . . . You shall not . . . live after the infinite Law that is in you, . . . you must accept *our* interpretations; and take his portrait as the vulgar draw it.

The injustice of the vulgar tone of preaching is not less flagrant to Jesus, than to the souls which it profanes. The preachers do not see that they make his gospel not glad, and shear him of the locks of beauty and the attributes of heaven. . . .

The second defect of the traditionally and limited way of using the mind of Christ is a consequence of the first; this, namely, that the Moral Nature, that Law of laws, whose revelations introduce greatness,—yea, God himself—into the open soul, is not explored as the fountain of the established teaching in society. Men have come to speak of the revelation as somewhat long ago given and done, as if God were dead. The injury to faith throttles the preacher; and the goodliest of institutions becomes an uncertain and inarticulate voice.

The spirit only can teach. . . . Only he can give, who has, he only can create, who is. The man on whom the soul descends, through whom the soul speaks, alone can teach. Courage, piety, love, wisdom, can teach; and every man can open his door to these angels, and they shall bring him the gift of tongues. But the man who aims to speak as books enable, as synods use, as the fashion guides, and as interest commands, babbles. Let him hush. . .

It is my duty to say, that the need was never greater of new revelation than now. From the views I have already expressed, you will infer the sad conviction, which I share, I believe, with numbers, of the universal decay and now almost death of faith in society. . . .

It is time that this ill-suppressed murmur of all thoughtful men against the famine of our churches;—this moaning of the heart because it is bereaved of the consolation, the hope, the grandeur, that come alone out of the culture of the moral nature,—should be heard through the sleep of indolence and, over the din of routine. . . . In how many churches, by how many prophets, tell me, is man made sensible that he is an infinite Soul; that the earth and heavens are passing into his mind; that he is drinking forever the soul of God? Where now sounds the persuasion, that by its very melody imparadises my heart, and so affirms its own origin in heaven? . . . The test of the true faith, certainly, should be its power to charm and command the soul, as the laws of nature control the activity of the hands—so commanding that we find pleasure and honor in obeying. The faith should blend with the light of rising and of setting suns, with the flying cloud, the singing bird, and the breath of flowers. But now the priest's Sabbath has lost the splendor of nature; it is unlovely; we are glad when it is done.

Whenever the pulpit is usurped by a formalist, then is the worshiper defrauded and disconsolate. We shrink as soon as the prayers begin, which do not uplift, but smite and offend us. . . .

It is still true, that tradition characterizes the preaching of this country; that it comes out of the memory, and not out of the soul; that it aims at what is usual, and not at what is necessary and eternal; that thus historical Christianity destroys the power of preaching, by withdrawing it from the exploration of the moral nature of man; where the sublime is. . . . The pulpit is losing sight of this Law, loses it reason, and gropes after it knows not what. And for want of this culture, the soul of the community is sick and faithless. . . .

I have heard a devout person, who prized the Sabbath, say in bitterness of heart, "On Sundays, it seems wicked to go to church." And the motive, that holds the best there, is now only a hope and a waiting. . . .

My friends, in these two errors, I think, I find the causes of a decaying church and a wasting unbelief. . . .

And now, my brothers, you will ask, what in these desponding days can by done by us? The remedy is already declared in the ground of our complaint of the Church. . . . It is the office of a true teacher to show us that God is, not was; that He speaketh, not spake. The true Christianity,—a faith like Christ's in the infinitude of man,—is lost. None believeth in the soul of man, but only in some man or person old and departed. Ah me! . . . Once leave your own knowledge of God, your own sentiment, and take secondary knowledge, as St. Paul's, or George Fox's, or Swedenborg's, and you get wide from God with every year this secondary form lasts, and if, as now, for centuries . . . men can scarcely be convinced there is in them anything divine.

Let me admonish you, first of all, to go alone; to refuse the good models, even those which are sacred without mediator or veil. Friends enough you shall find who will hold up to your emulation Wesleys and Oberlins, Saints and Prophets. Thank God for these good men, but say, "I also am a man." Imitation cannot go above its model. The imitator dooms himself to hopeless mediocrity. . . .

Yourself a newborn bard of the Holy Ghost, cast behind you all conformity, and acquaint men at first hand with Deity. Look to it first and only, that fashion, custom, authority, pleasure, and money, are nothing to you,—are not bandages over your eyes, that you cannot see. . . .

Society's praise can be cheaply secured, and almost all men are content with those easy merits; but the instant effect of conversing with God will be to put them away. . . .

I look for the hour when the supreme Beauty which ravished the souls of those Eastern men, and chiefly of those Hebrews, and through their lips spoke oracles to all time, shall speak in the West also. The Hebrew and Greek Scriptures contain immortal sentences, that have been the bread of life to millions. But they have no epical integrity; are fragmentary; are not shown in their order to the intellect. I look for the new Teacher that shall follow so far those shining laws that he shall see them come full circle; shall see their rounding complete grace; shall see the world to be the mirror of the soul; shall see the identity of the law of gravitation with purity of heart; and shall show that the Ought, that Duty, is one thing with Science, with Beauty, and with Joy.

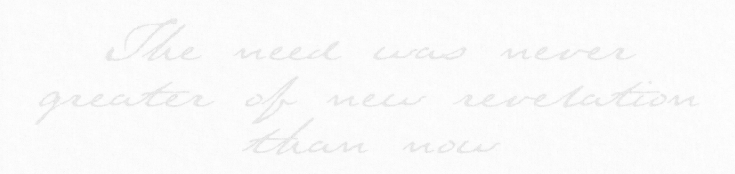

The need was never greater of new revelation than now

AN ERA OF
STATES' RIGHTS

In 1833, the United States Supreme Court unanimously ruled in *Baron vs. Baltimore* that the Constitutional protections guaranteed in the Bill of Rights did not apply to the states, only to the federal government. In speaking for the court, Chief Justice John Marshall proclaimed that state constitutions protected residents from the abusive actions of state officials. But what if the governor was part of the problem? Neither the ruling nor the prevailing views of the nature of government at this time provided a satisfactory answer, as the Mormons learned following their expulsion from Missouri.

Because their new nation was a work in progress with little experience and no previous models to draw upon, Americans during the early part of the nineteenth century were still trying to implement the federalist model they had created. Since the tenth amendment specifies that "powers not delegated to the United States by the Constitution . . . are reserved to the States," the prevailing view was that the federal government and the states operated in "separate spheres of dual sovereignty," their powers mutually exclusive. The federal government could get involved in state affairs—but only at the request of the governor.

Of the two spheres, the power reserved to the states was generally regarded as greater than that delegated to the United States. Reflecting Founding Fathers' concerns that freedom and virtue were incompatible with centralized power, the doctrine of "states' rights" formalized during this time proclaimed that states could unilaterally "nullify" federal acts. Given how most Americans viewed the relationship between the states and federal government, it is not surprising that Young America viewed the phrase "the

United States are" as the correct way to refer to the nation rather than "the United States is."

Although the Founding Fathers focused much of their attention on the potential dangers of big government, subsequent experience showed that abuse of power on the state and local governments could be equally dangerous. Joseph Smith reminded his followers in an 1839 letter from Missouri's Liberty Jail that any individual with power could create problems: "We have learned by sad experience that it is the nature and disposition of almost all men, as soon as they get a little authority, as they suppose, they will immediately begin to exercise unrighteous dominion" (D&C 121:39).

The abuses suffered by the Mormons in Missouri and Illinois are unimaginable today, but not completely out of the ordinary for the time. What the Founding Fathers feared might transpire on a national level happened on the state level, frequently in the name of "states' rights." With fewer checks and balances than their federal cousins, excesses occurred on the state level. "The states rights doctrine [is] what feeds mobs," Joseph rightly observed.

Joseph Smith's recital of President Martin Van Buren's reply to the Latter-day Saints' request for redress for their sufferings in Missouri reflected the reality that chief executives faced in the Era of States' Rights: "What can I do? I can do nothing for you! If I do anything, I shall come in contact with the whole state of Missouri." Given the prevailing view of the Constitution, for Van Buren and other presidents during the time to uphold their oath of office required them to allow the states their rights, no matter how egregious their actions.

Joseph Smith, however, was among the minority of Americans who viewed the Constitution as both allowing and demanding action from the president in cases such as the Mormons had experienced. His position regarding the relationship between the federal government and the states, while commonplace today, was ahead of the vast majority of Americans in the 1840s. So strong were his feelings in this regard that his 1844 presidential platform advocated the death penalty for federal officials who refused their duty to assist any oppressed group. Given Joseph's feelings, it is not surprising that his followers later changed President Van Buren's words to reflect a self-serving, callous person who wouldn't act in their behalf, not one who *couldn't* offer help: "Your cause is just, but I can do nothing for you. If I take up for you I shall lose the vote of Missouri."

In spite of Mormon efforts to spin President Van Buren's actions differently, the fact remains that the prevailing Constitutional interpretation prevented his involvement in the matter. When the Supreme Court revisited *Baron* in 1845 *(Permoli vs. New Orleans)*, it upheld its previous ruling: States remained free to operate under rules different from those applied to the federal government.

The position that Joseph and others advocated regarding presidential power would eventually be adopted, but not before events forced many in the nation to reevaluate their stance on the issue. Increasingly, the states' rights doctrine became nearly synonymous with the defense of slavery. By the 1830s, slavery was at the heart of the most notable clashes between the states and the federal government. As calls to abolish slavery increased, states' rights opponents became more aggressive. When South Carolina in the 1832 "Nullification Crisis" threatened to veto tariffs imposed by Congress, its stance was motivated in part by fears that enhanced federal power might next be turned against slavery. During much of the 1840s gag rules were in place in Congress that prohibited the discussion of the south's "peculiar institution." For many, it was no longer the federal government that needed to be feared, but the states.

Eventually, the relationship between the federal government and the states was resolved by the Civil War. The details, however, still had to be worked out.

Three years after the end of the Civil War, the Fourteenth Amendment directly addressed abuses at the state level: "No state shall make or enforce any law which shall . . . deprive any person of life, liberty, or property, without due process of law; nor deny to any person within its jurisdiction the equal protection of the laws." Nearly sixty years after that important development, the United States Supreme Court overturned *Baron* by ruling in 1925 (*Gitlow vs. New York*) that the restraints and guarantees of the Bill of Rights also applied to states.

Finally, more than one hundred years after Joseph Smith's death, his view of presidential power was affirmed in 1957 when President Dwight Eisenhower sent troops to segregate Little Rock, Arkansas, schools against the wishes of that state's governor.

TALES OF TWO CITIES

Founded more than a generation apart during America's westward expansion, Cincinnati, Ohio, and Nauvoo, Illinois, were two of the nation's frontier boom towns. They existed for different reasons. Cincinnati was primarily a commercial center, while Nauvoo was founded as a place of gathering. By the time Nauvoo was being settled in 1839, Cincinnati fully epitomized Alexander Hamilton's vision of America. Throughout its brief existence, Mormon Nauvoo largely exemplified Thomas Jefferson's view. Hamilton wanted the United States to become another Great Britain in terms of trade, cities, and manufacturing. Jefferson believed that farmers were the backbone of the nation. "Cultivators of the earth are the most valuable citizens," he proclaimed.

Alexis de Tocqueville, during his famous visit to America, wondered what circumstances gave birth and growth to cities.

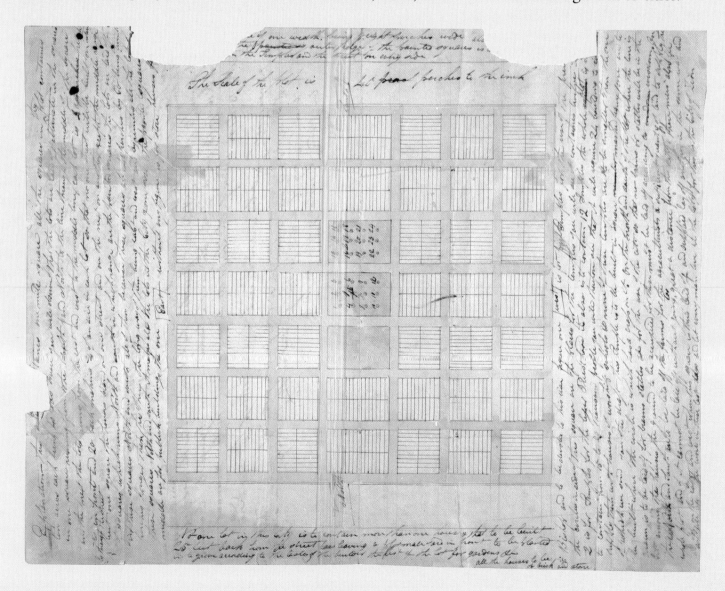

Plat for the City of Zion, 1833

ance, he concluded, especially e "accident" of geography, yed a major factor. Cincinnati urished because of a prime tion in an extraordinarily tile valley.

Nauvoo, on the other hand, se on land few wanted. The e was procured cheaply, an ractive feature for people ced to flee their previous mes. As with most frontier communities, survival was the top priority. In 1843, Orson Hyde observed that Nauvoo's residents were "devoted to opening new farms, building habitations, and to supplying themselves with food." Henry Lewis concluded in his 1845 *Valley of the Mississippi,* "There is little hope for worldly prosperity in Nauvoo. The city is neither a commercial mart in itself, nor does it supply the markets of others. It is to a certain extent quite isolated, and has absolutely no principle of aggregation—if we except that of accumulating population."

When Frances Trollope reached Cincinnati in 1828, she observed that "in a single quarter of a century Cincinnati had risen from an inconsiderable village, to an opulent city of 19 or 20,000 inhabitants." Three years later Gustave de Beaumont wrote, "I don't believe there exists anywhere on earth a town which has had a growth so prodigious. Thirty years ago the banks of the Ohio were a wilderness. Now there are 30,000 inhabitants in Cincinnati. During the last five years the population had doubled."

Although Nauvoo never reached the size of Cincinnati, it initially grew faster than "the Queen City of the West." When Heber C. Kimball left Nauvoo on a mission in 1839, "there were not more than thirty buildings." When he returned two years later, there were "twelve hundred, and hundreds of others in progress." By the time the Latter-day Saints were forced from Nauvoo in 1846, the population was estimated at fifteen thousand.

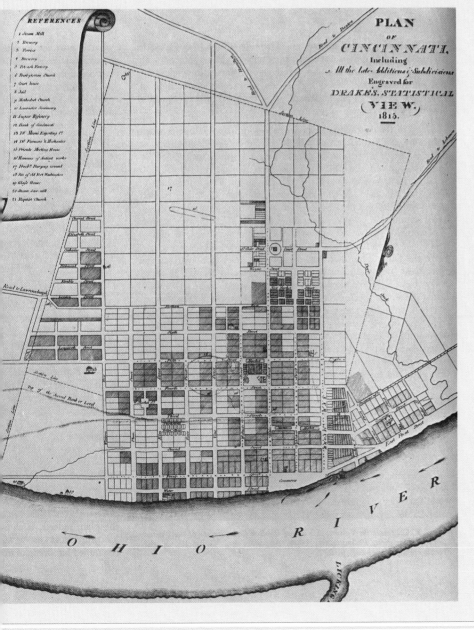

This 1815 plan of Cincinnati, Ohio, was ignored by later settlers

Tocqueville found Cincinnati to be "a city which seems to want to rise too quickly for people to have any system or plan about it. Great buildings, thatched cottages, streets encumbered with debris, houses under construction, no names on the streets, no numbers on the houses, no outward luxury, but the image of industry and labour obvious at every step."

Nauvoo, on the other hand, was praised for its order and beauty. In an era when cities tended to spring up, and city planning was infrequently practiced, Nauvoo stood out. While most cities grew haphazardly around a natural feature such as a harbor, or some previously established business such as a mill, Joseph Smith's efforts at city planning were quite unusual. Following a plan first outlined for the City of Zion in Jackson County, Missouri, in 1833, Joseph laid out Nauvoo in a regular grid pattern built around a temple. Streets crossed each other at right angles and were both wide and named. City blocks and building lots were of uniform size. All houses, even those for farmers, were to be built within the city boundaries, where all could enjoy the company of neighbors. Farm land was cultivated outside the city proper. Joseph declared that his plat for the City of Zion was given him by revelation.

An 1844 visitor to Nauvoo reported in the *Springfield* (Massachusetts) *Republican* that the city "has no rival for beauty and eligibility for the site of a city in any other town on the Mississippi river. I have seen no spot that resembles it near so much as the ground on which the city of Washington is built. . . . The flat alluvial part embraces perhaps one-third of the city, contains the principal part of the stores, and the most of the public-houses. This embraces Main-street, with a broad avenue, 1½ miles long, and several parallel streets, and others crossing them at right angles. The city then rises an easy grade to the level of the prairies, say 150 feet above the river. On this elevation the Temple is situate[d]." Although many of Nauvoo's buildings were small and of wood, a Methodist minister visiting from nearby Carthage stated, "They bore the marks of neatness which I have not seen equaled in this country."

Tocqueville observed that "the population of Ohio is made up of very dissimilar elements." Initial settlers from New England were later joined by emigrants from all regions of the United States and Europe. "All these diverse peoples find themselves amalgamated together, and their combination creates a moral being whose portrait it would be hard to draw," he wrote. Perhaps, Beaumont concluded, "the character" of America "is that of having none."

Although Nauvoo also drew settlers from the same diverse backgrounds, its visitors had less trouble drawing an integrated portrait. Part of the genius of Joseph's plan was that its design enhanced the cooperation and unity envisioned in the term *Zion*—the establishment of people who were "of one heart and one mind." As shown in Nauvoo, the "Plat of Zion" could easily accommodate a rapidly increasing population in an orderly way and in a short period of time.

Brigham Young employed Joseph's distinctive pattern of city planning in establishing settlements in the Great Basin. Time and again Mormon settlers in the last half of the nineteenth century laid out their own "City of Joseph," although they would call their communities by different names. During the twentieth century, Joseph's city plan readily adapted itself to enhanced urbanization. The wide roads easily handled large quantities of motorized traffic without expensive modification, and the large blocks readily allowed for downtown development.

"I HAVE BEEN AN INSTRUMENT IN HIS HANDS"

Joseph Smith was often asked to recount his story along with the history of The Church of Jesus Christ of Latter-day Saints. Portions of the best-known account, written in 1839 shortly after he was released from the jail at Liberty, Missouri, have been included in the Doctrine and Covenants as Joseph Smith—History. In 1842, he produced another history for Chicago newspaper editor John Wentworth, who had requested the same to be included in a history of New Hampshire being written by Wentworth's friend George Barstow. Although the account was never published by Barstow, it appeared in the 1 March 1842 *Times and Seasons* and concluded with a statement of beliefs that have come to be known as the Articles of Faith.

Among the least known of Joseph's accounts is one of his last. In September 1843, Joseph responded to a letter from I. Daniel Rupp requesting information about the Latter-day Saints. Rupp, who wanted to publish a volume containing the history and doctrines of the country's religions, had presented to each denomination the "opportunity of telling its own story . . . in its own way."

By early June 1844, Joseph had obtained a copy of Rupp's *An Original History of the Religious Denominations at Present Existing in the United States.*

The account that the Mormon prophet provided evidenced the optimism that characterized his life. For instance, his estimate of Church population was substantially less than the actual number for 1843, but it was an accurate reflection of Church membership at the time of John Taylor.

On 5 June 1844, Joseph wrote Rupp regarding his published volume. Assassins' bullets, however, ended the Prophet's life before Rupp likely received the following letter and its offer of further assistance:

I feel very thankful for so valuable a treasure. The design, the propriety, the wisdom of letting every sect tell its own story, and the elegant manner in which the work appears, have filled my breast with encomiums upon it, wishing you God speed. Although all is not gold that shines, any more than every religious creed is sanctioned with the so eternally sure word of prophecy, satisfying all doubt with "Thus said the Lord;" yet "by proving contraries," truth is made manifest, and a wise man can search out "old paths," wherein righteous men held communion with Jehovah, and were exalted through obedience. I shall be pleased to furnish further information at a proper time, and render you such further as the work and vast extension of our Church may demand for the benefit of truth, virtue and holiness.

LATTER DAY SAINTS

By Joseph Smith, Nauvoo, Illinois

The Church of Jesus Christ of Latter Day Saints, was founded upon direct revelation, as the true church of God has ever been, according to the scripture (Amos, iii, 7, and Acts i, 2.) And through the will and blessings of God, I have been an instrument in his hands, thus far, to move forward the cause of Zion. Therefore, in order to fulfil the solicitation of your letter of July last, I shall commence with my life.

I was born in the town of Sharon, Windsor county, Vermont, on the 23d of December, A.D. 1805. When ten years old, my parents removed to Palmyra, New York, where we resided about four years, and from thence we removed to the town of Manchester, a distance of six miles.

My father was a farmer, and taught me the art of husbandry. When about fourteen years of age, I began to reflect upon the importance of being prepared for a future state; and upon inquiring the place of salvation, I found that there was a great clash in religious sentiment; if I went to one society they referred me to one place, and another to another; each one pointing to his own particular creed as the "summum bonum" of perfection. Considering that all could not be right, and that God could not be the author of so much confusion, I determined to investigate the subject more fully, believing that if God had a church, it would not be split up into factions, and that if he taught one society to worship one way, and administer in one set of ordinances, he would not teach another principles which were diametrically opposed. Believing the word of

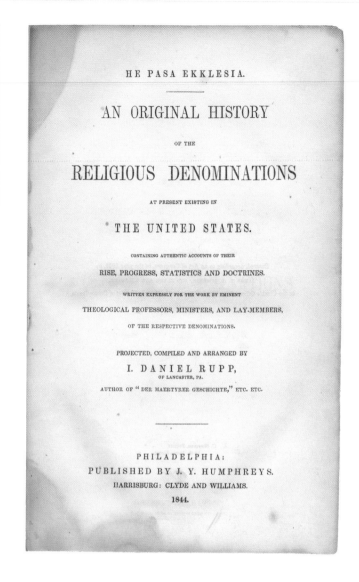

HE PASA EKKLESIA.

AN ORIGINAL HISTORY

OF THE

RELIGIOUS DENOMINATIONS

AT PRESENT EXISTING IN

THE UNITED STATES.

CONTAINING AUTHENTIC ACCOUNTS OF THEIR

RISE, PROGRESS, STATISTICS AND DOCTRINES.

WRITTEN EXPRESSLY FOR THE WORK BY EMINENT

THEOLOGICAL PROFESSORS, MINISTERS, AND LAY-MEMBERS,

OF THE RESPECTIVE DENOMINATIONS.

PROJECTED, COMPILED AND ARRANGED BY

I. DANIEL RUPP,

OF LANCASTER, PA.

AUTHOR OF " DER MAERTYRER GESCHICHTE," ETC. ETC.

PHILADELPHIA:
PUBLISHED BY J. Y. HUMPHREYS.
HARRISBURG: CLYDE AND WILLIAMS.
1844.

God, I had confidence in the declaration of James, "If any man lack wisdom let him ask of God, who giveth to all men liberally and upbraideth not, and it shall be given him."

I retired to a secret place in a grove, and began to call upon the Lord. While fervently engaged in supplication, my mind was taken away from the objects with which I was surrounded, and I was enrapt in a heavenly vision, and saw two glorious personages, who exactly resembled each other in features and likeness, surrounded with a brilliant light, which eclipsed the sun at noonday. They told me that all the religious denominations were believing in incorrect doctrines, and that none of them was acknowledged of God as his church and kingdom. And I was expressly commanded to "go not after them," at the same time receiving a promise that the fulness of the gospel should at some future time be made known unto me.

On the evening of the 21st September, A.D. 1823, while I was praying unto God and endeavouring to exercise faith in the precious promises of scripture, on a sudden a light like that of day, only of a far purer and more glorious appearance and brightness, burst into the room; indeed the first sight was as though the house was filled with consuming fire. The appearance produced a shock that affected the whole body. In a moment a personage stood before me surrounded with a glory yet greater than that with which I was already surrounded. This messenger proclaimed himself to be an angel of God, sent to bring the joyful tidings, that the covenant which God made with ancient Israel was at hand to be fulfilled; that the preparatory work for the second coming of the Messiah was speedily to commence; that the time was at hand for the gospel in all its fulness to be preached in power, unto all nations, that a people might be prepared for the millennial reign.

I was informed that I was chosen to be an instrument in the hands of God to bring about some of his purposes in this glorious dispensation.

I was informed also concerning the aboriginal inhabitants of this country, and shown who they were, and from whence they came;—a brief sketch of their origin, progress, civilization, laws, governments, of their righteousness and iniquity, and the blessings of God being finally withdrawn from them as a people, was made known unto me. I was also told where there was deposited some plates, on which was

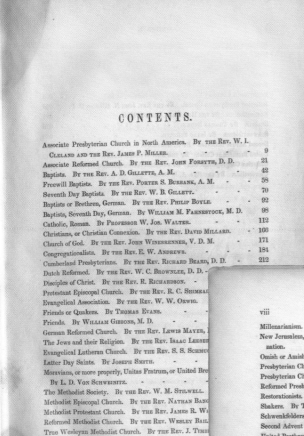

Table of contents, *An Original History of the Religious Denominations*

engraven an abridgment of the records of the ancient prophets that had existed on this continent. The angel appeared to me three times the same night and unfolded the same things. After having received many visits from the angels of God, unfolding the majesty and glory of the events that should transpire in the last days, on the morning of the 22d of September, A.D. 1827, the angel of the Lord delivered the records into my hands.

These records were engraven on plates which had the appearance of gold; each plate was six inches wide and eight inches long, and not quite so thick as common tin. They were filled with engravings in Egyptian characters, and bound together in a volume, as the leaves of a book, with three rings running through the whole. The volume was something near six inches in thickness, a part of which was sealed. The characters on the unsealed part were small and beautifully engraved. The whole book exhibited many marks of antiquity in its construction, and much skill in the art of engraving. With the records was found a curious instrument which the ancients called "Urim and Thummim," which consisted of two transparent stones set in the rim of a bow fastened to a breastplate.

Through the medium of the Urim and Thummim I translated the record, by the gift and power of God.

In this important and interesting book the history of an ancient America is unfolded, from its first settlement by a colony that came from the tower of Babel, at the confusion of languages, to the beginning of the fifth century of the Christian era.

We are informed by these records, that America, in ancient times, has been inhabited by two distinct races of people. The first were called Jaredites, and came directly from the tower of Babel. The second race came directly from the city of Jerusalem, about six hundred years before Christ. They were principally Israelites, of the descendants of Joseph. The Jaredites were destroyed, about the time that the Israelites came from Jerusalem, who succeeded them in the inheritance of the country. The principal nation of the second race fell in battle towards the close of the fourth century. The remnant are the Indians who now inhabit this country. This book also tells us that our Savior made his appearance upon this continent after his resurrection; that he planted the gospel here in all its fulness, and richness, and power, and blessing; that they had apostles, prophets, pastors, teachers, and evangelists; the same order, the same priesthood, the same ordinances, gifts, powers, and blessings, as was enjoyed on the eastern continent; that the people were cut off in consequence of their transgressions; that the last of their prophets who existed among them was commanded to write an abridgment of their prophecies, history, &c., and to hide it up in the earth, and that it should come forth and be united with the Bible, for the accomplishment of the purposes of God, in the last days. For a more particular account, I would refer to the Book of Mormon, which can be purchased at Nauvoo, or from any of our traveling elders.

As soon as the news of this discovery was made known, false reports, misrepresentation and slander flew, as on the wings of the wind, in every direction; my house was frequently beset by mobs, and evil designing persons; several times I was shot at, and very narrowly escaped, and every device was made use of to get the plates away from me; but the power and blessing of God attended me, and several began to believe my testimony.

On the 6th April, 1830, the "Church of Jesus Christ of Latter Day Saints," was first organized, in the town of Manchester, Ontario, Co., State of New York. Some few were called and ordained by the Spirit of revelation and prophecy, and began to preach as the Spirit gave them utterance, and though weak, yet were they strengthened by the power of God; and many were brought to repentance, were immersed in the water, and were filled with the Holy Ghost by the laying on of hands. They saw visions and prophesied, devils were cast out, and the sick healed by the laying on of hands. From that time the work rolled forth with astonishing rapidity, and churches were soon formed in the States of New York, Pennsylvania, Ohio, Indiana, Illinois, and Missouri; in the last named state a considerable settlement was formed in Jackson county; numbers joined the church and we were increasing rapidly; we made large purchases of land, our farms teemed with plenty, and peace and happiness were enjoyed in our domestic circle and throughout our neighbourhood; but as we could not associate with our neighbours,—who were, many of them, of the basest of men, and had fled from the face of civilized society to the frontier country, to escape the hand of justice—in their midnight revels, their sabbath-breaking, horse-racing, and gambling, they commenced at first to ridicule, then to persecute, and finally an organized mob assembled and burned our houses, tarred and feathered and whipped many of our brethren, and finally drove them from their habitations; these, houseless and homeless, contrary to law, justice, and humanity, had to wander on the bleak prairies till the children left the tracks of their blood on the prairie. This took place in the month of November, and they had no other covering but the canopy of heaven, in that inclement season of the year. This proceeding was winked at by the government; and although we had warrantee deeds for our land, and had violated no law, we could obtain no redress. There were many sick who were thus inhumanly driven from their houses, and had to endure all this abuse, and to seek homes where they could be found. The result was, that a great many of them being deprived of the comforts of life, and the necessary attendance, died; many children were left orphans; wives, widows; and husbands, widowers. Our farms were taken possession of by the mob, many thousands of cattle, sheep, horses, and hogs were taken, and our household goods, store goods, and printing press and types were broken, taken, or otherwise destroyed.

Many of our brethren removed to Clay county, where they continued until 1836 (three years); there was no violence offered, but there were threatenings of violence. But in the summer of 1836 these threatenings began to assume a more serious aspect; from threats, public meetings were called, resolutions were passed, vengeance and destruction were threatened, and affairs again assumed a fearful attitude; Jackson county was a sufficient precedent, and as the authorities in that county did not interfere, they boasted that they would not in this; which on application to the authorities we found to be too true; and, after much violence, privation, and loss of property, we were again driven from our home.

We next settled in Caldwell and Davies counties, where we made large and extensive settlements, thinking to free ourselves from the power of oppression by settling in new counties, with a very few inhabitants in them; but here we were not allowed to live in peace; and in 1838 were again attacked by mobs; an exterminating order was issued by Governor Boggs, and under the sanction of law, an organized banditti ravaged the country, robbing us of our cattle, sheep, horses, hogs, &c.; many of our people were murdered in cold blood, the chastity of our women was violated, and we were forced to sign away our property at the point of the sword; and after enduring every indignity that could be heaped upon us by an inhuman, ungodly band of marauders,—from twelve to fifteen thousand souls, men, women, and children, were driven from their own firesides, and from lands for which they had warrantee deeds, to wander houseless, friendless, and homeless, (in the depth of winter,) as exiles on the earth, or to seek an asylum in a more genial clime, and among a less barbarous people.

Many sickened and died in consequence of the cold and hardships they had to endure, many wives were left widows, and children orphans and destitute.

It would take more time than I am able to devote to your service, at present, to describe the injustice, the wrongs, the murders, the bloodshed, thefts, misery and wo that have been committed upon our people by the barbarous, inhuman, and lawless proceedings of the State of Missouri. And I would refer you, and the readers of your history who may be desirous of further information on this topic, to the evidence taken on my recent trial before the Municipal Court of Nauvoo, on Saturday, July 1st, 1843, on a writ of habeas corpus, which is published in pamphlet form by Messrs. Taylor & Woodruff, of this city.

After being thus inhumanly expelled by the government and people from Missouri, we found an asylum and friends in the State of Illinois. Here, in the fall of 1839, we commenced a city called Nauvoo, in Hancock county, which, in December 1840, received an act of incorporation from the Legislature of Illinois, and is endowed with as liberal powers as any city in the United States. Nauvoo, in every respect, connected with increase and prosperity, has exceeded the most sanguine expectations of thousands. It now contains near 1500 houses, and more than 15,000 inhabitants. The charter contains, amongst its important powers, privileges, or immunities, a grant for the "University of Nauvoo," with the same liberal powers of the city, where all the arts and sciences will grow with the growth, and strengthen the strength of this beloved city of the "saints of the last days." Another very commendatory provision of the charter is, that that portion of the citizens subject to military duty are organized into a body of independent military men, styled the "Nauvoo Legion," whose highest officer holds the rank, and is commissioned lieutenant-general. This legion, like other independent bodies of troops in this republican government, is at the disposal of the Governor of this State, and President of the United States. There is also an act of incorporation for an agricultural and manufacturing association, as well as the Nauvoo House Association.

The temple of God, now in the course of erection, being already raised one story, and which is 120 feet by 80 feet, of stone, with polished pilasters, of an entire new order of architecture, will be a splendid house for the worship of God, as well as an unique wonder for the world, it being built by the direct revelation of Jesus Christ for the salvation of the living and the dead.

Since the organization of this church its progress has been rapid, and its gain in numbers regular. Besides these United States, where nearly every place of notoriety has heard the glad tidings of the gospel of the Son of God, England, Ireland, and Scotland, have shared largely in the fulness of the everlasting gospel, and thousands have already gathered with their kindred saints, to this the corner-stone of Zion. Missionaries of this church have gone to the East Indies, to Australia, Germany, Constantinople, Egypt, Palestine, the Islands of the Pacific, and are now preparing to open the door in the extensive dominions of Russia.

There are no correct data by which the exact number of members composing this now extensive, and still extending, Church of Jesus Christ of Latter Day Saints can be known. Should it be supposed at 150,000, it might still be short of the truth.

Believing the Bible to say what it means and mean what it says; and guided by revelation according to the ancient order of the fathers to whom came what little light we enjoy; and circumscribed only by the eternal limits of truth: this church must continue the even tenor of her way, and "spread undivided, and operate unspent."

We believe in God the Eternal Father, and in his son Jesus Christ, and in the Holy Ghost.

We believe that men will be punished for their own sins and not for Adam's transgression.

We believe that through the atonement of Christ all men may be saved by obedience to the laws and ordinances of the gospel.

We believe that these ordinances are: 1st, Faith in the Lord Jesus Christ; 2d, Repentance; 3d, Baptism by immersion for the remission of sins; 4th, Laying on of hands for the gift of the Holy Ghost.

We believe that a man must be called of God by "prophecy, and by laying on of hands," by those who are in authority to preach the gospel and administer in the ordinances thereof.

We believe in the same organization that existed in the primitive church, viz. apostles, prophets, pastors, teachers, evangelists, &c.

We believe in the gift of tongues, prophecy, revelation, visions, healing, interpretation of tongues, &c.

We believe the Bible to be the word of God as far as it is translated correctly; we also believe the Book of Mormon to be the word of God.

We believe all that God has revealed, all that he does now reveal, and we believe that he will yet reveal many great and important things pertaining to the kingdom of God.

We believe in the literal gathering of Israel, and in the restoration of the Ten Tribes. That Zion will be built upon this continent. That Christ will reign personally upon the earth, and that the earth will be renewed and receive its paradisiacal glory.

We claim the privilege of worshipping Almighty God according to the dictates of our conscience, and allow all men the same privilege, let them worship how, where, or what they may.

We believe in being subject to kings, presidents, rulers, and magistrates; in obeying, honouring, and sustaining the law.

We believe in being honest, true, chaste, benevolent, virtuous, and in doing good to all men; indeed we may say that we follow the admonition of Paul; "we believe all things: we hope all things:" we have endured many things, and hope to be able to endure all things. If there is any thing virtuous, lovely, or of good report, or praiseworthy, we seek thereafter. ❧

H. Lewis

Plate 48. NAUVOO, ILLINOIS

H. Lewis

Plate 49. THE MORMON TEMPLE

"HE CHEERED OUR HEARTS"

❧

As the Saints made their way eastward to Illinois during the bitter winter of 1838–1839, they were not always able to avoid contact with hostile Missourians. Lucy Mack Smith related her son Samuel's harrowing escape from Missouri. Forced to leave his family, he joined with other brethren, and they "suffered very much with hunger on their route, as they were pursued by their enemies, and they considered it unsafe to be seen by the inhabitants of the country. Game being very scarce, they soon lacked for provisions and finally ran out altogether, yet they pursued their journey, until they became so faint that they were almost in despair." After praying and receiving the Lord's guidance, the group came upon an Indian woman who fed them and indicated that "more of their friends were in the woods far off. . . . After this the brethren traveled on and succeeded in getting sufficient food to sustain them so that none of the company perished. In a short time they separated and took different routes . . . for Quincy."

Hyrum Smith described his family's experience during the time he languished with his brother in Liberty Jail as a period of "suffering every privation." He wrote, "Our enemies carried off nearly everything of value, until my family were left almost destitute. My wife had been but recently confined and had to suffer more than tongue can describe; and then in common with the rest of the people, had to move, in the month

Detail:
"A View of the Mississippi near Quincy"

of February, a distance of two hundred miles, in order to escape further persecutions and injury." He also shared the bitter personal toll the events of Missouri cost him, as, he later wrote, it left "my body broken down and my health very much impaired, from the fatigue and afflictions which I have undergone, so that I have not been able to perform any labor since I have escaped from my oppressors. The loss of property which I sustained in the state of Missouri would amount to several thousand dollars."

Regarding her own experience, Emma Smith poignantly wrote to the imprisoned Joseph, "No one but God, knows the reflections of my mind and the feelings of my heart when I left our house and home, and almost all of everything that we possessed excepting our little children, and took my journey out of the State of Missouri, leaving you shut up in that lonesome prison. But the reflection is more than human nature ought to bear, and if God does not record our sufferings and avenge our wrongs on them that are guilty, I shall be sadly mistaken."

Providentially, the Latter-day Saints found refuge among the citizens of Quincy, Illinois, who compassionately aided the indigent Saints. After observing Mormons making their way across the Mississippi River, O. H. Brown was so moved he wrote with anguish, "Great God! have I not seen it? Yes, my eyes have beheld the blood-stained traces of innocent

In our interview with the President [Martin Van Buren], he interrogated us wherein we differed in our religion from the other religions of the day. Brother Joseph said we differed in mode of baptism, and the gift of the Holy Ghost by the laying on of hands. We considered that all other considerations were contained in the gift of the Holy Ghost.

—Joseph Smith and Elias Higbee to Hyrum Smith, 5 December 1839.

women and children, in the drear winter, who had traveled hundreds of miles barefoot, through frost and snow, to seek a refuge from their savage pursuers. 'Twas a scene of horror sufficient to enlist sympathy from an adamantine heart." The *Quincy Argus* openly condemned what had transpired: "We know of no language sufficiently for the expression of our shame and abhorrence of her [Missouri's] recent conduct."

The spirits of the Saints were further boosted by Joseph Smith's arrival at Quincy on 22 April 1839. When Wilford Woodruff visited the Prophet shortly afterward, he joyfully wrote that Joseph was "frank, open & familiar as usual. Sister Emma was truly happy."

After arriving at Quincy, Joseph's priority was the

Nauvoo, the City Beautiful

establishment of a place to begin anew the gathering of the Saints. In early May, the village of Commerce, Illinois, fifty miles north of Quincy, was chosen.

The dark, woeful exodus from Missouri blossomed into a bright, hopeful period for the Saints. Life in the Mississippi River town of Commerce, which the Saints built into an impressive city they renamed Nauvoo in August 1839, proved to be a golden era in their political, economic, and social life and a period of great religious enlightenment. The name change, which became official the following year when the federal government renamed the post office, was explained in a statement by the First Presidency: "The name of our city (Nauvoo) is of

1840

The Postmaster General changed the name of the post office at Commerce to Nauvoo; Gov. Lilburn W. Boggs demanded that Joseph Smith be extradited to Missouri; Joseph first preached baptism for the dead at the funeral of Seymor Brunson

The first dental school in America, the Baltimore College of Dental Surgery, was founded

Richard Henry Dana published his classic account of life at sea, *Two Years before the Mast*; revolted by the cruelty of floggings, he was later instrumental in having the practice outlawed on U.S. vessels

The world's first postage stamp ("Penny Black") was issued in England

The population of Great Britain was 18.5 million; of the U.S., 17 million; Ireland, 8 million; London, 2.2 million; New York City, 312,710

U.S. abolitionists Lucretia Mott and Elizabeth Cady Stanton were refused admittance to the world anti-slavery convention in London, England, because they were women

William Henry Harrison was elected the ninth U.S. president

Currier and Ives began producing lithographic prints

Belgium resident Adolphe Sax invented the saxophone

Martin Van Buren implemented a ten-hour workday for federal employees

Hebrew origin, and signifies a beautiful situation, or place, carrying with it, also, the idea of rest; and is truly descriptive of this most delightful situation."

There was much physical work to be done before the location accurately reflected the optimism of the new name. The Prophet initially described the Saints' new home as "literally a wilderness. The land was mostly covered with trees and bushes, and much of it was so wet that it was with the utmost difficulty a footman could get through, and totally impossible for teams. Commerce was so unhealthful, very few could live there; but believing that it might become a healthful place by the blessing of heaven to the Saints, and no more eligible place presenting itself, I considered it wisdom to make an attempt to build up a city."

It was on this land at a bend in the Mississippi River that the Prophet determinedly set forth to build a new Zion. What the Saints could not accomplish in Missouri, they largely created in Illinois. During its brief existence, Nauvoo came close to fulfilling how the Lord had defined Zion in March 1831. Not only was the city largely settled by people "with one heart and one mind," but it was also "a land of peace, a city of refuge, a place of safety for the saints of the Most High God; and the glory of the Lord shall be there. . . . It shall be called Zion."

The Reverend George Peck described Nauvoo's humble, inauspicious beginnings "as a very singular encampment. Multitudes of people, men, women and children, ragged, dirty, and miserable generally, seemed to be living in tents and covered wagons for lack of better habitation. This strange scene presented itself along the shore for a mile or more. We were informed that they were Mormons who had recently fled from Missouri."

As the physically and emotionally exhausted Saints started to settle Nauvoo and its twin city of Montrose, Iowa, across the Mississippi River, during the late spring and early summer of 1839, malaria broke out among them. Wilford Woodruff wrote, "It was a very sickly time; Joseph had given up his home in Commerce to the sick, and had a tent pitched in his dooryard and was living in that himself." According to Elizabeth Ann Whitney, the Saints "were only just barely able to crawl around and wait upon each other." Joseph and Emma opened their hearts and arms to the Saints and worked to bring them comfort and aid, with Joseph eventually also becoming ill.

In the midst of this suffering, there occurred what Wilford Woodruff described as a "day of God's power." In his journal entry for 22 July 1839, he wrote, "There was many sick among the saints on both sides of the river and Joseph went through the midst of them taking them by the hand and in a loud voice commanding them in the name of Jesus Christ to arise from their beds and be made whole and they leaped from their beds made whole by the power of God." Elijah Fordham was one among the number, and he

---

Virtue is one of the most prominent principles that enables us to have confidence in approaching our Father who is in heaven in order to ask wisdom at his hand therefore if thou wilt cherish this principle in thine heart thou mayest ask with confidence before him and it shall be poured out upon thine head and thou shalt not lack any thing that thy soul desires in truth and again the Lord shall bless this house and none of them shall fail because they turned not away the servents of the Lord from their doors even so Amen.

—Notation made by Joseph Smith in the Wilkison Family autograph book, Philadelphia, Pennsylvania, in February 1840, while returning to Nauvoo, Illinois, from his visit to Washington, D.C.

ABRAHAM, MARTIN, AND JOSEPH

The difficulties the Latter-day Saints experienced in Missouri brought Joseph Smith directly into contact with a sitting president of the United States, indirectly with a future American president, and led him to declare himself a candidate for the presidency. In 1839, Joseph journeyed from Nauvoo, Illinois, to Washington, D.C., to meet with the eighth president of the United States, Martin Van Buren. In 1843, he was at Springfield, Illinois, where the nation's sixteenth president, Abraham Lincoln, was then a relatively obscure lawyer and politician. In 1844, Joseph declared himself a candidate to become the eleventh president of the United States.

On 28 November 1839, Joseph, in company with Elias Higbee, arrived in the nation's capital. "We spent the most of that day in looking up a boarding house," he wrote, "which we succeeded in finding. We found as cheap boarding as can be had in this city."

The following day, 29 November, they "proceeded to the house of the President" to request Martin Van Buren's help in redressing the wrongs the Saints had experienced when driven from Missouri the previous winter. Concerning their visit to the building that would later be named the White House, the pair wrote, "We found a very large and splendid palace, surrounded with a splendid enclosure, decorated with all the fineries and elegancies of this world. We went to the door and requested to see the President, when we were immediately introduced into an upper apartment, where we met the President, and were introduced into his parlor, where we presented him with our letters of introduction." The result of their journey was much less than they had hoped for. In an era of States' Rights, their plea for help went unanswered.

Abraham Lincoln, ca. 1847

Three years later, Joseph appeared before the U.S. Circuit Court at Springfield. An attempt had been made on the life of ex-governor Lilburn Boggs in May 1842. Missouri officials immediately charged Joseph as an accessory to the crime. Shortly after newly elected Governor Thomas Ford took over as Illinois's chief executive in early December 1842, he expressed a willingness to extradite Joseph to Missouri. Habeas corpus proceedings were held in early January 1843 to address the issue.

Courts were a form of entertainment in the 1800s and frequently attracted large crowds. Joseph's case, however, attracted additional attention. Several people came from Nauvoo, including members of the twelve. The case dealt with a constitutional question that likely would have caught the attention of the community's lawyers and citizens. Joseph's fame also brought out the curious. The courtroom was so crowded that a number of Springfield women sat on either side of Judge Nathaniel Pope. Included in this group was a young Mary Todd Lincoln, who was marking her two-month wedding anniversary to Abraham Lincoln on the day the proceedings began.

The uniqueness of the situation prompted Joseph's counsel, Justin Butterfield, the United

President Martin Van Buren, ca. 1839

States attorney for Illinois, to wryly observe in his opening remarks, "May it please the Court, I appear before you to-day under circumstances most novel and peculiar. I am to address the 'Pope' (bowing to the Judge), surrounded by angels, (bowing still lower to the ladies), in the presence of the holy Apostles, in behalf of the Prophet of the Lord."

Butterfield then earnestly argued that neither the Constitution nor existing laws would permit Illinois to return Joseph to Missouri. The only contingency upon which he could legally be extradited—he had committed a crime in that state and subsequently fled from justice—was not supported by Missouri's affidavit, Butterfield contended. The *Sangamo Journal* agreed, stating that Missouri's warrant was "manifestly defective" and that "the arguments presented by the counsel for Smith were conclusive."

The following day, 5 January, Judge Pope, again flanked by several women, rendered his verdict before a crowded courtroom:

> The importance of this case, and the consequences which may flow from an erroneous precedent, affecting the lives and liberties of our citizens, have impelled the court to bestow upon it the most anxious consideration. . . . This case presents the important question arising under the Constitution and laws of the United States, whether a citizen of the state of Illinois can be transported from his own state to the state of Missouri, to be tried for a crime, which, if he ever committed, was committed in the state of Illinois. . . . The court can alone regard the facts set forth in the affidavit of Boggs as having any legal existence. The mis-recitals and over-statements in the requisition and warrant are not supported by oath, and cannot be received as evidence to deprive a citizen of his liberty and transport him to a foreign state for trial. For these reasons Smith must be discharged.

The *Journal* published Pope's opinion in its entirety, proclaiming, "We have been long of the opinion that the requisition for Smith has been held over his head for sinister purposes. In the correctness of his decision, there is a universal acquiescence."

A year later, in January 1844, leading Mormons urged Joseph to enter the U.S. presidential race. Having previously written to five possible candidates to ascertain what would be their "rule of action relative to us as a people, should fortune favor your ascension to the chief magistracy," Church leaders were disappointed in the responses they received. Like Van Buren before him, John C. Calhoun stated that the Mormons' problems in Missouri did not fall under the jurisdiction of the federal government. Henry Clay, while sympathizing with the Mormons' plight, indicated that he would not make promises to any particular people.

By 7 February 1844, Joseph had completed his platform, which was published in a pamphlet entitled *Views of the Powers and Policy of the Government of the United States*. His proposals, ranging from common sense to idealistic, included revoking imprisonment for debt, turning prisons into seminaries of learning, putting felons to work on roads and other public projects, and economizing on national and state governments as a means of lowering taxes. Several of his proposals were doomed in an era of State's Rights, including the reestablishment of a national bank, with branch offices in each state. More idealistic were proposals to end slavery by 1850, with slave holders being reimbursed from the sale of public lands, and to expand presidential powers so that federal troops could be sent to a state to suppress mobs without the formal request of the governor.

At the time of Joseph's martyrdom, a number of Latter-day Saints were in the eastern United States campaigning for Joseph's presidency, including Brigham Young and the other members of the Twelve, except for John Taylor and Willard Richards, who were with the Prophet at Carthage Jail.

Nauvoo

with the rest of the sick rose from his bed and followed Joseph "from house to house and it was truly a time of rejoicing." Wilford Woodruff later recalled, "The words of the Prophet were not like the words of man, but like the voice of God. It seemed to me that the house shook on its foundations."

As the Saints recovered, they enthusiastically resumed the task of building a city, a Zion, a place to gather. Quickly, the swampy, raw wilderness became abuzz with human activity as they laid out lots in four-acre squares according to Joseph's plan, cut and improved roads, planted gardens and orchards, dug ditches, erected homes and barns, and opened bakery, tanner, blacksmith, tailor, and cooper shops. A grist-mill and sawmill as well a match factory and gunsmith were soon in business.

Visitors to frontier Nauvoo were amazed by what they saw. Bostonian J. H. Buckingham wrote that one could not visit "Nauvoo and come away without a conviction that . . . the body of the Mormons were an industrious, hard-working, and frugal people. In the history of the whole world there cannot be found such another instance of so rapid a rise of a city out of the wilderness—a city so well built, a territory so well cultivated." Some non-Mormon religious leaders revealed a jealousy of Nauvoo's hard-earned success. Reverend Samuel Prior flatly admitted, "Sadly was I disappointed" at what he saw. Rather than finding the hoped-for "miserable log cabins and mud hovels," he wrote, " . . . I was surprised to see one of the most romantic places that I had visited in the West. The buildings, though many of them were small and of wood, yet bore the marks of neatness which I have not seen equaled in this country."

The success of Nauvoo did not surprise Joseph. From its very founding, Joseph prophesied that he "would build up a city and the [old] inhabitants prophesied that I could not." By 1 October 1842,

Be assured, beloved brethren, that I am no disinterested observer of the things which are transpiring on the face of the whole earth; and amidst the general movements which are in progress, none is of more importance than the glorious work in which you are now engaged. . . .

Beloved brethren, you must be aware in some measure of my feelings, when I contemplate the great work which is now rolling on, and the relationship which I sustain to it, while it is extending to distant lands, and thousands are embracing it. I realize in some measure my responsibility, and the need I have of support from above, and wisdom from on high, that I may be able to teach this people, which have now become a great people, the principles of righteousness, and lead them agreeably to the will of Heaven; so that they may be perfected, and prepared to meet the Lord Jesus Christ when He shall appear in great glory. Can I rely on your prayers to our heavenly Father on my behalf, and on all the prayers of all my brethren and sisters in England, (whom having not seen, yet I love), that I may be enabled to escape every stratagem of Satan, surmount every difficulty, and bring this people to the enjoyment of those blessings which are reserved for the righteous?

—Joseph Smith to the Traveling High Council and Elders of The Church of Jesus Christ of Latter-day Saints
in Great Britain, 19 October 1840.

Joseph Smith was able to note, "It is one of the few comforts of the saints in this world, to be settled in peace, and witness the rap[i]d growth of their infant city, as a place of safety and gathering for the last days. For three or four miles upon the river and about the same distance back in the country, Nauvoo presents a city of gardens, ornamented with the dwellings of those who have made a covenant by sacrifice, and are guided by revelation, an exception to all other societies upon the earth."

As the Saints were striving to establish Nauvoo, Joseph also turned his focus to spreading the gospel. By the end of the summer of 1839, Joseph again sent members of the Quorum of the Twelve to Great Britain in an effort to further expand the Church's missionary effort. It was a great sacrifice for ill and destitute men who left behind ill and destitute families. In fact, as the missionaries journeyed, their appearance caused one stranger to wonder "who had been robbing the burying ground—so miserable was their appearance through sickness." The sympathetic prophet promised the brethren, "Your family shall know that the mind of God is in calling you to go and preach the Gospel of life and salvation in a perishing world." In fifteen months of proselyting, they converted some four thousand people and distributed five thousand copies of the Book of Mormon. In the following years, as the number of British conversions continued to

Moved that the inhabitents of this City shall keep their children at home except on lawful business on sundays and from skayting on the ice and from marauding upon their neighbours property and any persons refuseing to do the same shall pay five dollars fine for every offence for the same &c.

—Successful resolution Joseph Smith presented to the Nauvoo City Council, 5 March 1842.

A WELL REGULATED
MILITIA

During America's early colonial days, survival frequently depended upon every settler being both soldier and farmer. Borrowing a long-established European tradition, these colonists organized themselves into militias for protection. In later colonial times, the experience of having to house British troops intensified American disdain for standing armies. Victories by militiamen, better known as minutemen, over these same British regular army troops during the American Revolution further elevated the status of militias in the American mind.

Following the war, militias became a key democratic institution for the new nation. They were viewed as a safeguard against despotism, since the men and officers were locally selected and paid. Fearing that leaders of their new government might adopt the excesses of monarchies, the Bill of Rights addressed this issue: "A well regulated Militia, being necessary to the security of a free State, the right of the people to keep and bear Arms shall not be infringed." In 1792, Congress passed a law requiring all free, able-bodied white males between the ages of eighteen and forty-

Local militia drills ca. 1832

five to serve in their local militia. In the South these were usually organized by counties, in the North, by towns. Not only were militias cheaper than standing armies—militiamen usually provided their own weapons, which they already had—but they also sent a clear message that citizens in a democracy had both the right and the responsibility to bear arms in defense of freedom, law, and order.

This law, however, went unenforced in many areas. Where it was implemented, the results were frequently less than hoped for. Annual musters were often farcical, although one young girl remembered the day as one of her favorites during the year because of its festive-like atmosphere.

During the early 1800s, the need for professional soldiers became evident as experience proved that militias were better situated to protect local citizens' rights and property than to engage in long-term fighting. During the War of 1812, militiamen frequently performed poorly, except when led by able military officers as with the defense of Baltimore and during the Battle of New Orleans. Following the war, the nation's leaders expanded the size of the standing army to help protect its borders and deal with situations beyond the scope of militias.

As the army grew, some officials came to view militias as unnecessary. In 1840, Massachusetts abolished mandatory militia service. Other states, largely in the east, soon followed. In the west, universal service continued, although noncompliance was frequently winked at. On the frontier, however, safety concerns usually resulted in western settlers' organizing themselves into military units, often with little or no assistance from state authorities.

When the Latter-day Saints arrived at Commerce (later renamed Nauvoo) in 1839, it was a frontier river town. On the other side of the river was sparsely settled Iowa Territory. Although neighboring communities shared longstanding concerns of Indian attack, the experience of the Mormons in Missouri convinced them their enemy might also be their white neighbors. When the city of Nauvoo was incorporated in 1840, provision was made for the establishment of a militia—the Nauvoo Legion. Because Nauvoo was substantially larger than the other towns in the vicinity—in spite of popular myth, it never exceeded Chicago in terms of population—and because city leaders insisted upon universal service, the Nauvoo Legion was larger than most of the surrounding militias.

During Nauvoo's 4 July 1843 celebration, Joseph addressed the issue of the Nauvoo Legion: "When we came here the state required us to bear arms and do military duty according to the law," he explained. In response to concerns about establishing a militia, Joseph "told the Saints that though I was clear from military duty by law, in consequence of lameness in one of my legs, yet I would set them the example and would do duty myself. They then said they were willing to do duty, if they could be formed into an independent company, and I could be at their head. This is the origin of the Nauvoo Legion." The ordinance creating the Nauvoo militia authorized the rank of lieutenant general for its commanding officer, a rank that exceeded every other military officer in the United States.

As was the case in other countries before it, the professional soldier ultimately replaced the citizen-soldier as a result of war. Although the American army numbered around five thousand at the outbreak of the Civil War, within a short time millions of men were fighting on both sides. Mustered and organized on a local basis, regiments such as the Massachusetts 54th and Michigan 7th were frequently local militias revived and transposed into long-term combat units. As a result, the male population of some towns was nearly decimated during the war. Following the Civil War, professional soldiers assumed the primary role of defense of the nation while the concept of the local militia lives on today with the National Guard.

Vol. 2.]   "GO AHEAD!!"   [No. 3.

THE CROCKETT ALMANAC 1841.

Tussel with a Bear. See page 9.

Containing Adventures, Exploits, Sprees & Scrapes in the West, & Life and Manners in the Backwoods.

Nashville, Tennessee. Published by Ben Harding.

Popular writing promoted and exaggerated the exploits of frontier heroes

increase, some five thousand converts crossed the Atlantic to settle in and around Nauvoo. As a result of their successes, Joseph grew closer to the Twelve and expanded their ecclesiastical responsibilities.

Although the Saints rejoiced at what was taking place, other religionists feared and warned of the Mormon influence. In their 1841 annual report, the American Home Missionary Society listed the hazards awaiting Americans who moved to the frontier: "Mormonism is there to delude them. Popery is there to ensnare them. Infidelity is there to corrupt and debase them. And Atheism is there, to take away their God as they go on to the grave, and to blot out every ray of hope that may beam on them from beyond."

One for whom the warning "came too late" was John S. Fullmer, who joyfully wrote in a 15 February 1841 letter about his conversion and about Nauvoo:

We are comfortably, not splendidly situated. . . . Our place is rich and beautiful; half prairie, and susceptible, by proper management, of supporting stock to almost an unlimited extent. But what is of infinitely more importance is that we reside within two miles of the City of Nauvoo, a place founded by the church of Latter-day Saints with whom we became acquainted, and after an impartial and thorough investigation of their

1841

Nauvoo Charter took effect; Nauvoo Legion established, with Joseph Smith serving as lieutenant-general; converts from England began arriving at Nauvoo; Joseph sustained as trustee-in-trust of the Church; elected city councilman in Nauvoo's first municipal elections; presided over laying of cornerstones for the Nauvoo Temple; answered Nauvoo mayor's request to use the Nauvoo Legion to remove a grog shop kept in town; opened his red-brick store; appointed Hyrum Smith to serve as patriarch to the Church; taught members of the Twelve Apostles about plural marriage

The United States had three presidents this year: William Henry Harrison succeeded Martin Van Buren but died one month later; John Tyler then became the first vice president to ascend to the presidency

John Lloyd Stephens published *Incidents of Travel in Central America*, adding greatly to the accuracy and amount of information available regarding ancient Mesoamerica

New Zealand became a British Colony

Edgar Allen Poe's "The Murders in the Rue Morgue" was published; a new literary genre, the detective story, was born

Massachusetts transcendentalists established the utopian community of Brook Farm

Boston Unitarian clergyman Theodore Parker proclaimed that Christinity grew from the rational truths of Jesus' teaching rather than his personal authority; an outcry ensued

Upper and Lower Canada united to create the Province of Canada

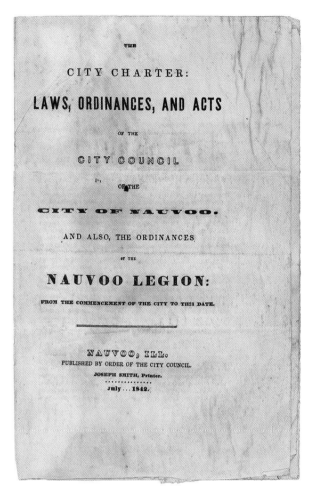

Title page of "The City Charter: Laws, Ordinances, and Acts. . . . ," July 1842

Nauvoo Temple

principles have united ourselves in Christian fellowship. . . . If you ever heard anything, be assured it was either a gross misrepresentation or perhaps an utter falsehood. They have, to be sure, been driven from the state of Missouri, two years ago, by the force of arms, but certainly not for any criminal act . . . but because there is a prophet at their head and because the church places implicit confidence in what he teaches. Equally with the primitive Christians, this church professes to have the same priesthood, together with the same power and gifts.

In January 1841, the First Presidency announced that an important step had been taken in the development of Nauvoo, as the state of Illinois had approved the "Nauvoo Charter": "The legislators of this state . . . freely, openly, boldly, and nobly, have come forth to our

assistance, owned us as citizens and friends, and took us by the hand, and extended to us all the blessings of civil, political, and religious liberty, by granting us, under the date of December 16, 1840, one of the most liberal charters, with the most plenary powers ever conferred by a legislative assembly on free citizens, 'The City of Nauvoo,' the 'Nauvoo Legion,' and the 'University of the City of Nauvoo.'"

With the temporal foundation for Nauvoo securely in place, Joseph turned his attention to building another temple. In March 1841, construction on the Nauvoo Temple began. It occupied much of the Saints' emotional, spiritual, and physical energies for the next five years. Women, men, and children donated to the completion of their temple. Many willingly gave up the few comforts they had. Elizabeth Kirby later

THE GLORIOUS FOURTH

Few days were as important to Americans in Joseph Smith's lifetime as the Fourth of July. Throughout the nation, the Glorious Fourth was celebrated with speeches, parades, and fireworks, although the anniversary of American independence was more commonly celebrated in the North than in the South.

By many accounts, the first time Americans joined in a unified celebration of Independence Day was during its fiftieth anniversary in 1826. Before that time, political parties held competing, partisan celebrations that were known to degenerate into violent confrontations that frequently included fisticuffs and occasionally ended in murder. While partisan celebrations diminished after 1826, they did not entirely disappear.

In July 1833, long-standing differences between the Latter-day Saints and their western Missouri neighbors erupted into violence, resulting in the Mormons being driven from their homes in Jackson County. "July, which once dawned upon the virtue and independence of the United States, now dawned upon the savage barbarity and mobocracy of Missouri," proclaimed a Latter-day Saint account of these events.

Lieutenant-General Joseph Smith Reviewing the Nauvoo Legion

As a result of what happened in July 1833, Joseph spent Independence Day 1834 in western Missouri. Upon learning of what transpired, Joseph petitioned the Lord for both solace and counsel. Through revelation Joseph was commanded to organize what is known as "Zion's Camp" to help Missouri officials return the Latter-day Saints to their Jackson County homes. Numbering nearly two hundred men when fully organized, the main body of Zion's Camp left Kirtland, Ohio, in May 1834, reaching western Missouri the following month.

In spite of Zion's Camp, the Latter-day Saints were not returned to their homes. On 22 June 1834, Joseph received another revelation declaring that Zion would not be redeemed at that time because the Latter-day

Saints had failed to live the "Law of Consecration": "Were it not for the transgressions of my people, speaking concerning the church and not individuals, they might have been redeemed even now. . . . Zion cannot be built up unless it is by the principles of the law of the celestial kingdom." The Lord further taught Joseph and his followers that He would not always fight their battles: "My people must needs be chastened until they learn obedience, if it must needs be, by the things which they suffer. . . . Therefore, in consequence of the transgressions of my people, it is expedient in me that mine elders should wait for a little season for the redemption of Zion." The Saints were instructed to "talk not of judgements, neither boast of faith nor of mighty works," counsel some settlers would soon forget with tragic consequences. On 30 June 1834, Joseph officially disbanded Zion's Camp, although he would not start for Ohio until after the Glorious Fourth.

Joseph spent the following year's Fourth of July at Kirtland, where the arrival of Michael Chandler the previous day, 3 July 1835, was causing great excitement. Chandler had brought several

Egyptian mummies, along with papyrus scrolls containing hieroglyphics that he hoped the Prophet might be able to translate. Joseph later proclaimed that they contained writings by the Old Testament prophet Abraham. In March 1842, Joseph published the Book of Abraham, containing an account of young Abraham's escape from Egypt to the land of Ur and inspired truths God taught Abraham concerning the relationship of God, man, and the universe.

At Nauvoo, Illinois, on 4 July 1842, the Nauvoo Legion, of which Joseph was the commanding general, remained "on parade" throughout the day. That evening several visitors to the town took advantage of an invitation to address the troops.

On Independence Day 1843, Joseph addressed an audience at Nauvoo estimated at fifteen thousand during an eight-hour celebration that also included addresses by Orson Hyde and Parley P. Pratt. Three times the festivities were interrupted by the arrival of steamers, whose occupants were escorted to their seats by members of the Nauvoo Legion and were welcomed by the firing of cannons. One visitor from Quincy, Illinois, moved by the experience, reported:

The large concourse of people assembled to celebrate the day which gave birth to American Independence, convinced me that the Mormons have been most grossly slandered, and that they respect, cherish and love the free institutions of our country, and appreciate the sacrifice and bloodshed of those patriots who established them. I never saw a more orderly, gentlemanly and hospitable people than the Mormons, nor a more interesting population, as the stirring appearance of their city indicates.

Not all Independence Day celebrations produced such positive results for the Saints. The 1838 celebration stands out in this regard. This was a time of renewed tensions between the Mormons and their frontier Missouri neighbors, and the Latter-day Saints at Far West spent the Fourth of July "celebrating the Declaration of Independence of the United States of America." However, with the outrages committed against Church members by Jackson County mobocrats still fresh in their minds, and with problems arising anew with their current neighbors, Latter-day Saints also made "a 'Declaration of Independence' from all mobs and persecutions which have been inflicted upon them . . . until they could bear it no longer." In his oration, Sidney Rigdon made several ill-advised and vehemently bitter comments. Caught up in the fervor, he threatened a "war of extermination" if mobs again arose to plague the Saints and state officials failed to protect them in their civil and religious liberties.

Prior to Rigdon's oration, the Latter-day Saints had laid cornerstones for a temple at Far West as part of their Fourth of July observance. The Saints, however, would not remain in Missouri long enough to build their temple. Later that fall, Rigdon's war challenge was answered when Governor Lilburn Boggs issued his infamous extermination order in October 1838.

The Fourth of July in 1839 found Joseph and his followers in Illinois, working hard to carve Nauvoo, their "City Beautiful," out of a swamp. Back at Far West on that Glorious Fourth, the four solitary temple cornerstones kept a silent watch over the Saints' former home.

> *Although I do wrong, I do not the wrongs that I am charged with doing; the wrong that I do is through the frailty of human nature, like other men. No man lives without fault. Do you think that even Jesus, if He were here, would be without fault in your eyes? His enemies said all manner of evil against Him—they all watched for iniquity in Him.*
>
> —Remarks of Joseph Smith, 31 August 1842.

recounted, "It was taught in our meetings that we would have to sacrifice our idols in order to be saved. I could not think of anything that would grieve me to part with in my possession, except Francis Kirby's [her late husband's] watch. So, I gave it to help build the Nauvoo Temple and everything else that I could possibly spare and the last few dollars that I had in the world, which altogether amounted to nearly $50."

A year after beginning work on the temple, the Prophet "assisted in the organization" of the Female Relief Society on 17 March 1842, saying, "I now turn the key to you in the name of God and this Society shall rejoice and knowledge and intelligence shall flow down from this time." He also admonished that

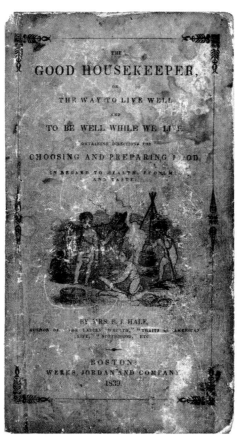

Author and editor Sarah Hale dedicated her life to improving, educating, and promoting the status of women

"the Society of Sisters might provoke the brethren to good works in looking to the wants of the poor—searching after objects of charity, and in administering to their wants to assist; by correcting the morals and strengthening the virtues of the female community." The twenty women present chose Emma Smith as president, and she selected two counselors, Sarah Cleveland and Elizabeth Ann Whitney. Emma challenged the women that their "duties to others were to seek out and relieve the distressed—that each member should be ambitious to do good . . . and be very careful of the character and reputation of the members." By 1844, there were more than thirteen hundred members. The last recorded Relief Society meeting in Nauvoo was

1842

Joseph Smith served for a time as editor of the *Times and Seasons*, during which time he published the Wentworth letter and the first portion of the book of Abraham, organized the Female Relief Society, administered the endowment for the first time, was selected by the city council to fill the Nauvoo mayoral vacancy, divided Nauvoo into ten ecclesiastical wards, and wrote epistles to the Saints regarding baptism for the dead (D&C 127 and 128)

English agronomist John Bennet Laws patented the first artificial fertilizer

Austrian physicist C. J. Doppler published "On the Colored Light of the Binary Stars" (the Doppler effect)

British paleontologist Richard Owen coined the term *dinosaur*

American physician Crawford Long became the first to use ether as a surgical anesthesia

Massachusetts limited the workday of children under 12 years of age to 10 hours

The U.S. and Canada settled the question of America's northeastern boundary through the Webster-Ashburton Treaty; the U.S. obtained about 7,000 of 12,000 square miles disputed in the Aroostook region

NAUVOO, FROM THE MISSISSIPPI, LOOKING DOWN THE RIVER.

As for the perils which I am called to pass through, they seem but a small thing to me, as the envy and wrath of man have been my common lot all the days of my life; and for what cause it seems mysterious, unless I was ordained from before the foundation of the world for some good end, or bad, as you may choose to call it. Judge ye for yourselves. God knoweth all these things, whether it be good or bad. But nevertheless, deep water is what I am wont to swim in. It all has become a second nature to me; and I feel, like Paul, to glory in tribulation; for to this day has the God of my fathers delivered me out of them all, and will deliver me from henceforth; for behold, and lo, I shall triumph over all my enemies, for the Lord God hath spoken it (D&C 127:2).

—Joseph Smith to the Latter-day Saints at Nauvoo, 1 September 1842.

YOU OUGHT TO HAVE
YOUR HEAD EXAMINED

When someone in Young America said you needed to have your head examined, they were not calling you crazy. Rather, they were suggesting that you see a phrenologist.

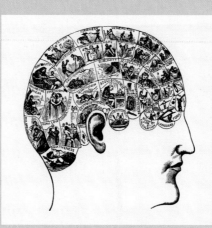

Developed by Viennese physician Franz Gall in the 1790s, phrenology taught that the brain was composed of multiple, innate faculties, each with its own seat or "organ." The shape of one's skull was determined by the development of the organ that lay directly beneath. Since the strength or weakness of each trait affected the topography of the skull, phrenologists believed they could determine a person's personality and intellectual capacity by "reading" the shape of the skull. Strong characteristics produced bumps; weak characteristics left depressions.

The greatest traits, such as benevolence and parental love, were believed to be situated in the frontal lobes, while animal drives such as appetite and combativeness were located at the base of the head. Thus, according to phrenology, the best men would have large heads and noble brows, while the basest men possessed small heads and meager brows.

Phrenology had its heyday in the United States during the 1830s and 1840s. Americans, eager for anything new and instructive, readily accepted its premises, and it enjoyed greater popularity there than in other areas of the world. It became fashionable for Americans to have their heads examined. After receiving flattering analyses, such figures as Daniel Webster, Henry Ward Beecher, and Andrew Jackson, their heads obviously swollen by praise, endorsed the "science."

Although the idea of reading character traits from the skull has been discredited, phrenology's basic assumption that functions are localized in the brain is now commonplace. Some personality and speech disorders correlate to specific atrophied regions of the brain. Frequent talk is made of "left brain" and "right brain" individuals.

Phrenology also called attention to the idea of individual differences rather than a collective mind and served as an impetus for new theories about the brain. It further paved the way for modern psychology by emphasizing that man could alter his personality and develop his brain by training. One phrenologist reported that an infidel who had a depression where "devotion" resided developed a prominent bump after turning to God.

During the summer of 1842, a phrenologist visited Nauvoo, in part because "a large number of persons in different places have manifested a desire to know the phrenological developments of Joseph Smith's head." Joseph agreed to have his head read, and in July an analysis "showing the development of his much-talked-of brain" was published. Of the forty traits for which Joseph was measured, the vast majority were highly developed, including a "great power of analysis" and "the ability to think and reason clearly." On the other extreme, the phrenologist found that while Joseph had a "love of music," he was "without quickness to catch or learn tunes by ear." He further concluded that Joseph "views the approach of death without fear," which he interpreted to mean that Joseph had an "indifference to life." Joseph allowed his chart to be published "for the gratification of the curious, and not for [any] respect [I entertain for] phrenology."

> *Brethren, shall we not go on in so great a cause?*
> *Go forward and not backward. Courage, brethren: and on, on to the victory!*
> *(D&C 128:22)*
>
> —Joseph Smith to The Church of Jesus Christ of Latter-day Saints, 6 September 1842.

in Nauvoo was held on 16 March 1844 as growing difficulties at Nauvoo led to cessation of Relief Society activities. However, in 1867 the organization, which still exists today, was revived on a church-wide basis by President Brigham Young.

During the Saints' time in Nauvoo, Joseph Smith brought forth additional inspired teachings. He wrote the Articles of Faith, published the Book of Abraham, explained and expounded upon the origins and eternal destiny of mankind, introduced baptism for the dead, instructed the Saints about eternal marriage, and introduced and taught the temple endowment.

The Prophet also inspired the Lord's people through his example, love, and selfless concern, in addition to his teachings. Given the trials, tribulations, and dangers he frequently encountered, it would be easily understood, and even forgivable, if Joseph had been austere and gloomy. Instead, he purposefully avoided the pompous, overblown sobriety of ministers. He was sociable, animated, approachable, and candid about his humanity. Simply put, Joseph Smith loved life and lived it exuberantly. "Happiness is the object and design of our existence," he proclaimed, "and will be the end thereof if we pursue the path that leads to it."

> *Be shure you are right and then go ahead David Crocket like*
>
> —Joseph Smith's response to an inquiry from William Clayton in October 1842. The famous hero, frontiersman, and politician had adopted "Be always sure you are right, and then go ahead" as his motto.

Joseph's dynamic personality drew people to him. William Henrie wrote, "You could not be in his presence without feeling the influence and Spirit of God, which seemed to flow from him almost as heat does from a stove." Emma later recalled of her prophet husband, "I never wanted him to go into the garden to work, for if he did, it would not be fifteen minutes before there would be three or four, or sometimes a half dozen men round him and they would tramp down the ground faster than he could hoe it up."

Illinois governor Thomas Ford, who knew Joseph Smith during the worst of times, later noted, "It must not be supposed that he was a dark and gloomy person, with a long beard, a grave and severe aspect, and a reserved and saintly carriage of his person; on the contrary, he was full of levity, even to boyish romping."

Indeed, he was a playful, physical man who loved athletic games. Benjamin F. Johnson remembered the Prophet Joseph as

> kind, generous, and mirth loving, and, at times, even convivial. . . . For amusements, he would sometimes wrestle with a friend, or ofttimes would test strength with others by sitting upon the floor with feet together and stick grasped between them. . . . Jokes, rebuses, matching couplets in rhymes, etc., were not uncommon. But to call for the singing of one or more of his favorite songs was more frequent. Of those, 'Wives, Children and Friends,' 'Battle of River Russen,' 'Soldier's Tear,' 'Soldier's Dream' and 'Last Rose of Summer' were most common.

April Conference, 1844, Nauvoo.

I told them I was but a man, and they must not expect me to be perfect; if they expected perfection from me, I should expect it from them; but if they would bear with my infirmities and the infirmities of the brethren, I would likewise bear with their infirmities.

—Joseph Smith's comments to some newly arrived Church members from the British Isles at Nauvoo, 29 October 1842. On another occasion Joseph told the Saints, "Brethren and sisters if I were as perfect as some of you wanted me to be, I could not stop in your midst."

Joseph also had a sense of humor and a quick wit—which at times could seem quite pointed. Millen Atwood remembered, "The first time I ever shook hands with a prophet he was easy, free & sociable, with all, he said that he rejoist to see us being Yankees for, said he, 'I was born in the State of Vermont.' Br. Robert Pierce was present and said to Br. Joseph why don't you hold your head up as I do—Br. Joseph said to him haven't you past by a field of wheat when it was ripe and seen some heads stand strait as yours does and others down as mine does[?] Yes sire said Br. Pierce. Well sayes Br. Joseph the full heads lop, the empty or blasted head with not much in them stand strait up like yours does. Joseph with all present had a good harty laugh at his expence[;] he comforted our hearts."

WHAT MIGHTY DIFFERENCES

While early 1840s America was mostly rural and its frontier was just beginning to push beyond the Mississippi River, teeming cities such as New York were experiencing geographic and population growth. Urban expansion also brought on a darker side of city life, as pointed out by prosperous and socially connected lawyer Richard Henry Dana. In his private journal, Dana, author of the classic *Two Years before the Mast*, recorded observations made in New York City during a January 1843 business trip:

Richard Henry Dana
(1815–1882)

> Passing down Broadway, the name of Anthony street, struck me, and I had a sudden desire to see that sink of iniquity and filth, the "Five Points." Following Anthony street down, I came upon the neighborhood. It was about half past ten, & the night was cloudy. The buildings were ruinous for the most part, as well as I could judge, & the streets & sidewalks muddy & ill lighted. Several of [the] houses had wooden shutters well closed & in almost [each] such case I found by stopping & listening, that there were many voices in the rooms & sometimes the sound of music & dancing. On the opposite side of [the] way I saw a door opened suddenly & a woman thrust into the street with great resistance & most foul language on her part. She seemed to be very drunk & threatened the life of one woman who was in the house, calling upon them to turn her out too, & saying "I'll watch for you." Her oaths were dreadful, & her drunken screeches & curses were so loud that they could be heard several squares off. As I passed on I still heard them behind me. Next there passed me a man holding up under his arm a woman who was so drunk that she could not walk alone & was muttering senseless words to herself. Men & women were passing on each side of the street, sometimes in numbers together, & once or twice a company of half a dozen mere girls ran rapidly, laughed & talking loud, from one house into another. These I gradually found were dancing houses. Grog shops, oyster cellars & close, obscure & suspicious looking places of every description abounded.
>
> Passing out of Anthony street, at the corner of one next to it, a girl who was going into a small shop with a shawl drawn over her head stopped & spoke to me. She asked me where I was going. I stopped & answered that I was only walking about a little, to look round. She said "I am only doing the same," & came down from the doorstep towards me. I hastened my pace & passed on. Turning round, I found she had followed me a few steps & then gone back to the shop.
>
> The night was not cold, & some women were sitting in the doorways or standing on the sidewalks. From them I received many invitations to walk in & see them, just to sit down a minute, &c., followed usually by laughter & jeers when they saw me pass on without noticing them. . . . From these dark, filthy, violent, & degraded regions, I passed into Broadway, where were lighted carriages with footmen, numerous well dressed passers by, cheerful light coming from behind curtained parlor windows, where were happy, affectionate & virtuous people connected by the ties of blood & friendship & enjoying the charities & honors of life. What mighty differences, what awful separations, wide as that of the great gulf & lasting for eternity, do what seem to be the merest chances place between human beings, of the same flesh & blood.

Joseph Smith preaching in the wilderness

Fourteen-year-old Goudy Hogan, who walked with his family eight miles to attend the 6 April 1844 conference, recounted an aspect of Joseph that continued to impress him in later life. An estimated twenty thousand people attended the meeting held in "the grove not far from the temple." Hogan recalled of that meeting, "I with a few other boys climbed up on some boards behind the stand that was temporary so that I could hear every word that was said. I was sitting close behind the Prophet Joseph Smith so that I nearly touched his clothes. I had not been long in the church and was somewhat superstitious and took particular notice of his manner of dress and action. I remember that he had on a light colored linen coat with a small hole in each elbow of his coat sleeve. I remember thinking that he was not a proud man and that this very noble experience inspired me with great confidence and faith that he was a great prophet of the Lord." Indeed, Joseph's understanding of his mission instilled in him a humility that allowed him to focus his mind and spirit on the higher purpose of continuing the restoration of the gospel for the benefit of others.

The Prophet's immense compassion for people often surfaced in spontaneous acts of simple but profound kindness. Mercy Thompson, a widow, remembered Joseph Smith's "tender sympathy and brotherly kindness he ever showed toward me and my fatherless child. When riding with him and his wife Emma in their carriage I have known him to alight and gather prairie flowers for my little girl."

Margarette Burgess remembered going to school on a day after it had rained, "causing the ground to be very muddy. . . . My brother Wallace and I both got fast in the mud and could not get out, and, child-like, we began to cry, for we thought we would have to stay there. But looking up, I beheld the loving friend of children, the Prophet Joseph, coming to us. He soon had us on higher and drier ground. Then he stooped down and cleaned the mud from our little, heavy-laden shoes, and took his handkerchief from his pocket and wiped our tear-stained faces. He spoke kind and cheering words to us, and sent us on our way to school rejoicing."

If any person should ask me if I were a prophet, I should not deny it, as that would give me the lie; for, according to John, the testimony of Jesus is the spirit of prophecy; therefore, if I profess to be a witness or teacher, and have not the spirit of prophecy, which is the testimony of Jesus, I must be a false witness; but if I be a true teacher and witness, I must possess the spirit of prophecy, and that constitutes a prophet; and any man who says he is a teacher or a preacher of righteousness, and denies the spirit of prophecy, is a liar, and the truth is not in him.

—Comments of Joseph Smith, 30 December 1842.

ADVOCATE FOR THE HELPLESS, THE FORGOTTEN, AND THE INSANE

When Dorothea Dix began teaching a Sunday school at the East Cambridge, Massachusetts, jail in 1841, she found several people who were mentally ill kept in misery in an unheated room. Thus a lifelong crusade was born. At a time when few worried about the treatment of the insane and those in prison, Dix became their advocate.

In January 1843, after an extensive statewide study, Dix went to the state capital to outline the appalling treatment of the insane, many of whom were frequently confined in jails and almshouses, often in chains: "Gentlemen, I come to present the strong claims of suffering humanity. I come to place before the Legislature of Massachusetts the condition of the miserable, the desolate, the outcast. I come as the advocate of helpless, forgotten, insane and idiotic men and women; of beings sunk to a condition from which the most unconcerned would start with real horror; of beings wretched in our prisons, and more wretched in our almshouses." She reported "insane persons confined within this Commonwealth, in cages, closets, cellars, stalls, pens! Chained, naked, beaten with rods, and lashed into obedience." In conclusion she stated, "Men of Massachusetts. . . . Become the benefactors of your race, the just guardians of the solemn rights you hold in trust. Raise up the fallen, succor the desolate, restore the outcast, defend the helpless, and for your eternal and great reward receive the benediction, 'Well done, good and faithful servants, become rulers over many things!'" Spurred to action by her scathing report, the Massachusetts legislature appropriated funds for a state mental hospital.

Except for the time she spent as an army nurse during the Civil War, Dix devoted the rest of her life to reforming the care of the insane, improving jails, and building hospitals for the mentally ill. For more than thirty years she traveled at home and abroad, visiting asylums and prisons, and writing and lecturing about them. The changes were slow in coming, but they came. By 1852, eleven additional states had established institutions for the insane. At the time of her death in 1887, her reform ideas had taken root in every state. Her single-minded focus allowed her to accomplish more changes through politics than any other woman of her era.

CHRISTMAS

"Shall we have Christmas?" was a question one Pennsylvanian asked in 1810. That same year the *Philadelphia Democratic Press* reported that few of Pennsylvania's residents celebrated Christmas. The Quaker State was not alone in this regard. The question of whether to have Christmas, and then how to celebrate the day, challenged Americans throughout Joseph's lifetime. During this time, Americans slowly started elevating this day until it began to acquire prominence as a holiday in the 1840s. The increasing diversity of American culture also began to be reflected in their Christmas celebrations.

Many of Joseph's contemporaries experienced little of Christmas during their youth. Henry Ward Beecher knew virtually nothing of Christmas until 1843, when he was thirty. "To me Christmas was a foreign day," he recalled. "When I was a boy I wondered what Christmas was." Two other New Englanders, Elizabeth Cady Stanton and Samuel Goodrich, recalled the Fourth of July, Thanksgiving, and "training day" for the local militia as the only "great festivals" of their early-nineteenth-century youths. In 1832 English actress Fanny Anne Kemble noted that Christmas in America "is no religious day and hardly a holiday with them." Newspapers made little mention of Christmas. The only reference the *Providence* (Rhode Island) *Gazette* made to Christmas in 1823 was a note about prevailing disagreements over the exact date of Christ's birth.

Couples frequently chose 25 December to wed. In the nation's cities, Christmas differed little from any other workday of the year. One person reported attending court in 1823; another the official opening of a bridge in 1828. On the frontier, Christmas was more frequently celebrated. The tradition of a Christmas Day "turkey shoot," popular in colonial America, continued in many parts of rural America during the first half of the nineteenth century.

In 1828 the United States' first ambassador to Mexico, Dr. Joel Poinesett, brought back a native Mexican plant that the locals called "flower of the blessed night" because it resembled the Star of Bethlehem. By the time of his death in 1851, the poinsettia, named in his honor, had become a part of American holiday decorations.

During the 1840s, decorated Christmas trees began to appear regularly. In the 1820s, a number of Pennsylvania's German immigrants ("Deutsche" was mistranslated by Americans as "Dutch") continued a tradition started by Martin Luther of decorating the trees surrounding their homes. In December 1842, a recently arrived political exile from Hesse is claimed to have been the first person in America to cut and trim an indoor tree. These same immigrants traditionally observed two days of Christmas, one devoted to religious sentiments, the other to more temporal pleasures.

Throughout this period, women's magazines disseminated and popularized Christmas practices. They also helped convince many that Christmas could be both a holy day and a festive holiday.

In 1837, Louisiana became the first state to declare Christmas an official holiday; the following year Arkansas became the second. By 1860, fourteen other states had joined the list, but Illinois was not numbered among them.

Little reference is made to how Joseph Smith spent the majority of his Christmases. On Christmas Day 1832 while residing at Kirtland, Ohio, he received a revelation (now section 87 of the Doctrine and Covenants) prophesying of "the wars that will shortly come to pass, beginning at the rebellion of South Carolina, which will eventually terminate in the death and misery of many souls." The prophecy also spoke of a time when "war will be poured out upon all nations." Nearly thirty years later, the prophecy began to be fulfilled when shots were fired at Ft. Sumter in Charleston, South Carolina, in April 1861 to open America's Civil War.

Concerning Christmas Day 1835 Joseph wrote, "Enjoyed myself at home with my family, all day, it being Christmas, the only time I have had this privilege so satisfactorily for a long time." Joseph's 1838 Christmas, however, was not so joyful. He, along with other Church leaders, including his brother Hyrum, spent the day as they would every other day of December 1838, imprisoned in Liberty, Missouri. Emma, who had been permitted to visit Joseph a few days before Christmas, spent the day at Far West with their children. So also did Hyrum's wife, Mary Fielding, and her one-month-old son, Joseph F. Smith.

In 1843 England was introduced at Christmas to a "Ghostly little book" in which author Charles Dickens intended "to raise the Ghost of an Idea" and not put his "readers out of humour with themselves, with each other, with the season, or with me." Shortly

A Christmas Carol would become a best-seller in America as well. Back in Illinois in 1843, Joseph Smith's Christmas celebration reflected the "Christmas Present" activities of Ebenezer Scrooge's nephew rather than those of the aging miser. However, like Scrooge, Joseph's Christmas sleep was also disturbed, although the visitors he reported differed greatly from those that haunted Scrooge:

> This morning, about one o'clock, I was aroused by an English sister, Lettice Rushton, widow of Richard Rushton, Senior, (who, ten years ago, lost her sight,) accompanied by three of her sons, with their wives, and her two daughters, with their husbands, and several of her neighbors, singing, "Mortals, awake! With angels join," &c., which caused a thrill of pleasure to run through my soul. All of my family and boarders arose to hear the serenade, and I felt to thank my Heavenly Father for their visit, and blessed them in the name of the Lord.

The greater part of 25 December 1843 was a mixture of pleasure and business for Joseph. During the morning, several brethren from "Morley Settlement" sought his counsel. In the early afternoon "about fifty couples" shared a Christmas feast. Their meal was interrupted by a couple who had come to be married. Since Joseph was busy as host, Brigham Young performed the ceremony. Joseph also approved a plan that encouraged the sisters of Nauvoo to give "a small weekly subscription for the benefit of the Temple" in the amount of "one cent per week." In the evening, Joseph wrote, "a large party supped at my house, and spent the evening in music, dancing, &c., in a most cheerful and friendly manner." The party was made even more joyful by the arrival of Orrin Porter Rockwell, who had spent nearly a year in a Missouri jail, where he had been held without a trial on the attempted murder of ex-Missouri Governor Lilburn Boggs.

The Prophet also found creative ways to help those less fortunate and in need of a helping hand. As mayor of Nauvoo, Joseph was asked to render a judgment on a black man named Anthony who was illegally selling liquor. Anthony begged for leniency, pointing out that he needed the money to secure the freedom of his child, who was a slave in a southern state. Joseph told him, "I am sorry, Anthony, but the law must be observed and we will have to impose a fine." The next day the Prophet gave Anthony a fine horse to sell toward the purchase of the child's freedom.

One Nauvoo resident looked with satisfaction on Joseph's labors on the outside of his house, for he kept his yard clean and his woodpile neatly stacked. This same man, however, did not look favorably upon the Prophet's willingness to help with domestic chores inside the house. He did not think a great man should build a kitchen fire, carry out ashes, bring in wood and water, and assist in the care of children. To fetch and carry flour, he told Joseph, was "too terrible a humiliation for you who are the head, and you should not do it." The Prophet quietly listened and then answered, "If there be humiliation in a man's house who but the head

> *I . . . visited with a brother and sister from Michigan, who thought that "a prophet is always a prophet;" but I told them that a prophet was a prophet only when he was acting as such.*
>
> —Comments of Joseph Smith, 8 February 1843.

of that house should or could bear that humiliation?"

Susan Johnson Martineau, who lived in nearby Ramus, recalled that "Joseph with Heber C. Kimball, Jedediah M. Grant and some others from Nauvoo, whose names I do not now remember, partook of a Christmas dinner at my father's; and standing at the head of the table he carved the turkey. Fearing that his clothing might accidentally be soiled, my step-mother, Susan Bryant Johnson tied a long apron upon him. He laughed and said it was well for he did not know what might happen to him. My brother Seth and I were in the room, admiring, in our childish way, him whom we thought the greatest man on earth."

Like all men, even great ones, Joseph was mortal. As if anticipating his impending death, he began to ensure that the Church was properly organized, and he expanded his greatest teachings during the last few months of his life. By 1844, the Twelve had assumed a greater role in helping with Church leadership, Joseph Smith purposely tutoring them in their role as "a quorum, equal in authority and power to the three presidents [First Presidency]" (D&C 107). In March 1844, the Prophet held a series of meetings in which he gave

1843

Joseph Smith attended court in Springfield on a writ of habeas corpus; was elected mayor in the municipal election; obtained half interest in the Maid of Iowa steamship; met with Stephen A. Douglas, prophesying that Douglas would aspire to the presidency but feel the hand of the Almighty upon him if he turned his hand against the Latter-day Saints; recorded a revelation previously received pertaining to the new and everlasting covenant (D&C 132); was arrested while visiting his sister at Dixon, Illinois, but was saved from being kidnapped and taken to Missouri by his friends; moved into the Mansion House and opened it as a hotel

Charles Dickens published *A Christmas Carol*

The first powdered laundry soap, Benjamin Babbitt's Best Soap, was sold

Explorer John C. Fremont began a year-long exploration of the West, resulting in an accurate survey of the emigrant route to Oregon and a better understanding of California and the Great Basin

The Mansion of Happiness became a popular new board game; players had to avoid financial ruin and imprisonment to achieve love, spiritual enrichment, and the ultimate goal: eternal happiness

Ulysses S. Grant graduated from West Point, ranking in the middle of his class

The first matinee was offered at Mitchell's Olympic Theater in New York City

Skiing as a sport began at Tromso, Norway

I do not govern the people. I teach them correct principles and they govern themselves.

—Erastus Snow, recounting Joseph Smith's response to a question from United States senator Stephen A. Douglas during a May 1843 visit to Nauvoo. Douglas expressed surprise at the ease with which Joseph managed the Latter-day Saints. "We cannot do it," Douglas noted. "What is the secret of your success?"

the keys of the kingdom to the Twelve Apostles, laying a foundation for succession. After Joseph's murder, Brigham Young testified, "Joseph conferred upon our heads all the keys and powers belonging to the Apostleship which he himself held before he was taken away, and no man or set of men can get between Joseph and the Twelve. . . . Joseph said to the Twelve, 'I have laid the foundation and you must build thereon, for upon your shoulders the kingdom rests.'"

In a 7 April 1844 talk honoring Church member King Follett, who died the previous month, the Prophet Joseph gave the world a clear and hope-filled understanding of the creation, the nature and character of God, mankind's potential for eternal progression, and the bonds between generations. Joseph asked the congregation, "What kind of a being is God? . . . I want you to know Him and to be familiar with Him. . . . Open your ears and hear, all ye ends of the earth. . . . I say, if you were to see him today, you would see him like a

man in form—like yourselves in all the person, image, and very form as a man." He consoled "those who mourn for the loss of their friends," asking, "Is there nothing to be done?—no preparation—no salvation for our fathers and friends who have died without having had the opportunity to obey the decrees of the Son of Man?" The Prophet powerfully declared, "God hath made a provision that every spirit in the eternal world can be . . . saved unless he has committed unpardonable sin." Continuing his oration, Joseph taught, "We have reason to have the greatest hope and consolations for our dead of any people on the earth; for we have seen them walk worthily in our midst, and seen them sink asleep in the arms of Jesus; and those who have died in the faith are now in the celestial kingdom of God."

In May 1844, at a Nauvoo political convention, Joseph Smith was officially nominated to run for U.S. president, and Sidney Rigdon was picked to run for vice-president. In early February 1844, Joseph had published

All the power that I desire or have sought to obtain has been the enjoyment of the constitutional privilege for which my fathers shed their blood, of living in peace in the society of my wife and children, and enjoying the society of my friends and that religious liberty which is the right of every American citizen, of worshiping according to the dictates of his conscience and the revelations of God. . . . If it has been demonstrated that I have been willing to die for a "Mormon," I am bold to declare before Heaven that I am just as ready to die in defending the rights of a Presbyterian, a Baptist, or a good man of any other denomination; for the same principle which would trample upon the rights of the Latter-day Saints would trample upon the rights of the Roman Catholics, or of any other denomination who may be unpopular and too weak to defend themselves.

—Comments of Joseph Smith, 4 and 9 July 1843.

West view of the Capitol, Washington, D.C., 1839

West front of the Capitol, Washington, D.C., 1828

his platform in a pamphlet titled *Views of the Powers and Policy of the Government of the United States*. The 7 February 1844 issue of the *Nauvoo Neighbor* enthusiastically endorsed Joseph's candidacy when it declared that "General Joseph Smith" was the answer to "who should be our next president?" Brigham Young at April Conference informed the Saints, "It is now time to have a President of the United States. Elders will be sent to preach the Gospel and electioneer. The government belongs to God." Hyrum Smith added, "We want a President of the U.S., not a party President, but a President of the whole people." As part of his platform, Joseph advocated a strong federal government with power to protect people from the abuses of state and local government. He also actively campaigned for the abolition of slavery, a national bank, and the annexation of Oregon and Texas. Soon Church leaders left Nauvoo to campaign throughout the United States, while Rigdon ran his campaign from Pennsylvania, where he had previously moved.

During the winter and spring of 1844, neighboring gentiles were growing particularly anxious and becoming antagonistic of Nauvoo prosperity under Joseph Smith's increasingly centralized political and religious power—he simultaneously served as ecclesiastical leader, land agent, merchant, mayor, and head of the municipal militia, the Nauvoo Legion. Threats and fear of physical violence prompted the Prophet to warn in a December 1843 speech to the Nauvoo police, "There are speculators in this State who want to sell revolving pistols to us, in order to fight Missourians, and at the same time inciting the Missourians to fight us. Don't buy: it would be better to buy ploughshares and raise corn with them."

Joseph Smith, "General Smith's Views of the Powers and Policies of the Government"

Additional dissension and tension grew as rumors spread of Smith and selected associates teaching and practicing polygamy. In the spring of 1844, a band of excommunicated Mormons, alienated Mormons, and hostile non-Mormons united to publish the inflammatory *Nauvoo Expositor* in an effort to undermine Joseph. At the same time, the 29 May issue of the *Warsaw Signal* warned that "Joe Smith, is not safe out of Nauvoo. We would not be surprised to hear of his death by violent means in a short time. He has deadly enemies. . . . The feeling in this country is now lashed to its utmost pitch, and it will break forth in fury upon the slightest provocation."

Less than two weeks later, on 10 June 1844, the Nauvoo City Council, at Joseph's urging, declared the *Nauvoo Expositor* a public nuisance and ordered it destroyed. The next day, Vilate Kimball reported that Nauvoo was a "scene of great confusion last night, some hundred of the Brethren turned out and burned the printing press, and all the aparatus pertaining to the office of the opposite party. . . . They have sworn revenge, and no doubt will have it." Indeed, the *Warsaw Signal* rallied its readers to respond to the destruction of the *Expositor*: "Arise, one and all!!! Can you stand by, and suffer such infernal devils! to rob men of their property and rights, without avenging them? We have no time for comment; every man will make his own. Let it be made with powder and ball!"

Following the destruction of the *Expositor*, Illinois governor Thomas Ford ordered Joseph Smith to stand trial for treason against the state of Illinois. Later in the evening of 22 June 1844, Joseph and his brother Hyrum crossed the Mississippi River to seek refuge in the West. The following morning the pleas of family and friends brought them back to Nauvoo. Governor Ford promised their safety if they went to the county seat and submitted themselves to arrest, but Joseph prophesied prior to leaving for Carthage on 24 June, "I am going like a lamb to the slaughter."

Lt. Gen. Joseph Smith in full dress uniform of Nauvoo Legion

Destruction of the *Nauvoo Expositor*, 1844

BUSY AS BEES

As towns and cities grew in Young America, the social structure of the nation changed, including how Americans found recreation. While life on the farm usually required contributions of all family members from the youngest to the oldest to meet the seemingly never-ending work, many "city folk" found themselves freed from the constant toil. As leisure time grew during the early nineteenth century, an increasing number of American children living in cities and towns became the first generation for which playing and toys were an integral part of childhood. City life further provided regular entertainment opportunities for all ages in the form of theaters, concerts, and other public amusements. Throughout the country, traveling entertainment troupes, such as "Showboats" that began plying America's waterways in 1831, drew large crowds. Physical activities were also a popular pastime. "Rounders," or "town ball," was a favorite diversion, although it was frequently played differently from location to location until Abner Doubleday codified rules that led to baseball as we know it today. Gymnasiums were also established in larger cities.

The changes were not entirely welcomed. In the late 1820s, Lydia Maria Child decried in her *Frugal Housewife* some of what she saw:

> There is one kind of extravagance rapidly increasing in this county, which, in its effects on our purses and our habits, is one of the worst kinds of extravagance; I mean the rage for travelling, and for public amusements. The good old home habits of our ancestors are breaking up— it will be well if our virtue and our freedom do not follow them! It is easy to laugh at such prognostics,—and we are well aware that the virtue we preach is considered almost obsolete,—but let any reflecting mind inquire how decay has begun in all republics, and then let them calmly ask themselves whether we are in no danger, in departing thus rapidly from the simplicity and industry of our forefathers.

In rural America, however, Child's ideals largely remained intact. Frontier families still had overwhelming amounts of work to accomplish. "Country folk" generally provided their own subsistence as well as most of their own entertainment. Since much of their time was spent isolated from other people, they looked forward to any event that brought them together with neighbors in a social setting and provided new entertainment. Religious revivals, such as those held in western New York around 1820, helped fill the bill. Many attended for the social and recreational aspect rather than the spiritual benefit. The Fourth of July, election day, and the annual militia muster were also events that incorporated social components.

Given the seemingly unending work, Americans also found ways to turn work into play through such favorite activities as barn raisings and husking and quilting bees. These "bees" buzzed with the sound of gossip and laughter. Homes and barns were raised, corn was husked, and quilts were made, all in a social setting.

A man finding a red ear of corn during a husking bee was entitled to a kiss from the girl of his choice. Concerning quilting bees, one person wrote, "There is, indeed, nothing to compare to a country quilting bee for the simple and unaffected happiness which it affords all parties. . . . No debts, nor duns, nor panics, nor poverty, nor wealth disturbs their thoughts or mars the joyousness of the hour. Serene as a summer's day, and cloudless as the skies in June, the moments hurry by, as they ply their nimble needles and sing their simple songs, or whisper their tales of love, heedless of the great world."

Noah Webster's efforts to create standardized, simplified spellings led to the establishment in the 1800s of a uniquely American event—the spelling bee. Thanks to Webster and his dictionary, a girl living on an isolated farm could compete on an equal footing with one attending a city school.

Joseph Smith frequently found recreation in the homemade fun of the frontier. He joined in games of "town ball" and pulled sticks against all comers. He loved to wrestle; some claim he was never bested.

Joseph also intertwined play and work. After gathering a group of boys together for a game of ball, Joseph then led his fellow ballplayers to the home of one of Nauvoo's widows who needed help.

While dancing and other "worldly entertainments" were frowned upon by many religions, Joseph encouraged dancing, the performance of stage plays, and concerts by bands and orchestras, such as the Nauvoo Brass Band. These activities were not inherently evil, he taught, but became evil only when used for evil purposes. Like Thomas Jefferson before him, Joseph did not like dining alone and took great delight in entertaining guests at his home.

A BOY'S THANKSGIVING

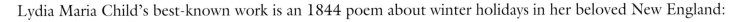

Lydia Maria Child's best-known work is an 1844 poem about winter holidays in her beloved New England:

Over the river, and through the wood,
to Grandfather's house we go;
the horse knows the way to carry the sleigh
through the white and drifted snow.

Over the river, and through the wood,
to Grandfather's house away!
We would not stop for doll or top,
for 'tis Thanksgiving Day.

Over the river, and through the wood—
oh, how the wind does blow!
It stings the toes and bites the nose,
as over the ground we go.

Over the river, and through the wood,
with a clear blue winter sky.
The dogs do bark and the children hark,
as we go jingling by.

Over the river, and through the wood,
to have a first-rate play.
Hear the bells ring, "Ting a ling ding!"
Hurray for Thanksgiving Day!

Over the river, and through the wood—
no matter for winds that blow;
Or if we get the sleigh upset
into a bank of snow.

Over the river, and through the wood,
to see little John and Ann;
we will kiss them all, and play snowball
and stay as long as we can.

Over the river, and through the wood,
trot fast, my dapple gray!
Spring over the ground like a
*   hunting-hound!*
For 'tis Thanksgiving Day.

Over the river, and through the wood
and straight through the barnyard gate.
We seem to go extremely slow—
it is so hard to wait!

Over the river, and through the wood—
Old Jowler hears our bells;
he shakes his paw with a loud bow-wow,
and thus the news he tells.

Over the river, and through the wood—
when Grandmother sees us come,
she will say, "O, dear, the children are here,
bring pie for everyone."

Over the river, and through the wood—
now Grandmother's cap I spy!
Hurrah for the fun! Is the pudding done?
Hurrah for the pumpkin pie!

AMERICA'S DA VINCI

Samuel F. B. Morse has been called "the American Leonardo" because, like the great Italian, he was an artist with wide-ranging interests in many areas, particularly scientific pursuits. Although few would place Morse's art in the category of *The Last Supper*, the American's contributions to science eclipsed those of his more famous counterpart. Because da Vinci's inventions were remarkably ahead of their time, they seldom advanced beyond the theoretical stage. Morse, on the other hand, showing the American genius of adopting ideas, built upon the work of others and implemented new, beneficial technology.

As a child in Massachusetts, Morse had a great interest in painting. If he had been born at an earlier time, he might have reached his stated goal "to rival the genius of a Raphael, a Michelangelo or a Titian." But after studying at the London Royal Academy, he found little interest in his historical canvases. He therefore turned to the growing practice of portrait painting, plying his trade on both sides of the ocean. Two of his best-known portraits were of Danish sculptor Betel Thorvaldsen, whose most famous work is the *Christus*, and of the Marquis de Lafayette, the much-beloved Frenchman who helped the United States win its War of Independence. A professor of painting and sculpture at the University of the City of New York, he also found time to invent a new water pump for fire

Samuel F. B. Morse

engines and a machine for sculpting marble, neither of which were profitable to him.

The seed for his most famous invention, the electronic telegraph, was planted in 1832 when he overheard a discussion about the recent discovery of electromagnets while returning from Europe. By 1835, he had built an experimental version of the telegraph, only four years after the discovery of the laws of magnetic induction. The following year he began working full-time on his idea after he failed to obtain the expected commission to paint the United States Capitol rotunda. During this time, he perfected a circuit relay that allowed transmission of electrical impulses over great distances.

In 1838, he devised the code that bears his name—the dots and dashes of which were based largely on semaphore signals. At that time, Congress was considering the establishment of a semaphore telegraph system to communicate long distances, and Morse proposed the electronic telegraph as a better alternative. Although he would receive a United States patent for his telegraph in 1840, it would be several more years before money was appropriated for a test.

Finally, on 24 May 1844, after twelve years of working out details and getting wires strung between Washington, D.C., and Baltimore, a group of dignitaries gathered in the Supreme Court chambers in the Capitol in Washington D.C. as Samuel F. B. Morse typed out the first message to be sent over his newly constructed electronic telegraph line. At the other end of the line, at the Baltimore and Ohio railroad depot at Baltimore, Maryland, Morse's message was successfully deciphered: "What hath God wrought?"

Although he had spent years trying to make his idea work, Morse felt that this first message, a quotation from Numbers 23:23, was apropos. He had come to recognize that the principles behind the telegraph had existed since the planet's creation. He believed that God had worked the miracle by constituting matter as He did, although He had left it to others to discover the principles and to Morse to figure out how to combine them to send messages.

After the first message was sent, someone observed that it would now be possible for Maine to talk to Florida. "Yes, but has Maine anything to say to Florida?" Ralph Waldo Emerson jokingly asked. The answer seemed to be a resounding yes. Within seconds of Henry Clay's nomination as Whig candidate for president in Baltimore later in the summer of 1844, the news was being spread through the nation's capital. Now people at a distance could communicate with each other almost as if in the same room.

After the initial demonstration, Congress refused to purchase Morse's patents or pay for additional lines. Government officials failed to see its potential, but others did not. Morse sold the patent rights to private companies, and telegraph lines quickly spread across the nation. By 1846 the major eastern United States cities were connected. By 1851 more than fifty telegraph companies were operating, including American Telegraph, which later became American Telegraph and Telephone (AT&T). In 1861 Ezra Cornell's Western Union company succeeded in stretching telegraph wires from coast to coast, with the last wires being connected in the Utah Territory. The Pony Express, which had been established only months earlier, was put out of business. With his profits, Cornell founded a university on his farmland in Ithaca, New York.

Morse's other major contribution, while less known, is no less important to Americans today. During an extended trip to Europe, where he had gone to demonstrate the telegraph to the Academy of Sciences and to obtain the European patents for it, the French government announced Louis Daguerre's invention of photography. Morse immediately showed an interest in the new technology, and in March 1839 Daguerre graciously agreed to meet with him. Possibly the first American to view a photograph, he was the first to describe photography in a letter to his brothers, which was published in the *New York Observer* the following month. Photography, Morse concluded, was "one of the most beautiful discoveries of the age."

After returning to the United States later that fall with information in hand on how to create a daguerreotype, he set to work adapting Daguerre's technology to his own interest in portraits. Initially the time needed to expose a photograph—upwards of an hour—seemingly made portraits out of the question. By the spring of 1840, Morse and a partner had found a way to shorten the time needed to create an image by concentrating the sun's rays on "sitters" by means of mirrors. Opening one of the earliest photographic "parlors," Morse used the profits from his daguerreotype studio to continue working on the telegraph.

As the father of American photography, Morse taught the art to many, including famed Civil War photographer Matthew Brady. Shortly before his death, Morse attended a service in 1871 to mark his eightieth birthday, during which his statue was unveiled in Central Park in New York City.

If, then, the hand of God in all these things that I have accomplished towards the salvation of a priest-ridden generation, in the short space of twelve years, through the boldness of the plan of preaching the Gospel, and the boldness of the means of declaring repentance and baptism for the remission of sins, and a reception of the Holy Ghost by laying on of the hands agreeably to the authority of the Priesthood, and the still more bold measures of receiving direct revelation from God, through the Comforter, as promised, and by which means all holy men from ancient times till now have spoken and revealed the will of God to men, with the consequent "success" of the gathering of the Saints, throws any "charm" around my being, and "points me out as the most extraordinary man of the age," it demonstrates the fact that truth is mighty and must prevail, and that one man empowered from Jehovah has more influence with the children of the kingdom than eight hundred million led by the precepts of men.

—Joseph Smith to James Arlington Bennett,
13 November 1843.

The Prophet Joseph surrenders

The Hamilton Hotel at Carthage Illinois

1844

Joseph Smith declared his candidacy for U.S. president; conferred the keys of the kingdom upon the Quorum of the Twelve; delivered his majestic King Follett discourse; as mayor of Nauvoo ordered the destruction of the *Nauvoo Expositor*; attempted to go west but instead went to Carthage at the request of his friends; was martyred at Carthage Jail along with his brother Hyrum

Alexandre Dumas published *The Three Musketeers*

The Baptist Church split into Northern and Southern conventions over the issue of slavery

The Dominican Republic gained independence from Haiti

James Polk was elected the eleventh U.S. president

The Young Men's Christian Association (YMCA) was founded in London, England

Having predicted the world's end would occur in April 1844, renowned revivalist William Miller proclaimed Christ's second coming for 22 October 1844

Black Canadian inventor Cyrus McCoy was born; his automatic lubricating system prompted people to insist their engines be equipped with "the real McCoy"

Joseph requested my father to lend him $100.00 to pay the lawyer who defended Porter Rockwell. He explained the situation, and father freely counted out the money. "This shall be returned within three days, if I am alive," said the Prophet, and departed. My aunt, father's sister, who was camped with us, was quite wrathy, and called my father very foolish and unwise.

"Don't you know, Thomas," said she, "you will never see a cent of that money again. Here are your family without a home, and you throw your money away."

"Don't worry, Katie," father replied, "if he cannot pay it, he is welcome to it."

This conversation was held before us children, and I thought seriously about it. Would he pay it, or would he not? But I had strong faith that he would. The day came when it was to be paid. A cold, wet, rainy day. The day passed. Night came; 9 o'clock, 10 o'clock, and we all retired for the night. Shortly after there was a knock at the door. Father arose and went to it, and there in the driving rain stood the Prophet Joseph.

"Here, Brother Thomas, is the money." A light was struck, and seated at the table, he counted out the $100.00 in gold. He said, "Brother Thomas, I have been trying all day to raise this sum, for my honor was at stake. God bless you."

—Recollections of Sarah M. Pomeroy.

During this time of excitement, Vilate Kimball witnessed the mood of Nauvoo and reported, "Hundreds have left the city since the fuss commenced. Most of the merchants on the hill have left." Yet the majority of the faithful held tight, not letting fear dictate their action—instead, feeling a "confidence in the Lord, that He would presurve us from the ravages of our enemies."

I never told you I was perfect; but there is no error in the revelations which I have taught. Must I, then, be thrown away as a thing of naught?

—Comments of Joseph Smith, 2 May 1944

Some say I do not interpret the Scripture the same as they do. . . . I have it from God, and get over it if you can.

—Comments of Joseph Smith, 16 June 1944.

On the morning of Thursday, 27 June, Dan Jones, after passing the night in jail with Joseph and Hyrum, left to inquire of the guards about a disturbance during the night. Jones later reported that several men had rushed the jail in the middle of the night but hesitated upon hearing movement in the room. "The Prophet with a 'Prophet's voice' called out 'Come on ye assassins we are ready for you, and would as willingly die now as at daylight,'" Jones wrote. The mobbers retreated. Frank A. Worrell, officer of the guards, spoke words to Jones that set the mood and predicted the course of the day: "We had too much trouble to bring old Joe here to let him ever escape alive, and unless you want to die with him you had better leave before sundown. . . . You'll see that I can prophesy better than Old Joe, for neither he nor his brother . . . will see the sun set today." Jones tried to return to the jail but was not allowed to do so.

Late Thursday afternoon on 27 June, a mob of about a hundred men gathered, disguised their faces, and then stormed the jailhouse, charging up the stairs and firing through the door into the room housing

Courthouse in Carthage, Illinois

Joseph, Hyrum, John Taylor, and Willard Richards. Shot in the face through the door, Hyrum fell to the ground a dead man. Joseph opened the door and fired into the narrow hallway crowded with assassins while Taylor and Richards attempted to deflect the muskets with their canes. Taylor tried to escape out a window but was shot five times before rolling under the bed. Joseph also went to the open window in an attempt to escape but was struck in the collarbone and chest. Fatally wounded, he fell out the window—his last words were "O Lord, my God!"

Joseph had previously prophesied that Richards would one day stand while bullets whizzed around him and would escape unharmed. Amazingly, Richards was not wounded, and at 8:05 P.M., after a coroner's inquest, he wrote a brief note communicating the shocking, haunting news to Nauvoo: "Joseph and Hyrum are dead. Taylor wounded. . . . I am well. Our guard was forced, as we believe, by a band of Missourians from 100 to 200. The job was done in an instant, and the party fled towards Nauvoo instantly. This is as I believe it. The citizens here are afraid of the Mormons attacking them. I promise them no!"

The hearts of the Saints, which the Prophet had so warmed, would grow cold with sadness as word of the martyrdom spread.

> *I am going like a lamb to the slaughter, but I am calm as a summer's morning. I have a conscience void of offense toward God and toward all men. If they take my life I shall die an innocent man, and my blood shall cry from the ground for vengeance, and it shall be yet said of me, He was murdered in cold blood!"*
>
> —Comments of Joseph Smith, 24 June 1844, prior to leaving for Carthage.

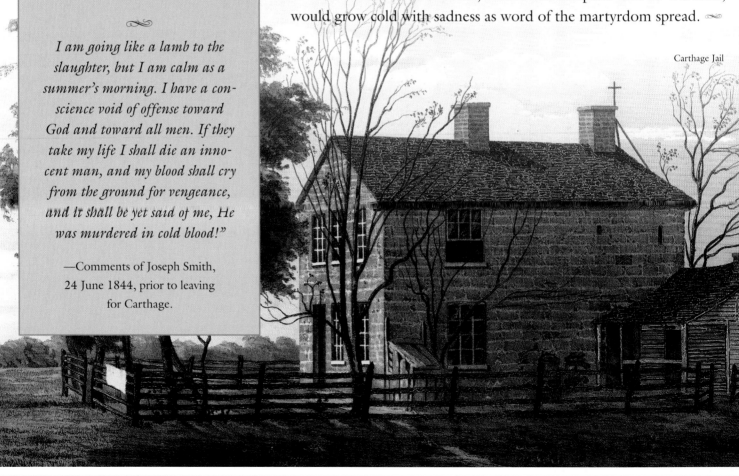

Carthage Jail

27 JUNE 1844

As spring began to glow with the promise of summer, unwelcome violence pointed to a clash pitting the ideals of liberty and equality against the latent reality of cultural and religious divisions in 1844 America. On May 8, Thomas Cope recorded in his diary the ominous eruptions near his neighborhood: "10 o'clock—fire engines out—State House bell ringing. A powerful light in the direction of St. Augustine, no doubt 'tis on fire. The flame ascends higher and the whole City is lighted up." The flames were evidence of the fear and misunderstanding that exploded into open warfare in the Philadelphia suburb of Kensington as Irish-Catholics and Protestants attacked each other. Protestant rioters set fire to St. Michael's Catholic Church and attacked the Sisters of Charity Seminary before turning their destruction to St. Augustine's Catholic Church in nearby Philadelphia. As the churches burned, the hate-filled rioters cheered. The violence, which Pennsylvania governor David R. Porter quieted by calling out the state militia, erupted again in July's searing heat.

The cause was rooted in Philadelphia's American-born Protestant community's decade-old fear that the increasing number of Catholic immigrants were gaining too much influence in politics, education, and values. This growing mutual distrust was played out in the Protestant-run public schools in which the Protestant King James Bible was used for required daily readings and the schools' textbooks contained anti-Catholic rhetoric. When Catholic leaders persuaded local school boards to allow reading from both Protestant and Catholic versions of the Bible, to stop using anti-Catholic textbooks, and to allow Catholic students to leave classrooms during certain religious exercises, rumors quickly spread about total cessation of Bible readings and the Catholic takeover of schools. Ultimately, the violence claimed twenty to thirty lives and caused more than $250,000 worth of property destruction. It also forced a community into deeper divisions as Protestants continued to ignore Catholic religious rights and the Catholics became more insular.

To the south of Philadelphia, more hopeful events were in the works. Communication distance became shorter on 24 May when inventor Samuel F. Morse's message "What hath God wrought!" was tapped in dots and dashes sent along a forty-four-mile telegraph line strung from Washington, D.C., to Baltimore, Maryland. Three days later, news that the Democratic National convention in Baltimore had nominated New York Senator Silas Wright for vice-president was reported to Washington over the new telegraph. On receiving the news, Mr. Wright declined the nomination by telegraph. The Convention, in disbelief, awaited a messenger on horseback from Washington to confirm Wright's telegraph.

America's frontier was shifting ever westward as "Oregon fever" intensified. In 1843, some one thousand men, women, and children braved the arduous two-thousand-mile journey from Missouri to Oregon in an effort to better their lives. In 1844, the move to Oregon continued as politician James Polk won the presidency by echoing expansionists' patriotic cry of "Fifty-four forty or fight!"—which referred to the northern latitude for the United States claim of Oregon land.

Although desirous of expansion in the southwest, on 8 June 1844, the United States Senate rejected (thirty-five to sixteen) the annexation treaty between the U.S. and Texas. After months of great effort and intense negotiations, Texas would become the twenty-eighth state on 29 December 1845.

Throughout the spring of 1844, anti-Mormons, excommunicated Mormons, and disenchanted members worked together to bring down the Prophet

Joseph Smith. They claimed he was a fallen prophet as they denounced and misinterpreted many of his teachings, including polygamy. To undermine the Prophet, the dissidents published the inflammatory *Nauvoo Expositor*. On 10 June, after long deliberation and at the Prophet's urging, the Nauvoo City Council declared the *Expositor* "to be a nuisance and ordered the city marshal to destroy it."

Following the destruction of the *Nauvoo Expositor*, Illinois governor Thomas Ford ordered the arrest of Joseph Smith on the charge of treason. On Sunday, 23 June, fearing for their lives, Joseph and Hyrum Smith, accompanied by Willard Richards and Orrin Porter Rockwell, crossed the Mississippi River, hoping to take refuge in the West. The accusations of cowardice and the pleas of family and friends caused Joseph to lament, "If my life is of no value to my friends, it is of none to myself." Seeking advice, he asked Rockwell, "What shall I do?" His friend replied, "You are the oldest and ought to know best; as you make your bed, I will be with you." Joseph, addressing his brother, inquired, "Brother Hyrum, you are the oldest, what shall we do?" Hyrum counseled that they return, give themselves up, and "see the thing out." The Prophet replied, "If you go back I will go with you, but we shall be butchered." Perhaps in an effort to ease his brother's fears, Hyrum puzzlingly responded, "No, no; let us go back and put our trust in God, and we shall not be harmed. The Lord is in it. If we live or have to die, we will be reconciled to our fate." As Joseph and his companions returned, he again warned, "We are going back to be slaughtered." The party returned to Nauvoo on the same day they left.

Early the next morning, with Governor Ford's promise of safety, the two brothers departed Nauvoo for Carthage. Passing the temple, Joseph slowed his horse to gaze upon it and the city, saying "This is the loveliest place and the best people under the heavens; little do they know the trials that await them."

ASSASSINATION OF JOSEPH SMITH.

Many years later, Eunice B. Snow recalled seeing Joseph leave for Carthage: "He passed our house with his brother Hyrum, both riding. My mother and I were standing in the dooryard, and as he passed he bowed with uplifted hat to my mother. Hyrum seemed like one in a dream, sad and despondent, taking no notice of anyone. They were on their way to Carthage Jail, and it was the last time I saw the Prophet alive."

On the morning of 27 June at 8:20 A.M., the Prophet addressed a letter to Emma in which he told her that Governor Ford "continues his courtesies, and permits us to see our friends." After giving her instructions on receiving and working with the governor, Joseph added a postscript: "Dear Emma, I am very much resigned to my lot, knowing I am justified, and have done the best that could be done. Give my love to the children and all my friends."

As the day progressed, friends and associates came and went:

11:30 A.M. A. W. Babbitt arrived to read a note from Oliver Cowdery,

12:20 P.M. Joseph wrote a memo to lawyer O.H. Browning to engage his services,

1:15 P.M. Joseph, Hyrum, and Willard Richards dined in their second-story room.

3:15 P.M. Guards became restless and threatening. Elder John Taylor sang *A Poor Wayfaring Man of Grief,* which he sang again at the Hyrum's request.

As John Taylor "was sitting at one of the front windows of the jail," he saw "a number of men, with painted faces, coming around the corner of the jail, and aiming towards the stairs." Shortly after 5:00 P.M., a mob of one to two hundred men gathered and encircled Carthage Jail. They muddied their faces as a disguise, stormed into the jail, charged up the stairs, and fired through the door into the room that held Joseph, Hyrum, John Taylor, and Willard Richards.

Willard Richards later described the scene: "A ball was sent through the door which hit Hyrum on the side of his nose, when he fell backwards, extended at length, without moving his feet. . . . As he struck the floor he exclaimed emphatically, 'I am a dead man.' Joseph looked towards him and responded, 'Oh! dear brother Hyrum!' and opening the door two or three inches with his left hand, discharged one barrel of a six shooter (pistol) at random in the entry. . . . While Mr. Taylor with a walking stick stood by his side and knocked down the bayonets and muskets which were constantly discharging through the doorway, while I stood by him, ready to lend any assistance, with another stick." Taylor tried to escape out a window but was shot five times. He then rolled under the bed. Miraculously, Richards was not wounded.

At an open window, Joseph was struck in the collarbone and the chest. Fatally wounded, he fell out the window, landing on his left side. His dying words were "O Lord, my God!" The mob cried out "He's leaped from the window!" The violent rabble descended the stairs and rushed the body of the Prophet. However, murderous group-think quickly changed into fear, and the mob fled in a panic as the warning "The Mormons are coming!" filled the air. A stunned Willard Richards woefully asked, "Oh! Brother Taylor, is it possible that they have killed both Brother Hyrum and Joseph? It cannot surely be, and yet I saw them shoot them.

"L'assassinat du Prophete Smith, 1844"

209

Oh Lord, my God, spare Thy servants! Brother Taylor, this is a terrible event."

After news of the murder spread, Reverend William G. Brownlow, in the *Jonesborough Whig* delightedly declared, "Three cheers to the brave company who shot him to pieces!" He continued his excited tirade, writing, "That blasphemous wretch Joe Smith, the Mormon Prophet . . . ought to have been dead ten years ago, and . . . those who at length deprived him of his life, have done the cause of God, and of the country, good service."

Typical Latter-day Saint reaction to the murder of the Smith brothers was conveyed by Luman Shirtliff: "This Caused the Greatest Mourning of anything that has ever taken place with this people. A cloud of g[l]oom was spread over the People and Sorrow depicted in every face. On the 28[th] When their

Boddies ware brought into Nauvoo Most of the inhabitants went out and met them and accompanied them to the Mansion. Verry few of the Saints [who] visited their remains . . . [had not] droped a tear over those most Beloved Brothers. On viewing them I could but Call to mind the many Prophets and wise men Whose Blood had bin spiled by Wicked men. . . . I would [have] rather Marched out with the L[e]gion with these men at our head onto the Prairie and faught the Whole United States . . . than to let these Brethren have Bin Murdered. . . . But the [Church] Authorities that ware left said be stil and see the Salvation of God."

The Mormons were suddenly without the guiding leadership of their charismatic prophet. Anti-Mormons hoped the murders would put an end to what they thought was now a leaderless church.

"THE KEYS OF THE KINGDOM ARE RIGHT HERE"

Shortly after 8:00 A.M. on the morning of Friday, 28 June 1844, two wagons piled high with bushes to protect the bodies of Joseph and Hyrum Smith from the blistering heat of the summer sun began the long, mournful journey over the dusty road that led from Carthage to Nauvoo. Among those accompanying the bodies were Willard Richards, who had survived the previous day's murderous barrage, and Samuel H. Smith, brother of the two martyrs. Within a month Samuel would become the third martyr. Having been weakened by a hard ride the previous day escaping from a mob; he soon contracted pneumonia, from which he never recovered. Behind the solemn procession, John Taylor remained in Carthage, which had been nearly deserted out of fear of Mormon retaliation, to recover

The Prophet Joseph

from his wounds. Ahead of them lay the grieving city of Nauvoo, whose residents had already learned of the martyrdom.

When the funeral cortege reached Mulholland Street in mid-afternoon, several thousand stunned residents lined the street, their hearts grieving almost beyond consolation. After the procession reached the Mansion House, the people were firmly instructed to peacefully return to their homes as the blood-covered bodies were taken inside to be prepared for burial. After Dimick and William Huntington and William Marks lovingly cleaned the martyrs, their bereaved widows and children were brought in to see the bodies.

Emma, who was four months pregnant at the time, screamed and fell back upon seeing her deceased

Joseph Smith, the Prophet and Seer of the Lord, has done more, save Jesus only, for the salvation of men in this world, than any other man that ever lived in it. In the short space of twenty years, he has brought forth the Book of Mormon, which he translated by the gift and power of God, . . . has sent the fulness of the everlasting gospel, which it contained, to the four quarters of the earth; has brought forth the revelations and commandments which compose this book of Doctrine and Covenants, and many other wise documents and instructions for the benefit of the children of men . . . and left a fame and name that cannot be slain. He lived great, and he died great in the eyes of God and his people; and like most of the Lord's anointed in ancient times, has sealed his mission and his works with his own blood; and so has his brother Hyrum. In life they were not divided, and in death they were not separated! (D&C 135:3).

husband, but she was caught and supported by Dimick Huntington. "Oh Joseph, Joseph! My husband, my husband! Have they taken you from me at last?" Going to Joseph, she kissed him, called him by name, and begged him to speak to her. She later had to be helped from the room.

Hyrum's wife, Mary, likewise kissed her husband's cheek as tears streamed down her own. "Oh Hyrum, Hyrum! Have they shot you, my dear Hyrum—are you dead? Oh! Speak to me my dear husband. I cannot think you are dead."

Nauvoo, Illinois, ca. 1846

As the long, hot summer day turned to night, a few close friends and relatives were also allowed into the Mansion House to grieve. The mother of the slain martyrs, Lucy Mack Smith, painted the pain of that night: "I had for a long time braced every nerve, roused every energy of my soul, and called upon God to strengthen me; but when I entered that room, and saw my murdered sons extended both at once before my eyes, and heard the sobs and moans of my family . . . it was too much, I sank back, crying to the Lord, in the agony of my soul, 'My God, My God, why hast thou forsaken this family!'" In response Lucy heard a voice reply, "I have taken them to myself, that they may rest."

The next day some ten thousand people viewed the bodies of Joseph and Hyrum. Dan Jones, who had spent time with the martyrs in Carthage Jail, described the scene: "Old, young, male and female together bewail the day—their much loved Prophet and Patriarch from their embraces by ruthless assassins were untimely torn—how can they be comforted?"

During the next several weeks, other Latter-day Saints experienced the sorrow felt at Nauvoo as word of the martyrdom made its way east. In early July,

Emma Smith, ca. 1860

> *Joseph Smith, claiming to be an inspired teacher, faced adversity such as few men have been called to meet, enjoyed a brief season of prosperity such as few men have ever attained, and, finally . . . went cheerfully to a martyr's death.*
>
> —Josiah Quincy, Figures of the Past, 1883.

John M. Horner was stumping for Joseph's presidential campaign in New Jersey. At the close of a speech, a man in the audience proclaimed, "I have one reason to give why Joseph Smith can never be President of the United States; my paper, which I received from Philadelphia this afternoon, says that he was murdered." Horner noted, "The grief and sadness of this heart was beyond the power of man to estimate."

While Latter-day Saints grieved, others rejoiced at the news, believing that with the death of its dynamic leader, the church that Joseph founded would become another flash-in-the-pan religious movement. The *New York Herald* ended its account of the murders with this prediction: "Thus ends Mormonism."

NEW-YORK MESSENGER.
NEW-YORK MESSENGER.
SATURDAY, SEPTEMBER 13, 1845.

The *Herald* was not alone in its bleak forecast. Other newspapers around the country made similar prognostications. Four years later, as the Mormons were establishing a new home and gathering place in the Salt Lake Valley, Thomas Ford, governor of Illinois at the time of the murders, again echoed in his *History of Illinois* what was widely claimed in 1844: "Thus fell Joe Smith, the most successful impostor in modern times; a man who, though ignorant and coarse, had some great natural parts which fitted him for temporary success, but which were so obscured and counteracted by the inherent corruption and vices of his nature that he never could succeed in establishing a system of policy which looked to permanent success in the future."

Sinless as celestial spirits—
Lovely as a morning flow'r,
Comes the smiling infant stranger
In an evil-omen'd hour.
Not to share a father's fondness—
Not to know its father's worth—
By the arm of persecution
'Tis an orphan at its birth!
Thou may'st draw from love and kindness
All a mother can bestow;
But alas! on earth, a father
Thou art destin'd not to know!

Emma Hale Smith holding her son
David Hyrum Smith, ca. 1845

This poem was written by Eliza R. Snow to honor the birth of David Hyrum Smith, the youngest son of Joseph and Emma Smith, born 17 November 1844, five months after his father's martyrdom.

Joseph once noted, "My family was kept in a continual state of alarm, not knowing when I went from home, that I should ever return again; or what would befall me from day to day." The toll of what Emma had endured is evident on her face as she holds her young son.

OF HEAVEN AND EARTH

"I . . . know more than all the world put together. The Holy Ghost does, anyhow, and He is within me, and comprehends more than all the world; and I will associate myself with Him," Joseph Smith boldly proclaimed at the April 1844 funeral of King Follett.

The message of hope Joseph delivered in the "King Follett Discourse" reveals that his knowledge had indeed surpassed the understanding of the theologians of his day. His inspired teachings concerning the nature and character of God, mankind's relationship to his Creator, and the possibilities that awaited King Follett and all mankind in the hereafter were in conflict with the Christian world's views of heaven and hell. When Joseph declared, "It is the first principle of the Gospel to know for a certainty the Character of God, and to know that we may converse with him as one man converses with another, and that he was once a man like us," most who heard his teachings regarding man's potential joyfully embraced them as pure truth. Others, however, viewed Joseph's words as blasphemy worthy of death, and they began plotting toward that end.

Another aspect of Joseph's discourse that went against the religious teaching of the time was his rejection of the traditional Christian belief that the world was created *ex nihilo*—out of nothing: "The learned men who are preaching salvation say that God created the heavens and the earth out of nothing. The reason is, that they are unlearned in the things of God," Joseph declared. "You ask the learned doctors why the world was made out of nothing; and they will answer, 'Doesn't the Bible say He created the world?' And they infer, from the word create, that it must have been made out of nothing." The biblical word "create" derived from *baurau,* which, Joseph explained,

means to organize; the same as a man would organize and use things to build a ship. Hence,

we infer that God Himself had materials to organize the world out of chaos—chaotic matter—which is element and in which dwells all the glory. Element had an existence from the time He had. The pure principles of element are principles that never can be destroyed. They may be organized and reorganized, but not destroyed. Nothing can be destroyed. They never can have a beginning or an ending; they exist eternally.

While Joseph's views on the creation differed dramatically from those of his fellow religionists, they harmonized with what nineteenth-century scientists were increasingly accepting as good science and what is held by the scientific community today as irrefutable law. Sixteen years after the King Follett Discourse, Herbert Spencer addressed the *ex nihilo* doctrine in his 1860 *First Principles:* "There was once universally current, a notion that things could vanish into absolute nothing, or arise out of nothing. . . . The current theology, in its teachings respecting the beginning and end of the world, is clearly pervaded by it. . . . All the apparent proofs that something can come of nothing, a wider knowledge has one by one cancelled."

Joseph gained much of his knowledge concerning the creation of the world through his work on two sets of ancient writings—the book of Moses and the book of Abraham. As early as 1829, the Lord declared to Joseph that "many plain and precious things" lost from the Bible would be restored. At the Lord's command, Joseph began work on an "inspired translation" of the Bible in June 1830. While working on the translation between June 1830 and February 1831, Joseph received through revelation additional writings of Moses. In July 1835, Joseph was given several Egyptian papyrus scrolls to translate, which he announced contained writings of Abraham. Both the book of Moses and the book of Abraham contain accounts of the creation that differ from that found in Genesis.

As with the Book of Mormon, critics have long branded the books of Moses and Abraham as fantasies from Joseph's fertile mind. Modern scientists, however, continue to verify statements concerning the heavens and earth contained in these records. Each book describes the heavens in terms that twenty-first-century astronomers with their powerful telescopes are only now discovering. Joseph had been able to obtain through spiritual eyes knowledge that far exceeded the abilities of nineteenth-century telescopes.

In the book of Abraham, the ancient prophet wrote, "There stood one among them that was like unto God, and he said unto those who were with him: We will go down, for there is space there, and we will take of these materials, and we will make an earth." In the book of Moses, the Lord told the ancient prophet, "Worlds without number have I created. . . . The heavens, they are many, and they cannot be numbered unto man; but they are numbered unto me, for they are mine. And as one earth shall pass away, and the heavens thereof even so shall another come; and there is no end to my works." When John Taylor later recounted to a celebrated group of European scientists what Joseph taught regarding the heavens, one astronomer reportedly responded that although "he had read and studied a great deal," it appeared he had "a good deal more yet to learn."

Scientists today have come to the same realization. In June 2003, astronomers reported the discovery of more than a hundred planets orbiting nearby stars, including one circling 51 Pegasus, a star much like our sun. "We know for certain there are . . . a lot of planets out there," one astronomer stated of the estimated 10 billion planets in our galaxy alone. Later that summer, astronomers released a new estimate of the number of stars in the universe—70 sextillion (70,000,000,000,000,000). One scientist succinctly noted of the number that there were "more stars in the sky than there are grains of sand in every beach and desert on Earth." In August 2004, astronomers announced the discovery of three planets similar in size to the earth, the size of planet believed to be the most advantageous to sustaining life. "It's a unique time in history, finding the first planets reminiscent of those in our own solar system," one astronomer proclaimed. Scientists believe they will soon discover planets with more "life-friendly" orbits.

Also in 2004, astronomers reported the discovery of an estimated ten thousand new galaxies. These galaxies, consisting of a wide range of sizes, shapes, and colors, are a far cry from the traditional spiral and elliptical galaxies previously known. Many of these galaxies are believed to be the youngest ever seen, and they reveal a time when order and structure were just beginning to emerge. They were found in an area approximately one-tenth the diameter of the moon as seen from the earth which was previously believed to be a desolate region because it looks "largely empty" from earth.

Joseph Smith anticipated such discoveries when he wrote to the Saints while imprisoned in Liberty Jail in March 1839:

> God shall give unto you knowledge by his Holy Spirit, yea, by the unspeakable gift of the Holy Ghost, that has not been revealed since the world was until now;
>
> Which our forefathers have awaited with anxious expectation to be revealed in the last times, which their minds were pointed to by the angels, as held in reserve for the fulness of their glory;
>
> A time to come in the which nothing shall be withheld, whether there be one God or many gods, they shall be manifest.
>
> All thrones and dominions, principalities and powers, shall be revealed and set forth upon all who have endured valiantly for the gospel of Jesus Christ. And also, if there be bounds set to the heavens or to the seas, or to the dry land, or to the sun, moon, or stars—
>
> All the times of their revolutions, all the appointed days, months, and years, and all the days of their days, months, and years, and all their glories, laws, and set times, shall be revealed in the days of the dispensation of the fulness of times (D&C 121:26–31).

Nauvoo, 1859

To the surprise and dismay of its enemies and critics, the Church did not die. Ultimately, Joseph Smith, who proclaimed that the Church he established would fill the world, proved a better prophet than the *New York Herald*, Governor Thomas Ford, and the dozens of others who predicted Mormonism's impending demise. What has transpired since that terrible day in June 1844 bears eloquent testimony of the divine work of a singularly remarkable man.

Nearly two weeks after the martyrdom, Brigham Young first heard the rumors of Joseph's death. One week later, on 16 July, he and Orson Pratt were in Petersboro, New Hampshire, when they listened to a letter from Nauvoo giving particulars of the martyrdom. "The first thing I thought of was whether Joseph had taken the keys of the kingdom with him from the earth," Young recalled. "Brother Orson Pratt sat on my left; we were both leaning back on

The object with me is to obey and teach others to obey God in just what He tells us to do. It mattereth not whether the principle is popular or unpopular, I will always maintain a true principle, even if I stand alone in it.
—Comments of Joseph Smith, 21 February 1844.

No man knows my history. I cannot tell it: I shall never undertake it. I don't blame any one for not believing my history. If I had not experienced what I have, I could not have believed it myself. . . . When I am called by the trump of the archangel and weighed in the balance, you will all know me then.

—Comments of Joseph Smith, 7 April 1844.

our chairs. Bringing my hand down on my knee, I said the keys of the kingdom are right here with the Church."

Brigham Young perfectly understood what Joseph himself comprehended prior to leaving for Carthage. The prophet knew that what he left behind was infinitely more important than what assassin's bullets could take away. The knowledge of God and the plan of salvation he had reintroduced to a world "ever seeking but never able to come to a knowledge of the truth," along with restored priesthood power and keys, were what was important. As William W. Phelps told the grieving Saints at Nauvoo during Joseph's funeral, "Be assured . . . the priesthood remains unharmed." Joseph was only the instrument that Jesus Christ had raised up to restore His church once again to the earth.

And that is the secret to understanding the prophet Joseph Smith. He was not about personal power but empowering others. His sole purpose was to help mankind realize its divine potential. "You have not as yet understood how great blessings the Father hath . . . prepared for you," one of his revelations proclaimed. "You cannot bear all things now; nevertheless, be of good cheer, for I will lead you along. The kingdom is yours and the blessings thereof are yours, and the riches of eternity are yours." On another occasion Joseph wrote, "And again I say, how glorious is the voice we hear from heaven, proclaiming in our ears, glory, and salvation, and honor, and immortality, and eternal life; kingdoms, principalities, and powers!"

Like the ancient prophets before him, Joseph Smith brought the word and the will of God to His people. His divine ministry renewed a long-lost vision of life—the bright, the hopeful, and the possible now replaced a world blighted with darkness and negativity. Nauvoo resident George Laub clearly explained what Joseph Smith's lifelong, hard-won efforts meant to him: "The prophet . . . spake with great power and assurance. He expounded the Scripture that it could not be misunderstood for plainness. He also told us the will of the Lord concerning our present situation and state. In this my soul found food, as a hungry man's body that sits to the luxuries of the Earth." Brigham Young proclaimed, "Joseph Smith, the Prophet of the last days, had a happy faculty of reducing the things of heaven to the capacity of persons of common understanding, often in a single sentence throwing a flood of light into the gloom of ages. He had the power to draw the spirits of the people who listened to him to his standard, where they communed with heavenly objects and heavenly principles, connecting the heavenly and the earthly together—in one blending flood of heavenly intelligence."

Joseph reconnected heaven and earth in an era when many, such as Ralph Waldo Emerson, felt

A SUBJECT THAT OUGHT
TO BE OF SURPASSING INTEREST

Thomas Cole

Thomas Cole and Joseph Smith were two Americans inspired by the natural beauty of the world around them.

English-born artist Thomas Cole (1801–1848) was trained as an engraver of woodblocks before his family immigrated to America. In 1818, he first tried his hand at landscape painting while designing patterns for his father's Steubenville, Ohio, wallpaper company. In 1825, his work gained the positive attention of New York City artists and patrons—after which his career as a landscape artist was assured. His romantic, spiritual, and intelligent expressions of nature heightened appreciation of American landscape and helped establish the Hudson River School of painting.

When Joseph Smith wrote his initial account of his first vision in 1832, he specified that his reflections upon nature helped him believe in a God who answered prayers. Written in his own hand, not dictated like later accounts, the spelling and syntax are typical Joseph:

From the age of twelve to fifteen I pondered many things in my heart concerning the sittuation of the world. . . . I looked upon the sun the glorious luminary of the earth and also the moon rolling in their magesty through the heavens and also the Stars Shining in their courses and the earth also upon which I stood and the beast of the field and the fowls of heaven and the fish of the waters and also man walking forth upon the face of the earth in magesty and in the Strength of beauty . . . and when I considered upon these things my heart exclaimed well hath the wise man Said it is a fool that Saith in his heart there is no God my heart exclaimed all these bear testimony and bespeak an omnipotent and omnipreasant power a being who makith Laws and decreeeth and bindeth all things in their bounds . . . and when I considered all these things . . . I cried unto the Lord for mercy for there was none else to whom I could go and obtain mercy and the Lord heard my cry in the wilderness.

Given the awe with which Joseph viewed the world and its creator, it is not surprising that the place he had "previously designed to go" to utter his first prayer was the same woods that helped inspire him to commune with God. It is also understandable that Joseph would later recall that "beautiful, clear day," made even more beautiful and clear by what transpired.

In 1843, Joseph, after recounting to the Saints the goodness of God as manifested in the plan of salvation and baptism for the dead, revisited the subject of nature: "Let the mountains shout for joy, and all ye valleys cry aloud; and all ye seas and dry lands tell the wonders of your Eternal King! And ye rivers, and brooks, and rills, flow down with gladness. Let the woods and all the trees of the field praise the Lord; and ye solid rocks weep for joy! And let the sun, moon, and the morning stars sing together, and let all the sons of God shout for joy! And let the eternal creatures declare his name forever and ever!" (D&C 128:23).

Joseph's simple and concise writing style stands in stark contrast to the style of his day, where complex sentences and flowery language were frequently held as the epitome of good writing. He put forth clear and precise views without a need to dress them up.

Typical of Young America is one of the renowned essays of the nineteenth century, Thomas Cole's classic expression of American aesthetics, "Essay on American Scenery," published in the January 1836 *Atlantic Monthly*. Like Joseph Smith in 1832 and 1843, Cole addressed the ability of nature to bring one closer to God. In this excerpt he also argued for the beauty of America and reflected the awe and pride many Americans felt for their country:

> The essay, which is here offered, is a mere sketch of an almost illimitable subject—American scenery; and in selecting the theme the writer placed more confidence in its overflowing richness than in his own capacity for treating it in a manner worthy of its vastness and importance.

> It is a subject that to every American ought to be of surpassing interest; for, whether he beholds the Hudson mingling waters with the Atlantic, explores the central wilds of this vast continent, or stands on the margin of the distant Oregon, he is still in the midst of American scenery—it is his own land; its beauty, its magnificence, its sublimity, all are his; and how undeserving of such a birthright if he can turn toward it an unobserving eye, an unaffected heart! . . .

> Poetry and Painting sublime and purify thought, by grasping the past, the present, and the future; they give the mind a foretaste of its immortality, and thus prepare it for performing an exalted part amid the realities of life. And rural nature is full of the same quickening spirit; it is, in fact, the exhaustless mine from which the poet and the painter have brought such wondrous treasures—an unfailing fountain of intellectual enjoyment, where all may drink and be awakened to a deeper feeling of the works of genius and a keener perception of the beauty of our existence. For those whose days are all consumed in the low pursuits of avarice, or the gaudy frivolities of fashion, unobservant of nature's loveliness, are unconscious of the harmony of creation. . . .

> The good, the enlightened of all ages and nations have found pleasure and consolation in the beauty of the rural earth. Prophets of old retired into the solitudes of nature to wait the inspiration of heaven. It was on Mount Horeb that Elijah witnessed the mighty wind, the earthquake, and the fire; and heard the "still small voice." That voice is yet heard among the mountains! St. John preached in the desert; the wilderness is yet a fitting place to speak of God. . . .

> The spirit of our society is to contrive but not to enjoy, toiling to produce more toil, accumulating in order to aggrandize. . . .

> I would have it remembered that nature has shed over this land beauty and magnificence . . . it has features, and glorious ones, unknown to Europe. . . .

> . . . Nature has spread for us a rich and delightful banquet. Shall we turn from it? We are still in Eden; the wall that shuts us out of the garden is our own ignorance and folly. . . . May we at times turn from the ordinary pursuits of life to the pure enjoyment of rural nature; which is in the soul like a fountain of cool waters to the way-worn traveler; and let us

> *Learn*
> *The laws by which the Eternal doth sublime*
> *And sanctify his works, that we may see*
> *The hidden glory veiled from vulgar eyes.*

219

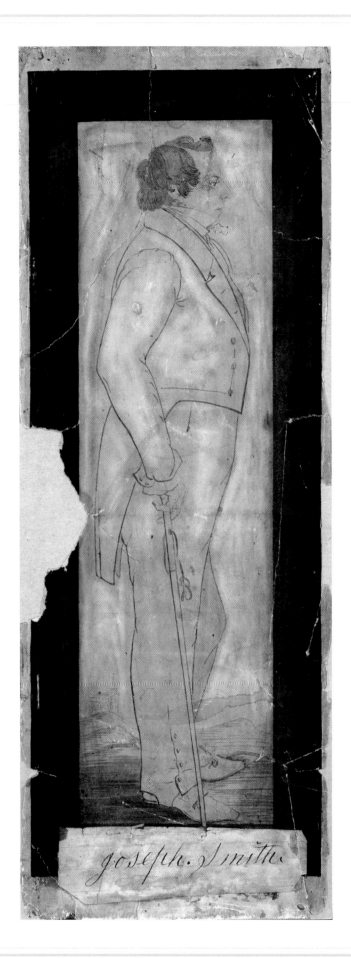

joseph. Smith

disconnected from God and therefore sought spiritual answers in other ways. Many fundamental truths taught in the Bible were denounced or ignored by the churches of the day. At a time when Christianity was coming under assault for having strayed from basic beliefs, Joseph Smith returned Christianity to its origins. His message was one of certainty in an era when uncertainty was the norm; it expressed an absolute belief at a time when competing doctrines and claims by various religions were multiplying.

Joseph was definitive in his pronouncements, sure in his steps. One modern admirer, Harold Bloom, has marveled at what he called the "sureness of [Joseph's] instincts, his uncanny knowing precisely what is needful for the inauguration of a new faith," and that Joseph "understood not only his own aims but the pragmatics of religion making, or what would work in matters of the spirit." To Joseph, there was little reason to wonder at what he accomplished. He had his errand from the Lord, then sought and obtained access to the mind of Deity. He knew that as long as God was directing him, he would continue on the path the Lord had established. With this assurance he moved ahead, in spite of opposition and his own limitations. He displayed honesty, courage, vitality, and a comprehensiveness that few have come close to matching.

Ultimately, it was revelation that set Joseph Smith apart from his contemporaries. He unequivocally proclaimed that the heavens were again open and that his knowledge was revealed from heaven, not agreed upon in a council or intuitively figured out. Modern revelation was needed to restore truth and understand the true meaning of Christ's doctrine. "Take away the Book of Mormon and the revelations, and where is our religion?" Joseph asked early in his ministry. His critics have recognized this point and tried unsuccessfully to explain his revelations away. But as Joseph forthrightly declared in June 1843, "Many of the sects cry out, 'Oh, I have the testimony of Jesus; I have the spirit of God; but away with Joe Smith; he says he is a prophet; but there are to be no prophets or revelators in the last days.' Stop, sir! The Revelator says that the testimony of Jesus is the spirit of prophecy; so by your own mouth you are condemned."

Joseph proclaimed not only that God talked to him but that revelation was available to all mankind. Having come to know God through the revelatory process, Joseph wanted others to enjoy the same knowledge. He was a conduit to heaven, but individuals did not have to take his word. Anyone could obtain through revelation the same knowledge he had received, no longer having to guess at the meaning of the scriptures. He also taught that as mankind came to understand their Heavenly Father, they would be empowered to accomplish His will. Joseph truly believed this—indeed, he was living proof.

JOSEPH SMITH,   HYRUM SMITH,
Founder of the Mormon Church.   Great Patriarch.
From the original painting in the palace of Brigham Young.

A STATESMANLIKE WORD

In the following selection from his 1883 *Figures of the Past*, Josiah Quincy reflected upon Joseph Smith's plan to end slavery. Although nearly twenty years had passed since the end of the Civil War, the horror of that national tragedy still burned bright in Quincy's mind. The cost to the country, both in terms of lives and money, led him to conclude with others that it would have been better to pay slave owners rather than suffer fratricidal war. Although others before Joseph had generally advocated that the government purchase slaves' freedom, the Boston Brahman continued to be impressed by the specific nature of the plan Joseph presented in his presidential platform:

It may be worth while to remark that Smith's plan was publicly advocated, eleven years later, by one who has mixed so much practical shrewdness with his lofty philosophy. In 1855, when men's minds had been moved to their depths on the question of slavery, Mr. Ralph Waldo Emerson declared that it should be met in accordance "with the interest of the South and with the settled conscience of the North. It is not really a great task, a great fight for this country to accomplish, to buy that property of the planter, as the British nation bought the West Indian slaves." He further says that the "United States will be brought to give every inch of their public lands for a purpose like this." We, who can look back upon the terrible cost of the fratricidal war which put an end to slavery, now say that such a solution of the difficulty would have been worthy a Christian statesman. But if the retired scholar was in advance of his time when he advocated this disposition of the public property in 1855, what shall I say of the political and religious leader who had committed himself, in print, as well as in conversation, to the same course in 1844? If the atmosphere of men's opinions were stirred by such a proposition when war clouds were discernible in the sky, was it not a statesmanlike word eleven years earlier, when the heavens looked tranquil and beneficent?

Joseph's view of God and man's relationship to his Creator further set him apart from other religionists of the day. We know Jesus Christ because Joseph understood the Savior better than other religionists. His life is an example of one who possessed mighty faith. Through his faith, Joseph as a young man proved the word of God. The moment of the first vision in 1820, the world became a significantly different place. Mankind once again could understand the true nature of God and the Godhead. Marion G. Romney observed,

> Some people have said that Joseph Smith was an unlearned man. He was an unlearned man in the things of the world, but the day he came out of the grove, following the first vision, he was the most learned person in the world in the things that count. When he came out of that grove, he knew more than all the world put together about the greatest question of the resurrection, which had been argued from the time man began to think seriously, because he had seen standing before him, the resurrected Christ. When he came out of that grove, he knew more about the nature of God than all the world. There had been many books written; philosophers had spent their lives trying to find out the nature of God, but when God took Joseph in hand to teach him he cut through all material things and taught Joseph the truth about these and many other things.

Unlike many whose accomplishments derived from their charisma, Joseph's success was based on the inspired truths he taught. He spoke of man's divine potential and the perfectibility of the individual. His stated desire was to bring mankind to Jesus Christ and then through Him to a loving and living Heavenly Father. "If men do not comprehend the character of God, they do not comprehend themselves. . . . I want you all to know him and be familiar with him," Joseph proclaimed shortly before his death. On another occasion he taught,

"When men begin to live by faith they begin to draw near to God; . . . and when faith is perfected they are like him; and because he is saved they are saved also; for they will be in the same situation he is in, because they have come to him; and when he appears they shall be like him, for they will see him as he is."

However, Joseph's message angered many and confounded others. Those who proclaimed that Joseph's death foreshadowed the demise of the Latter-day Saints failed to grasp how Joseph viewed himself. While his enemies tried to make Mormonism about Joseph, he proclaimed that it was about Jesus Christ—thus the name The Church of Jesus Christ of Latter-day Saints. "The fundamental principles" of Mormonism, he declared,

> are the testimony of the Apostles and Prophets, concerning Jesus Christ, that He died, was buried, and rose again the third day, and ascended into heaven; and all other things which pertain to our religion are only appendages to it. But in

connection with these, we believe in the gift of the Holy Ghost, the power of faith, the enjoyment of the spiritual gifts according to the will of God, the restoration of the House of Israel, and the final triumph of truth.

Many could not understand why Joseph would endure great difficulties and trials to start yet another church. Joseph did not view his work as simply providing yet another way for mankind to come to Christ. He proclaimed that it was the true, the perfect way—the only way. He was restoring the kingdom of God to the earth. That was the reason he was willing to endure all he went through. As was the case with Jesus Christ, Joseph lived his life for his fellowmen. The Lord raised him up for that very purpose.

Joseph made it very clear that it was not his teachings but Christ's doctrines that saved—doctrines that, as had been prophesied anciently, were no longer interpreted in the manner Jesus taught them. To obtain salvation, people had to completely understand that there was only "one faith, one Lord, one baptism," as the Apostle Paul taught.

Throughout his life and ministry, Joseph maintained a belief in the ultimate goodness and potential godliness of mankind. This belief did not falter, even in the face of never-ending persecution and ridicule. Rather than viewing people as "sinners in the hands of an angry God," he talked of mankind's relationship to its Maker as that of a child to a loving and just father. We come to God not out of fear, Joseph taught, but to experience His love so we might reach our divine potential. "Our heavenly Father is more liberal in His views, and boundless in His mercies and blessings, than we are ready to believe or receive," Joseph proclaimed.

Although Joseph taught perfection, he never claimed to be perfect. He did not claim a special sanctity, to have led a faultless life, or to be perfect in character. He was honest about his humanity, something that is frequently untrue of those wanting to fabricate falsehood, perpetrate fraud, or practice deceit. In his own life, the process of proving, reproving, and improving was evident. "I am a man of like passions with yourselves," William Clayton recalled Joseph stating. But, as Clayton concluded, "I wish I was such a man. . . . Joseph says, that when he is out preaching he always tells the people not to come here for ex-amples, but to set them and to copy from the Saviour, who is our pattern." Joseph explicitly proclaimed Jesus as "the prototype or standard of salvation," the only one against whom we measure our spiritual progress.

Because of his humanity, Joseph did not claim that every word he spoke was inspired. He did, however, claim that when he spoke by the power of the Spirit, it was as if God himself were speaking.

Joseph was asked to carry out apparently impossible tasks for which he did not seem to have the necessary skills. But he accomplished them, nevertheless. What came through Joseph was beyond him—as it was beyond most of his generation in terms of what was known about the early Americas, ancient Egypt, science, and astronomy, to name a few. Much of what is common knowledge today was in its infancy during Joseph's lifetime and understood by only a few. Nevertheless, his teachings are in conformity with increasing knowledge and scientific truth.

> *As brother Joseph used to say,*
> *"Yankee doodle do it."*
>
> —Heber C. Kimball in a 14 July 1852 discourse while discussing the opportunity the Latter-day Saints would soon have to build a temple at Salt Lake City.

The standard of truth has been erected: no unhallowed hand can stop the work from progressing; persecutions may rage, mobs may combine, armies may assemble, calumny may defame, but the truth of God will go forth boldly, nobly and independent till it has penetrated every continent, visited every clime, swept every country, and sounded in every ear, till the purposes of God shall be accomplished and the great Jehovah shall say the work is done.

—Joseph Smith in the "Wentworth Letter," 1842.

While many of Joseph's contemporaries made their name along one avenue, he successfully ventured down many streets. He reestablished the church of Jesus Christ on the earth. He also produced a book—the Book of Mormon—that continues to baffle critics, and he brought forth two other ancient books of scripture, the books of Moses and Abraham. He not only received but also published modern revelation. He restored the priesthood, the authority to act in the name of God for the salvation of mankind. He taught of the divine nature of all individuals. He reintroduced the concept of salvation for the dead, which practice had ceased shortly after the days of the New Testament apostles. He reintroduced temples and joyfully taught how mankind can be endowed with power from on high. He taught how families can be eternal units. He also proposed solutions to issues of his day, including health concerns and the abolition of slavery. He was also actively involved in community affairs.

Given the uniqueness of Joseph Smith and the wide range of his accomplishments during his thirty-eight years of mortality, it is little wonder that he continues to stand out in relation to his contemporaries and that he is known the world over by more than just scholars and academics. Parley P. Pratt, one of the twelve apostles at the time of Joseph's death, wrote of the martyred prophet, "Had he been spared a martyr's fate till mature manhood and age, he was certainly endowed with powers and ability to have revolutionized the world in many respects, and to have transmitted to posterity a name associated with more brilliant and glorious acts than has yet fallen to the lot of mortals. As it is, his works will live to endless ages, and unnumbered millions yet unborn will mention his name with honor, as a noble instrument in the hands of God, who, during his short and youthful career, laid the foundation of that kingdom spoken of by Daniel, the prophet, which should break in pieces all other kingdoms and stand forever."

William E. Berrett recounted that shortly after World War II, a prominent Russian who had spent a year studying in the United States was asked who were the great Americans. He replied, "You have had only one great American—Joseph Smith the Mormon Prophet. He is the only man in your culture who has given to the world ideas which if followed would revolutionize the human race."

The ends of the earth shall inquire after thy name, and fools shall have thee in derision, and hell shall rage against thee:

While the pure in heart, and the wise, and the noble, and the virtuous, shall seek counsel, and authority, and blessings constantly from under thy hand.

And thy people shall never be turned against thee by the testimony of traitors.

—From a revelation received by Joseph Smith while in Liberty Jail.

ETERNITY SKETCHED
IN A VISION

In February 1832 while working with Sidney Rigdon on the inspired translation of the Bible, Joseph Smith was profoundly moved by John 5:29: "And [they] shall come forth; they that have done good, unto the resurrection of life; and they that have done evil, unto the resurrection of damnation." Later he noted: "From sundry revelations which had been received, it was apparent that many important points touching the salvation of man had been taken from the Bible, or lost before it was compiled. It appeared self-evident from what truths were left, that if God rewarded every one according to the deeds done in the body, the term 'Heaven,' as intended for the Saints' eternal home, must include more kingdoms than one."

Joseph Smith and Sidney Rigdon petitioned the Lord for more knowledge; in response, they were permitted to behold the degrees of glory spoken of in the Bible. One who was present in the room during the vision recalled that "Joseph would, at intervals, say: 'what do I see?' . . . Then he would relate what he had seen or what he was looking at. Then Sidney replied, 'I see the same.' Presently Sidney would say, 'what do I see?' and would repeat what he had seen or was seeing, and Joseph would reply, 'I see the same.' This manner of conversation was repeated at short intervals to the end of the vision, and during the whole time not a word was spoken by any other person."

While still in the Spirit, Joseph and Sidney wrote what they had beheld, which is now Doctrine and Covenants section 76. Although Joseph concluded that "nothing could be more pleasing to the Saints upon the order of the kingdom of the Lord, than the light which burst upon the world through the foregoing vision," Brigham Young recalled that it was not universally joyously received: "It was a great trial for many, and some apostatized because God was not going to send to everlasting punishment heathens and infants."

The negative response to the revelation no doubt contributed to Joseph writing later in the year, "Oh Lord God deliver us in thy due time from the little narrow prison almost as it were totel darkness of paper pen and ink and a crooked broken scattered and imperfect language."

On 1 February 1843, the *Times and Seasons* published a short poem by William W. Phelps, and a long poetic response by Joseph Smith. Phelps's poem, Vade Mecum ("Go with Me"), was an appeal that he might go with the Prophet to the paradise of God. The first stanza reads:

> Go with me, will you go to the
>   saints that have died,—
> To the next, better world, where
>   the righteous reside;
> Where the angels and spirits in
>   harmony be
> In the joys of a vast paradise?
>   Go with me.

Joseph's response, entitled "The Answer," is a poetic rephrasing of section 76 that also contains interpretive commentary. In publishing Joseph's poem, John Taylor wrote that it was at "once both novel and interesting; for while the common landmarks of modern poetry are entirely disregarded; there is something so dignified and exalted conveyed in the ideas of this production."

SECTION 76

1. Hear, O ye heavens, and give ear, O earth, and rejoice ye inhabitants thereof, for the Lord is God, and beside him there is no Savior.

11. We, Joseph Smith, Jun., and Sidney Rigdon, being in the Spirit on the sixteenth day of February, in the year of our Lord one thousand eight hundred and thirty two—

12. By the power of the Spirit our eyes were opened and our understandings were enlightened, so as to see and understand the things of God—

13. Even those things which were from the beginning before the world was, which were ordained of the Father, through his Only Begotten Son, who was in the bosom of the Father even from the beginning.

14. Of whom we bear record; and the record which we bear is the fulness of the gospel of Jesus Christ, who is the Son, whom we saw and with whom we conversed in the heavenly vision.

16. Speaking of the resurrection of the dead, concerning those who shall hear the voice of the Son of man;

17. And shall come forth; they who have done good, in the resurrection of the just; and they who have done evil, in the resurrection of the unjust.

18. Now this caused us to marvel, for it was given unto us of the Spirit.

19. And while we meditated upon these things, the Lord touched the eyes of our understandings and they were opened, and the glory of the Lord shone round about.

20. And we beheld the glory of the Son, on the right hand of the Father, and received of his fullness;

22. And now, after the many testimonies which have been given of him, this is the testimony, last of all, which we give of him: That he lives!

"THE ANSWER"

I will go, I will go to the home of the Saints,
Where the virtue's the value, and life the reward;
But before I return to my former estate
I must fulfill the mission I had from the Lord.
Wherefore, hear, O ye heavens, and give ear O ye earth;
And rejoice ye inhabitants truly again;
For the Lord he is God, and his life never ends,
And besides him there ne'er was a Saviour of men.

I, Joseph, the prophet, in spirit beheld,
And the eyes of the inner man truly did see
Eternity sketch'd in a vision from God.
Of what was, and now is, and yet is to be.

Those things which the Father ordained of old,
Before the world was, or a system had run,—
Through Jesus the Maker and Savior of all;
The only begotten, (Messiah) his son.
Of whom I bear record, as all prophets have,
And the record I bear is the fulness,—yea even
The truth of the Gospel of Jesus—the Christ,
With whom I convers'd in the vision of heav'n.

I marvel'd at these resurrections, indeed!
For it came unto me by the spirit direct:—
And while I did meditate what it all meant,
The Lord touch'd the eyes of my own intellect:—
Hosanna forever! They open'd anon,
And the glory of God shone around where I was;
And there was the Son, at the Father's right hand,
In a fulness of glory, and holy applause.

And now after all of the proofs made of him,
By witnesses truly, by whom he was known,
This is mine, last of all, that he lives; yea he lives;
And sits at the right hand of God, on his throne.

227

23. *For we saw him, even on the right hand of God; and we heard the voice bearing record that he is the Only Begotten of the Father—*

24. *That by him, and through him, and of him, the worlds are and were created, and the inhabitants thereof are begotten sons and daughters of God.*

And I heard a great voice, bearing record from heav'n,
He's the Saviour, and only begotten of God—
By him, of him, and through him, the worlds were all made,
Even all that career in the heavens so broad.

40. *And this is the gospel, the glad tidings, which the voice out of the heavens bore record unto us—*

41. *That he came into the world, even Jesus, to be cruci-fied for the world, and to bear the sins of the world, and to sanctify the world, and to cleanse it from all unrighteousness;*

The myst'ry of Godliness truly is great:—
The past, and the present, and what is to be;
And this is the gospel—glad tidings to all,
Which the voice from the heavens bore record to me:
That he came to the world in the middle of time,
To lay down his life for his friends and his foes,
And bear away sin as a mission of love;
And sanctify earth for a blessed repose.

96. *And the glory of the celestial is one, evens as the glory of the sun is one.*

97. *And the glory of the terrestrial is one, even as the glory of the moon is one.*

98. *And the glory of the telestial is one, even as the glory of the stars is one; for as one star differs from another star in glory, even so differs one from another in glory in the telestial world.*

The glory celestial is one like the sun;
The glory terrestrial is one like the moon;
The glory telestial is one like the stars,
And all harmonize like the parts of a tune
As the stars are all different in lustre and size,
So the telestial region, is mingled in bliss;
From the least unto greatest, and greatest to least,
The reward is exactly as promis'd in this.

111. *For they shall be judged according to their works, and ever man shall receive according to his own works, his own dominion, in the mansions which are prepared.*

Ev'ry man shall be judg'd by the works of his life.
And receive a reward in the mansions prepar'd;
For his judgements are just, and his works never end,
As the prophets and servants have always decalr'd
But the great things of God, which he show'd unto me,
Unlawful to utter, I dare not declare;
They surpass all the wisdom and greatness of men,
And only are seen, as has Paul, where they are.
I will go, I will go, while the secret of life,
is becoming in heaven, and blasting in hell;
Is leaving on earth, and a budding in space:—
I will go, I will go, with you, brother, farewell.

"Monday, 24 June 1844, 4:15 A.M.: Beyond the Events"

PRAISE TO THE MAN

William Wines Phelps, 1792–1872

William W. Phelps, an early convert to Mormonism, became a confidant of Joseph Smith before turning against his fellow Latter-day Saints during the tumultuous summer of 1838. False charges he made against the Mormons contributed both to the long imprisonment of Joseph in Richmond and Liberty jails and the expulsion of the Latter-day Saints from Missouri. On 29 June 1840, after two years of estrangement from the Church, Phelps wrote Joseph asking for forgiveness. He concluded his letter by stating,

> I know my situation, you know it, and God knows it, and I want to be saved if my friends will help me. Like the captain that was cast away on a desert island; when he got off he went to sea again, and made his fortune the next time, so let my lot be. I have done wrong and I am sorry. The beam is in my own eye. I have not walked along with my friends according to my holy anointing. I ask forgiveness in the name of Jesus Christ of all the Saints, for I will do right, God helping me. I want your fellowship; if you cannot grant that, grant me your peace and friendship, for we are brethren, and our communion used to be sweet, and whenever the Lord brings us together again, I will make all the satisfaction on every point that Saints or God can require.

On 22 July 1840, Joseph poignantly responded to his friend,

> Dear Brother Phelps:
> I must say that it is with no ordinary feelings I endeavor to write a few lines to you in answer to yours of the 29th ultimo; at the same time I am rejoiced at the privilege granted me.
> It is true, that we have suffered much in consequence of your behavior—the cup of gall, already full enough for mortals to drink, was indeed filled to overflowing when you turned against us. One with whom we had oft taken sweet counsel together, and enjoyed many

refreshing seasons from the Lord—"had it been an enemy, we could have borne it." . . .

However, the cup has been drunk, the will of our Father has been done, and we are yet alive, for which we thank the Lord. And having been delivered from the hands of wicked men by the mercy of our God, we say it is your privilege to be delivered from the powers of the adversary, be brought into the liberty of God's dear children, and again take your stand among the Saints of the Most High, and by diligence, humility, and love unfeigned, commend yourself to our God, and your God, and to the Church of Jesus Christ.

Believing your confession to be real, and your repentance genuine, I shall be happy once again to give you the right hand of fellowship, and rejoice over the returning prodigal.

Your letter was read to the Saints last Sunday, and an expression of their feeling was taken, when it was unanimously

Resolved, That W. W. Phelps should be received into fellowship.

"Come on, dear brother, since the war is past,
For friends at first, are friends again at last."
Yours as ever,
Joseph Smith, Jun.

Following Joseph's death, Phelps, Joseph's friend, turned enemy, turned friend again, immortalized the martyred prophet in a much-beloved Mormon hymn:

Praise to the man who communed with Jehovah!
Jesus anointed that Prophet and Seer.
Blessed to open the last dispensation,
Kings shall extol him, and nations revere.

Hail to the Prophet, ascended to heaven!
Traitors and tyrants now fight him in vain.
Mingling with Gods, he can plan for his brethren;
Death cannot conquer the hero again.

Praise to his mem'ry, he died as a martyr;
Honored and blest be his ever great name!
Long shall his blood, which was shed by assassins,
Plead unto heav'n while the earth lauds his fame.

Great is his glory and endless his priesthood.
Ever and ever the keys he will hold.
Faithful and true, he will enter his kingdom,
Crowned in the midst of the prophets of old.

Sacrifice brings forth the blessings of heaven;
Earth must atone for the blood of that man.
Wake up the world for the conflict of justice.
Millions shall know "Brother Joseph" again.

Hail to the Prophet, ascended to heaven!

Death cannot conquer the hero again.

ACKNOWLEDGMENTS

First and foremost we express the heartfelt gratitude we owe to each of our families.

Chad: To my wife, Elizabeth, whose patience, insights, research, and words of encouragement helped raised this book to a higher level; to the magnificent seven—Amy, Laura, Spencer, Taylor, Jane, Louisa, and Bryce—you were the ideal target audience, and your wide range of contributions, from research to hugs, was greatly appreciated.

Bill: To my wife, Sheri, for her encouragement, patience, and help; and to Danielle for her assistance; and to Wes for his encouragement and willingness to listen.

We are indebted and grateful to the many people who helped shepherd this project from an idea to a book. We appreciate the efforts of Cory Maxwell, Richard Erickson, and Ann Sheffield at Deseret Book Company. We also thank Tom Hewitson, Shauna Gibby, Laurie Cook, Tonya Facemyer, Lisa Mangum, Amy Stewart, and Meridith Ethington. Particular gratitude goes to designer Sheryl Dickert Smith and editor Jack M. Lyon for their patience and their exceptional efforts to bring this volume to fruition. Thank you for sharing our vision of the final product.

We would like to thank all our colleagues and friends at the LDS Church Archives and Church History Library. In particular we express our appreciation to Ron Barney, Mel Bashore, Christy Best, Jay Burrup, W. Randall Dixon, Sharalyn Duffin, Chad Foulger, Jeff Johnson, Mike Landon, Leslie Parker, Kathryn Phillips, Jenny St. Clair, April Williamsen, and Ron Watt.

We also appreciate the thousands of librarians and archivists whose anonymous, day-in and day-out efficiency make the work of researchers and writers possible: the LDS Church Archives and Church History Library; the Daughters of the Utah Pioneers; Special Collections, J. Willard Marriott Library, University of Utah; L. Tom Perry Special Collections, Lee Library, Brigham Young University; the Library of Congress; the National Archives; Special Collections, Merrill Library, Utah State University; the Utah State Historical Society; and the Museum of Church History and Art.

Many individuals listened, gave insights, and encouraged us. Thank you again to Mark Thomas of Brigham Young University for his insights. Thanks also to Fred Woods, Richard Holzapfel, Marc Bohn, Heidi Swinton, Alan Morrell, Connie Disney, Gary Bergera, Jeffrey Cottle, Lee Groberg, Mark McConkie, Matthew Heiss, Larry DeMartini, Joe Glenn, Dave Rowe, Phil Plothow, Bill Larkin, Jon Tingey, Joe Robertson, and Briant Badger.

We also wish to express our great respect and appreciation for the work of our friends and colleagues who have produced inspirational and important essays, articles, and books on American and LDS Church history. Without their dedicated efforts, this and other books and works would not be possible.

PICTURE CREDITS

"TO EVERY THING THERE IS A SEASON"

Benjamin Franklin. Photographic print of portrait by Joseph-Siffrede Duplessis. Library of Congress.

Nathaniel Hawthorne. Frontispiece engraving, *Twice-Told Tales,* 1851.

Henry W. Longfellow. Engraving by H. B. Hall & Sons, New York, ca. 1880.

Lydia Maria Child. Frontispiece, *The American Frugal Housewife,* 1836.

Walt Whitman. Photographic print, original ca. 1849. Library of Congress.

Andrew Jackson. Watercolor lithograph by Albert Newsam, published by Lehman & Duval, Philadelphia, 1830. Library of Congress.

Thomas Jefferson. Color photomechanical print of painting by Rembrandt Peale. Library of Congress.

Lewis and Clark. Illustration from *A Journal of the Voyages and Travels of a Corps of Discovery,* by Patrick Gass. Philadelphia, 1810.

Jonathan Edwards. Delmarute Trust.

Queen Victoria. Color lithograph, Boussod Valadon & Co., ca. 1897. Library of Congress.

Fall of the Alamo. Woodcut from *Davy Crockett's Almanack,* 1837.

Parley P. Pratt. Daguerreotype by Marsena Cannon, ca. 1853. LDS Church Archives.

Sarah Josepha Hale. Engraving from *Godey's Lady's Book,* ca. 1870.

Fashion plate, ca. 1810. Library of Congress.

William Clayton. Photograph by unknown photographer. LDS Church Archives.

Benjamin F. Johnson. Photograph by Edward Martin, 1864. LDS Church Archives.

Joseph and Hyrum Smith. Martha Spence Heywood Autograph Book. LDS Church Archives.

Pass the Mustard. Delmarute Trust.

James Madison. Stipple engraving by W. H. Morgan, ca. 1813. Library of Congress.

James Monroe. Color lithograph by D. W. Kellog, ca. 1842. Library of Congress.

John Quincy Adams. Glass negative of Mathew Brady daguerreotype, ca. 1844. Brady-Handy Photograph Collection, Library of Congress.

John Tyler. Glass negative of daguerreotype, n.d. Brady-Handy Photograph Collection, Library of Congress.

Midwinter Vermont. Photograph by George Edward Anderson, 1908. LDS Church Archives.

Vermont. Photograph by George Edward Anderson, 1907. LDS Church Archives.

"A REMARKABLY QUIET, WELL-DISPOSED SON"

Map of Vermont, 1795.

New York City, 1797. Lithograph by Henry R. Robinson, ca. 1847. Library of Congress.

Rural scene, cabin. Engraving, *Columbia Magazine,* July 1788.

Nathan Smith. Engraving by S. S. Jocelyn and S. B. Munson, n.d. Library of Congress.

"My Early Home." Lithograph by Thayer and Co., Boston, ca. 1843. Library of Congress.

Lucy Mack Smith. Painting by Sutcliff Maudsley, ca. 1845. Museum of Church History and Art.

Frontier family. Engraving, ca. 1820. Delmarute Trust.

Noah Webster. Steel engraving, ca. 1867. Library of Congress.

Hyrum Smith. LDS Church Archives.

"A View of the Whale Fishery." Etching, n.d. Library of Congress.

The President's House. Aquatint color print by William Strickland, 1814. Library of Congress.

Evolution of a pioneer settlement. Engravings by Ebenezer Mix, in Orsamus Turner, *Pioneer History of the Holland Purchase of Western New York,* 1849.

New England schoolhouse. Print by L. Prang and Company, n.d. Library of Congress.

Fort McHenry. Lithograph cover illustration for "Our Country's Flag!" by George F. Cole. Baltimore: John Cole & Son, 1836.

Methodist preacher. In Frances Trollope, *Domestic Manners of the Americans,* 2 vols. London: Whittaker, Treacher and Co., 1832.

Methodist camp meeting. Hand-colored engraving by M. Dubourg, ca. 1819. Library of Congress.

Baptism. Engraving courtesy Delmarute Trust.

"The Jerking Exercise." Engraving by Lossing-Barrett, ca. 1840. Library of Congress.

"Venerate the Plough." Engraving, *Columbian Magazine,* November 1786.

Robert Fulton. Engraving by Johnson, Wilson & Co., New York, ca. 1874. Library of Congress.

United States Capitol. Daguerreotype by John Plumbe, ca. 1846, Library of Congress.

The Sacred Grove. Photograph by George Edward Anderson, 1907. LDS Church Archives.

"THIS GENERATION SHALL HAVE MY WORD THROUGH YOU"

"Inception of Mormonism—Joseph Smith's First Vision." Engraving from T.B.H. Stenhouse, *The Rocky Mountain Saints.* New York: D. Appleton and Company, 1873.

Map of New York State by William Williams, 1828.

Camp meeting. Lithograph by Kenney and Lucas Lithography, ca. 1829. Library of Congress.

"Merrimack Looms." Engraving, ca. 1830. Delmarute Trust.

The Angel Moroni delivering the Book of Mormon plates to Joseph Smith. Lithograph, 1897, based on C.C.A. Christensen painting. Library of Congress.

"Eastern View in Main-street, Palmyra." Engraving from John W. Barber and Henry Howe, *Historical Collections of the State of New York.* New York: S. Tuttle, 1841.

"The Mormon Hill"—Hill Cumorah. Engraving from Barber and Howe, *Historical Collections of the State of New York,* 1841.

View of landscape near Joseph Smith home in Harmony Pennsylvania. Photograph by George Edward Anderson, 1907.

Emma Hale Smith. Painting by Sutcliffe Maudsley, ca. 1842. Museum of Church History and Art.

"Popping the Question." Lithograph by Sarony and Major, ca. 1846. Library of Congress.

Martin Harris. Charles W. Carter Glass Negative Collection, 1870. LDS Church Archives.

The Erie Canal at Albany, New York. Engraving, *Frank Leslie's Illustrated Newspaper,* 22 November 1856.

Charles Anthon. Engraving from *Harper's Weekly,* 17 August 1867.

Thomas Jefferson. Aquatint print by Michal Sokolnicki, ca. 1808; based on painting by Tadeusz Koscinuszko. Library of Congress.

John Adams. Lithograph by Peter S. Duval, ca. 1846. Library of Congress.

Funeral Thoughts. Broadside. Library of Congress.

The Susquehanna River. Photograph by George Edward Anderson, 1907. LDS Church Archives.

Oliver Cowdery. Charles W. Carter Glass Negative Collection, n.d. LDS Church Archives.

The Three Witnesses. Engraving by H. B. Hall and Sons, 1883. Delmarute Trust.

The E. B. Grandin bookstore. Photograph. LDS Church Archives.

Book of Mormon copyright, 1829. Library of Congress.

Title page, *The American Frugal Housewife.* Boston: American Stationer's Company, 1836.

James Fennimore Cooper. Engraving, *New Monthly Magazine,* April 1831.

Girls playing games. Engravings from *The American Girl's Book.* Boston: Munroe and Francis, 1831.

Eli Whitney. Engraving by William Hoogland, ca. 1821. Library of Congress.

Slaves using a cotton gin. Wood engraving, *Harper's Weekly,* 18 December 1869.

Western Emigration. H. Trumbull, *Journal of Doctor Jeremiah Simpleton's Tour to Ohio.* Boston: S. Sewall, 1819.

Title page of the first edition of the Book of Mormon. Palmyra: E. B. Grandin, 1830.

Jackson election ticket, 1828. Library of Congress.

"LIKE THE ANCIENTS"

The Temple at Kirtland, Ohio. Engraving from T.B.H. Stenhouse, *The Rocky Mountain Saints,* 1873.

"Meeting in the African Church, Cincinnati, Ohio, 1830." Etching from *Illustrated News,* April, 1830.

Sidney Rigdon. Fox and Symons photograph of an original, n.d. LDS Church Archives.

Alexis de Tocqueville. Photomechanical print from Karl Werckmeister, ed., *Das Neunzehnte Jahrhundert in Bildnissen.* Berlin: Kunstverlag der Photographische Gesellschaft, 1901.

The drunkard's progress. Hand-colored lithograph by E. B. and E. C. Kellog, ca. 1846. Library of Congress.

The fruits of temperance. Hand-colored lithograph by Nathaniel Currier, Currier and Ives, ca. 1848. Library of Congress.

Samuel Francis Smith. Photograph by Soule Photograph Company, 1895. Library of Congress.

"Falling of Stars, Jackson County, Missouri." C. B. Hancock, ca. 1895. LDS Church Archives.

"United States Slave Trade." Engraving on wove paper, 1830. Library of Congress.

Abolitionist press demolished. Engraving, 1836, Library of Congress.

Ralph Waldo Emerson. Engraving by Stephen A. Schoff, 1878 (based on Samuel Rowse painting). Library of Congress.

Calisthenics with bar. Engraving, *Atkinson's Casket,* 1832.

Boys exercising. Engraving, *Family Magazine,* vol. 1, 1834–1835.

Tarring and feathering of Joseph Smith. Library of Congress.

Kirtland, Ohio. Photograph by George Edward Anderson, 1907. LDS Church Archives.

The Book of Commandments.

A Collection of Sacred Hymns.

Davy Crockett. Library of Congress.

The first passenger steam railroad. Color woodcut, ca. 1870. Library of Congress.

Kirtland Safety Society bank note. Courtesy LDS Church Archives.

Chesapeake & Ohio Canal Company bank note.

Canal at Lockport, New York 1836.

Political cartoon detailing the effects of the Financial Panic of 1837.

John Deere. Steel engraving, n.d. Library of Congress.

Unidentified blacksmith, ca. 1850. Daguerreotype, unknown photographer, ca. 1850. Library of Congress.

Sheet music cover, "The Village Blacksmith." Lithograph by E. W. Bouve, 1848.

Mormons fleeing Jackson County. C. B. Hancock, ca. 1895, LDS Church Archives.

"Mormon troubles in Missouri begin." Engraving from T.B.H. Stenhouse, *The Rocky Mountain Saints,* 1873.

Zion's Camp. Etching from T.B.H. Stenhouse, *The Rocky Mountain Saints,* 1873.

The Sale. Card. Library of Congress.

The Kneeling Slave. Engraving from *The Poetic Works of Elizabeth Margaret Chandler.* Philadelphia: Lemuel Howell, 1836.

Raffle poster. Broadside, n.d.

Lydia Maria Child. Photographic print, n.d. Library of Congress.

"Massacre of Mormons at Haun's Mill." Etching from T.B.H. Stenhouse, *The Rocky Mountain Saints,* 1873.

William Lloyd Garrison. Engraving by F. S. Stuart, n.d. Library of Congress.

Liberty Jail. Photograph by J. T. Hicks, ca. 1878. LDS Church Archives.

Joseph rebuking the guards. Painting by Danquart Weggeland, 1888. Museum of Church History and Art.

Frederick Douglass. Print from glass negative, n.d. Brady-Handy Photograph Collection, Library of Congress.

Ralph Waldo Emerson. Etching from *Massachusetts Magazine.*

Plat for the City of Zion. Ink on paper, marginal notes by Frederick G. Williams. LDS Church Archives.

Plan of Cincinnati, Ohio, 1815. Engraved for *Drake's Statistical View,* 1815.

"I HAVE BEEN AN INSTRUMENT IN HIS HANDS"

Portrait of Joseph Smith. Artist and date unknown. Community of Christ.

An Original History of the Religious Denominations, edited by L. Daniel Rupp. Philadelphia: J. Y. Humphreys, 1844.

"Nauvoo, Illinois" and "The Mormon Temple." Lithographs from Henry Lewis, *Das Illustrirte Mississippithal.* Dusseldorf: Arnz and Company, 1854–1857.

"HE CHEERED OUR HEARTS"

Detail: "A View of the Mississippi near Quincy." Lithograph from Henry Lewis, *Das Illustrirte Mississippithal.* Dusseldorf: Arnz and Company, 1854–1857.

Nauvoo, the City Beautiful. Illustration, Aus d. Kunstanst d. Bibl. Instit. in Hildbhsn [trans: From the Art Institution of the Biblical Institute of Hildburhausen], n.d.

Abraham Lincoln. Daguerreotype by Nicholas H. Shepherd, ca. 1847. Library of Congress.

Martin Van Buren. Engraving by Charles Fenderich, 1839. Library of Congress.

Joseph Smith. Engraving by Frederick W. Piercy. LDS Church Archives.

Nauvoo. Engraving from John W. Gunnison, *The Mormons or Latter-Day Saints.* Philadelphia: Lippincott, Granbo, and Co., 1852.

Local militia drills, ca. 1832. Lithograph by David Johnston, ca. 1832. Library of Congress.

The Crockett Almanac, 1841.

The City Charter: Laws, Ordinances, and Acts. Nauvoo: Published by Order of the City Council, 1842.

Nauvoo Temple. Lithograph by Charles Shober in Holmes and Arnold's *Map of Hancock County,* 1859.

"Lieutenant-General Joseph Smith Reviewing the Nauvoo Legion." Watercolor and ink on paper, Robert Campbell, 1845. Museum of Church History and Art.

The Good Housekeeper.

Nauvoo. Colored illustration, 1850, *Gleason's*

Pictorial Drawing-Room Companion.

Phrenology chart, ca. 1834. Library of Congress.

April Conference, 1844, Nauvoo. Hand-colored lithograph published by George Lloyd, ca. 1845. LDS Church Archives.

Richard Henry Dana. Delmarute Trust.

Joseph Smith preaching in the wilderness. Illustration from *Harper's New Monthly Magazine,* April 1853.

Dorothea Dix. Photograph print, n.d. Library of Congress.

West view of the Capitol, Washington, D.C. Watercolor drawing by Augustus Kollner, ca. 1839. Library of Congress.

West front of the Capitol, Washington, D.C. Watercolor drawing by John Rubens Smith, ca. 1828. Library of Congress.

Joseph Smith, "General Smith's views of the powers and policies of the Government." Pittsburgh: John E. Page, 1844.

Lt. Gen. Joseph Smith. Egg tempera and ink on paper, Sutcliffe Maudsley, ca. 1842.

Destruction of the *Nauvoo Expositor.* Engraving, T.B.H. Stenhouse, *The Rocky Mountain Saints,* 1873.

Samuel F. B. Morse. Photograph by Mathew Brady, ca. 1850. Library of Congress.

The Prophet Joseph surrenders. Illustration from T.B.H. Stenhouse, *The Rocky Mountain Saints,* 1873.

The Hamilton Hotel at Carthage, Illinois. From map of Hancock County, 1859.

Courthouse in Carthage, Illinois. Photograph by Granger and Thomas, Photographers, ca. 1860 LDS Church Archives.

Carthage Jail. Engraving by Frederick Piercy, ca. 1853.

The assassination of Joseph Smith. Illustration from Ann Eliza Webb Young, *Wife no. 19.* Hartford, Conn.: Dustin, Gilman & Co., 1876.

"L'assassinat du Prophete Smith, 1844." Illustration from Maurice Soulie, *Les Procès Célèbres des Etats-Unis.* Paris: Payot, 1932.

The assassination of Joseph Smith. C. B. Hancock, ca. 1895. LDS Church Archives.

"THE KEYS OF THE KINGDOM ARE RIGHT HERE"

The Prophet Joseph. Artist unknown, ca. 1920. LDS Church Archives.

Emma Smith. Photographer unknown, ca. 1860. LDS Church Archives.

Nauvoo, Illinois, ca. 1846. Charles W. Carter Collection, attributed to Lucian Foster. LDS Church Archives.

Joseph Smith. Illustration from *New York Messenger,* September 13, 1845.

Emma Hale Smith holding her son David Hyrum Smith. Photograph print of daguerreotype by unknown photographer, ca. 1845. Utah State Historical Society.

Nauvoo, 1859. Oil on canvas, Joh. Schroder. Museum of Church History and Art.

Joseph Smith. Detail of engraving by Frederick W. Piercy. LDS Church Archives.

Thomas Cole. Daguerreotype by Mathew Brady, ca. 1847. Library of Congress.

Joseph Smith. Drawing by Sutcliffe Maudsley, ca. 1844. Museum of Church History and Art.

Joseph and Hyrum Smith. Engraving. LDS Church Archives.

Joseph Smith portrait. Charles W. Carter Collection, n.d. LDS Church Archives.

Hyrum and Joseph Smith. Charles W. Carter collection, n.d. LDS Church Archives.

"Monday, 24 June 1844, 4:15 A.M.: Beyond the Events." Painting by Drago Pino, 1987. Museum of Church History and Art.

William Wines Phelps. Photograph by Savage and Ottinger, n.d. LDS Church Archives.

SELECTED BIBLIOGRAPHY

Allen, James B. and Glen M. Leonard. *The Story of the Latter-day Saints.* Second edition, revised and enlarged. Salt Lake City: Deseret Book, 1992.

Ambrose, Stephen E. *Undaunted Courage: Meriwether Lewis, Thomas Jefferson and the Opening of the American West.* New York: Touchstone, 1997.

Anderson, Richard Lloyd. *Joseph Smith's New England Heritage: Influences of Grandfathers Solomon Mack and Asael Smith.* Salt Lake City: Deseret Book, 1971.

Anderson, Richard Lloyd. *Investigating the Book of Mormon Witnesses.* Salt Lake City: Deseret Book Company, 1981.

Andrus, Hyrum L. and Helen Mae Andrus, eds. *They Knew the Prophet.* Salt Lake City: Deseret Book, 1999.

Backman, Milton V., Jr. *Joseph Smith's First Vision: The First Vision in its Historical Context.* Salt Lake City: Bookcraft, 1971.

Bennett, Evelyn. *Frederick Douglass and the War Against Slavery.* Brookfield, Conn.: The Millbrook Press, 1993.

Boyer, Paul S., ed. *The Oxford Companion to United States History.* New York: Oxford University Press, 2001.

Brinkley, Douglas. *American Heritage History of the United States.* New York: Viking Penguin, 1998.

Bushman, Richard L. *Joseph Smith and the Beginnings of Mormonism.* Urbana and Chicago: University of Illinois Press, 1984.

Cable, Mary, and the editors of American Heritage. *American Manners & Morals: A Picture History of How We Behaved and Misbehaved.* New York: American Heritage Publishing, Co., 1969.

Calkins, Carroll C. *The Story of America.* Pleasantville, New York: Reader's Digest Association, Inc., 1975.

Carruth, Gorton. *The Encyclopedia of American Facts and Dates.* Tenth Edition. New York: HarperCollins Publishers, Inc., 1997.

Child, Lydia Maria. *The American Frugal Housewife.* Boston: American Stationers' Company, 1836. Reprint edited and introduction by Alice M. Geffen. New York: Harper and Row Publishers, 1972.

Church Educational System. *Church History in the Fulness of Times: The History of The Church of Jesus Christ of Latter-day Saints.* Salt Lake City: The Church of Jesus Christ of Latter-day Saints, 1993.

Cobbett, William. *A Years Residence in the United States of America.* A reprint facsimile of the 1818–1819 edition. New York: Augustus M. Kelley, 1969.

Colbert, David. ed. *Eyewitness to America: 500 Years of American in the Words of Those Who Saw It Happen.* New York: Pantheon Books, 1997.

Cook, Lyndon W. *The Revelations of the Prophet Joseph Smith: A Historical and Biographical Commentary of the Doctrine and Covenants.* Provo, Utah: Seventy's Mission Bookstore, 1981.

Dahl, Larry E. And Donald Q. Cannon, eds. *The Teachings of Joseph Smith.* Salt Lake City: Bookcraft, 1997.

Dana, Richard Henry. *The Journal of Richard Henry Dana, Jr.* Edited by Robert F. Lucid. 3 Volumes. Cambridge: Harvard University Press, 1968.

Daniel, Clifton. *Chronicle of America.* New York: DK Publishing, 1997.

Davidson, James West and Kathleen Underwood. *American Journey: The Quest for Liberty to 1877.* Englewood Cliffs, New Jersey: Prentice Hall, 1992.

Degregorio, William A. *The Complete Book of U. S. Presidents.* Fifth edition. New York: Gramercy Books, 2001.

Douglass, Frederick. *Narrative of the Life of Frederick Douglass: An American Slave.* Cambridge: Belknap Press of Harvard University, 1960.

Downs, Robert B. *Books that Changes America.* New York: The Macmillan Co., 1970.

Ehat, Andrew and Lyndon Cook, eds. *The Words of Joseph Smith: The Contemporary Accounts of the Nauvoo Discourses of the Prophet Joseph.* Provo, Utah: Religious Study Center, Brigham Young University, 1980.

Fifteenth Annual Report of the American Home Missionary Society. New York, 1841.

Garraty, John A. *1,001 Things Everyone Should Know About American History.* New York: Doubleday, 1989.

Givens, George W. *In Old Nauvoo: Everyday Life in the City of Joseph.* Salt Lake City: Desert Book Company, 1990.

Goodman, Drew S. *The Fullness of Times: A Chronological Comparison of Important Events in Church, U. S. and World History.* Salt Lake City: Eagle Gate, 2001.

Hakim, Joy. *A History of Us.* Vols. 4–5, Third edition. New York: Oxford University Press, 2003.

Hill, Donna. *Joseph Smith: The First Mormon.* Garden City, N.Y.: Doubleday and Company, Inc., 1977.

Holzapfel, Richard N. and William W. Slaughter. *Prophets of the Latter Days.* Salt Lake City: Deseret Book Company, 2003.

Hoose, Phillip. *We Were There, Too! Young People in U. S. History.* Melanie Kroupa Books. New York: Farrar Straus Giroux, 2001.

Jessee, Dean C., ed. *The Papers of Joseph Smith.* Vol. 1, Autobiographical and Historical Writings. Salt Lake City: Deseret Book, 1989.

Jessee, Dean C., ed *The Papers of Joseph Smith.* Vol. 2, Journal, 1832–1842. Salt Lake City: Deseret Book, 1992.

Jessee, Dean C., ed. *Personal Writings of Joseph Smith.* Revised edition. Salt Lake City: Deseret Book, 2002.

Karcher, Carolyn L., ed *A Lydia Maria Child Reader.* Durham & London: Duke University Press, 1997.

Lamb, Brian. *Booknotes: Stories from American History.* New York: PublicAffairs, 2001.

Leonard, Glen M. *Nauvoo: A Place of Peace, A People of Promise.* Salt Lake City: Deseret Book Company and Provo: Brigham Young University, 2003.

Long, Robert Emmet. *James Fenimore Cooper.* New York: Continuum, 1990.

Ludlow, Daniel H., ed. *Encyclopedia of Mormonism: The History, Scripture, Doctrine and Procedure of the Church of Jesus Christ of Latter-day Saints.* 4 vols. New York: Macmillan Publishing Company, 1992.

Maier, Pauline and Merritt Roe Smith, Alexander Keyssar and Daniel J. Kevles. *Inventing America: A History of the United States.* New York: W. W. Norton & Co., 2003.

McCloud, Susan Evans. *Joseph Smith: A Photobiography.* Salt Lake City: Aspen Books, 1992.

McConkie, Mark L. *Remembering Joseph: Personal Recollections of Those Who Knew the Prophet Joseph Smith.* Salt Lake City: Deseret Book, 2003.

Mulder, William and A. Russell Mortensen, eds. *Among the Mormons: Historic Accounts by Contemporary Observers.* New York: Alfred A. Knopf, 1958.

Quincy, Josiah. *Figures of the Past From the Leaves of Old Journals.* Boston: Roberts Brothers, 1883.

Rae, Noel, comp. *Witnessing America: The Library of Congress Book of Firsthand Accounts of Life in America, 1600–1900.* New York: Penguin Reference, 1996.

Randall, Ruth Painter. *Mary Lincoln: Biography of a Marriage.* Boston: Little, Brown and Company, 1953.

Reader's Digest. *Strange Stories, Amazing Facts of America's Past.* Pleasantville, New York: The Reader's Digest Association, 1990.

Restad, Penne L. *Christmas in America: A History.* New York: Oxford University Press, 1996.

Richardson, Robert D., Jr. *Emerson: The Mind on Fire.* Berkeley: University of California Press, 1995.

Riegel, Robert E. *Young America, 1830–1840.* Norman: University of Oklahoma, 1949.

Schlesinger, Arthur M., Jr., Gen. ed. *The Almanac of American History.* A Bison Book. New York: Putnam Publishing Group, 1983.

Shenkman, Richard and Kurt Reiger. *One-night Stands with American History: Odd, Amusing, and Little-known Incidents.* New York: William Morrow & Co., 1980.

Slaughter, William W. *Life in Zion: An Intimate Look at the Latter-day Saints, 1820–1995.* Salt Lake City: Deseret Book, 1995.

Smith, Joseph. *History of the Church of Jesus Christ of Latter-day Saints.* Second edition revised, edited by B. H. Roberts, 7 Vols. Salt Lake City: Deseret Book Company, 1980.

Smith, Joseph Fielding, comp. *Teachings of the Prophet Joseph Smith.* Salt Lake City: Deseret Book Company, 1976.

Spiller, Robert E. *James Fenimore Cooper.* Minneapolis: University of Minnesota Press, 1965.

Swinton, Heidi. *American Prophet: The Story of Joseph Smith.* Salt Lake City: Shadow Mountain, 1999.

Thomas A. Bailey, David M. Kennedy and Lizabeth Cohen. *The American Pageant: A History of the Republic.* Lexington, Massachusetts: D. C. Heath and Company, 1998.

Trollope, Frances. *Domestic Manners of the Americans.* London: Whittaker, Treacher, and Co., 1832.

Whitcomb, John and Claire Whitcomb. *Oh Say Can You See: Unexpected Anecdotes About American History.* New York: William Morrow, 1987.